English File

Intermediate

Student Book B Units 6–10   with access to
EXAM CONFIDENCE

fifth edition

Christina Latham-Koenig   Clive Oxenden
Kate Chomacki   Jerry Lambert

Paul Seligson and Clive Oxenden are the original co-authors
of *English File 1* (published 1996) and *English File 2* (1997)

Contents

		GRAMMAR	VOCABULARY	PRONUNCIATION
6				
58	**A** Extra information	passive (all tenses)	cinema	regular and irregular past participles
62	**B** In the picture	modals of deduction: *might*, *can't*, *must*	the body	diphthongs
7				
68	**A** Term time	first conditional and future time clauses + *when*, *until*, etc.	education	the letter *u*
72	**B** House or home?	second conditional, choosing between conditionals	houses	sentence stress, the letter *c*
8				
78	**A** The right job for you	choosing between gerunds and infinitives	work	word stress
82	**B** Service with a smile?	reported speech: sentences and questions	making nouns from verbs	the letters *ai* and *air*
9				
88	**A** I was so lucky!	third conditional	making adjectives and adverbs	sentence rhythm, weak pronunciation of *have*
92	**B** Power cut	quantifiers	electronic devices	linking, *ough* and *augh*
10				
98	**A** Idols and icons	relative clauses: defining and non-defining	compound nouns	word stress
102	**B** And the murderer is…	question tags	crime	intonation in question tags

| 108 | **Communication** | 125 | **Writing Bank** | 135 | **Listening** | 150 | **Grammar Bank** |

READING & LISTENING	**SPEAKING & WRITING**	
		Revise and Check p.66
Reading identifying positive and negative connotation **Listening** focusing on content words for note-taking	**Speaking** talking about cinema **Writing** a film review	Revise and Check 5&6
Reading interpreting visual information **Listening** checking assumptions; understanding advice	**Speaking** talking about profile photos	
		Practical English p.76
Reading understanding points of view **Listening** checking predictions	**Speaking** talking about your education; organizing and presenting your opinions	**Pictures of you** Episode 4: *Together again?* **Practical English** making suggestions **Social English**
Reading understanding pros and cons; understanding biographical information **Listening** using visual information to understand biographical information	**Speaking** discussing pros and cons of living at home; talking about future possibility and imaginary situations (first and second conditionals); describing a dream home **Writing** describing a house or flat	
		Revise and Check p.86
Reading predicting from evidence **Listening** listening for note-taking	**Speaking** asking about somebody's job; explaining what happened; presenting a product **Writing** a covering email	Revise and Check 7&8
Reading understanding the main point in a short text; predicting the end of a story **Listening** understanding the order of events; understanding how to do something better	**Speaking** sharing personal experience; role-playing complaining	
		Practical English p.96
Reading identifying topic sentences **Listening** listening for retelling	**Speaking** talking about luck	**Pictures of you** Episode 5: *Ben's big show* **Practical English** asking indirect questions **Social English**
Reading understanding technical language **Listening** listening for note-taking	**Speaking** talking about power cuts; discussing digital habits **Writing** a 'for and against' essay	
		Revise and Check p.106
Reading understanding biographical facts **Listening** understanding biographical facts; listening for note-taking	**Speaking** asking questions using relative clauses; talking about things, people, and places you like or admire **Writing** a biography	Revise and Check 9&10
Reading reading for detail; understanding characters, places, and events in a short story **Listening** understanding evidence and opinion; making biographical notes	**Speaking** checking information (question tags)	

167 **Vocabulary Bank**   173 **Irregular verbs**   174 **Sound Bank**

Welcome to English File *fifth edition*

Student Book and Workbook

The **Student Book** contains all the language and skills you need to improve your English, with Grammar, Vocabulary, Pronunciation, and skills work in every File.

The **Workbook** contains Grammar, Vocabulary, and Pronunciation practice for every lesson.

Also available as an e-Book.

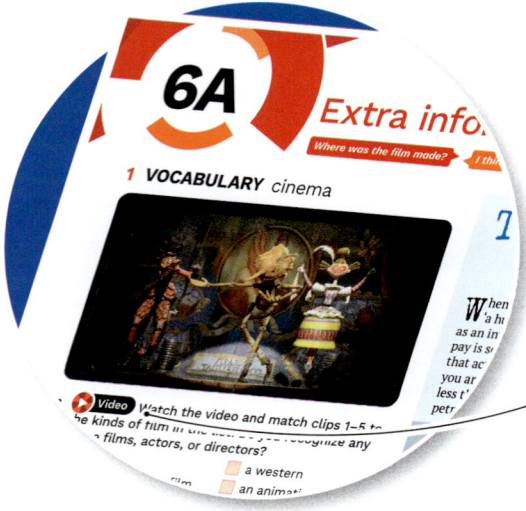

Bring language learning to life with new videos integrated into the lessons.

Look out for the ▶ Video icons in every File.

NEW EXAM CONFIDENCE

Develop your confidence in English with access to bite-size Reading, Listening, Speaking, and Writing practice that complements the course. Easily accessible from your mobile device, to use in your own time, at your own pace.

Access EXAM CONFIDENCE on Oxford English Hub.

 **NEW** Video-enhanced lessons

Grammar, Vocabulary, and Pronunciation

Complete the sentences using reported speech.
▶ Grammar practice

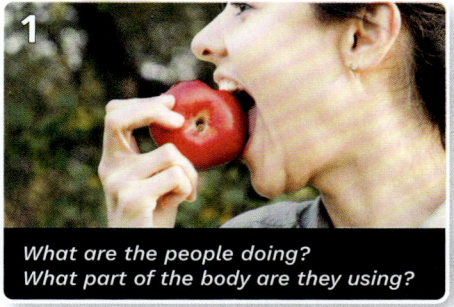
What are the people doing? What part of the body are they using?
▶ Vocabulary practice

Repeat the sounds and words.
▶ Pronunciation

Skills development

A product presentation
▶ Dramas

Handel Hendrix House
▶ Documentaries

Beata — *What rooms do the people show you?*
▶ Vox pops

NEW *Pictures of you* Season ❸

A brand new video drama story for the Practical English section.

Set in London, **Pictures of you** follows the story of Izzy and Ben and how their lives, careers, and relationships develop.

Oxford English Hub

Access all video and audio resources, and **EXAM CONFIDENCE** on Oxford English Hub.

Use the code in this book to get 2 years' access.

6A Extra information

G passive (all tenses)
V cinema
P regular and irregular past participles

Where was the film made? | I think it was shot in New York.

1 VOCABULARY cinema

a **Video** Watch the video and match clips 1–5 to the kinds of film in the list. Do you recognize any of the films, actors, or directors?
- ☐ a biopic
- ☐ a western
- ☐ a science fiction film
- ☐ an animation
- ☐ a musical

b **Vocabulary Bank** Cinema *p.167*

c With a partner, decide what the difference is between...
1 *a plot* and *a script*
2 *a musical* and *a soundtrack*
3 *the cast* and *the stars*
4 *a dubbed film* and *a film with subtitles*
5 *the set of a film* and *the film was set in...*
6 *a critic* and *a review*

2 READING

a You're going to read an article about being an extra for a film or on TV. In pairs, can you think of two positive and two negative things about being an extra?

b Read the article. Are your ideas there? Are the following things it mentions **P** (positive), **N** (negative), or **B** (both)?
1 the pay per day
2 the behaviour of the main actors
3 the weather
4 the food
5 waiting at mealtimes
6 having your hair cut
7 being on the screen
8 having a slightly bigger role

The secret life of an extra

When I first signed a contract to be an extra, or 'a human prop' as they are sometimes called, I saw it as an interesting way of earning a second income, but the pay is so bad that after a couple of jobs you soon realize that actually it's more like a hobby. On an average shoot, you are paid about £100 a day, but after tax you're left with less than half of that, not counting what you spend on petrol or train fares to get to each location.

You are not allowed to talk on set and you are not allowed to talk to any of the actors. In fact, the lead actors are not at all interested in you – they look down their noses or completely ignore you. Also, weather conditions tend to be either boiling hot or freezing cold. After spending an entire afternoon in March in the ruins of a castle, my hands were so cold I could hardly sign my name on the paperwork.

The best aspect of the work is the free catering: getting up at 4.00 a.m. isn't so bad when you can go straight in for coffee and a full English breakfast, and lunch almost always involves some sort of pudding with custard. Obviously, you aren't allowed to eat anything before the cast and then the crew, so you stand there while a long queue forms ahead of you.

For period dramas, you get the added benefit of a free haircut and shave, although this can be embarrassing if you've taken a day off sick from your day job and you go into the office the next day looking quite different. You also have the excitement of seeing yourself on screen even though you might not be recognizable to anybody except yourself. But that's your job – to just be part of the background.

There are times when you're chosen to play a bigger part in one scene, and suddenly you feel as if the difference between actor and extra isn't so huge after all. On the other

Adapted from The Guardian

c Read the article again. Choose a, b, or c.
 1 For a day's work as an extra you end up with _____ in your pocket.
   a about £100   b about £50   c less than £50
 2 The important actors _____ extras.
   a feel superior to
   b are curious about
   c are quite interested in
 3 The first people to get any food are _____.
   a camera operators   b extras   c actors
 4 If you have to have your hair cut for the film, _____.
   a you might get paid extra
   b you might have a problem at work
   c you might not recognize yourself on screen
 5 There are moments late at night when you realize that _____.
   a the actors work harder than you do
   b you deserve to be paid as much as the actors
   c the work is more enjoyable than you thought
 6 The writer would recommend working as an extra to _____.
   a someone who really wants to be an actor
   b someone who wants to earn a high salary
   c someone who just wants to be in a film

d Why do you think some people enjoy being extras? Would you like to be one? Why (not)?

hand, when you're finally allowed to go home at 2.00 a.m. after walking up and down 50 times wearing a heavy helmet on your head, and the actors still have hours more to go, the job doesn't seem quite so glamorous and you don't mind so much that they earn a lot more money than you.

Would I recommend becoming an extra? As a serious way of making money or getting into the industry, probably not. If, however, you like the idea of dressing up in a velvet suit on a hot summer's day and spending all afternoon in a room full of candles in order to be able to see yourself on the big screen for maybe three seconds and tell your family and friends how you've seen a famous actor up close eating vol-au-vents, then apply now.

3 GRAMMAR passive (all tenses)

a Read four fun facts about extras. What tense or form of the passive are the highlighted verbs?

- When a winter scene ¹is being filmed and actors are all in fur coats, it's usually 30 degrees, but the aircon has ²to be turned off because of the noise it makes.
- The last film to have large numbers of extras was *Gandhi*, when 300,000 extras ³were used in the funeral scene. Nowadays, big crowd screens are usually created digitally.
- Extras have to keep quiet. When a crowd scene ⁴was being filmed for the film *Jersey Girls*, the extras had to pretend to clap and cheer, but it was all done in silence.
- Phones ⁵aren't allowed on set and taking photos is strictly forbidden. An extra once posted photos of a set of a new film online. She ⁶has never been employed as an extra since then.

b **G** Grammar Bank 6A *p.150*

4 PRONUNCIATION regular and irregular past participles

a Look at the three groups of regular past participles. Match them to the sound pictures.

1   2   3 /ɪd/

☐ finished   released   based   looked
☐ recorded   directed   situated   acted
☐ filmed   used   dubbed   subtitled

b ▶ Video Watch and check. Then watch again and repeat the regular past participles.

c ▶ Video Watch the video and repeat the irregular past participles.

d How do you pronounce the past participles in the list? Is each pair the same or different? Write **S** or **D**. Then watch again and check.

paid–said ☐   grown–known ☐   done–gone ☐
bought–caught ☐   written–driven ☐

e ◉ 6.5 Listen and change the sentences into the present or past passive.

1 ◢ They shot the film in Poland. The film...
   The film was shot in Poland.

5 LISTENING

a Look at these film titles. What do they have in common?

*The Fabelmans   West Side Story   The BFG
Indiana Jones and the Kingdom of the Crystal Skull
Jurassic Park   Lincoln   ET   Jaws*

b Read about the film *Schindler's List*. Have you seen it? If yes, did you like it? If not, would you like to see it? What other Spielberg films have you seen and enjoyed?

> *Schindler's List* is a 1993 biopic directed by Steven Spielberg. The film is based on the true story of Oskar Schindler, a Czech businessman, who saved the lives of more than a thousand Polish-Jewish refugees during the Second World War. The film was shot in black and white. It stars Liam Neeson, Ralph Fiennes, and Ben Kingsley. It is often listed among the greatest films ever made, and it won seven Oscars, including Best Picture and Best Director.

c 🔊 6.6 Look at the photos of Dagmara Walkowicz and Spielberg. Where were they and what do you think Dagmara was doing in the black-and-white photo? Listen to Part 1 of an interview with Dagmara and check.

d Listen again and mark the sentences **T** (true) or **F** (false). Correct the **F** sentences.
1 When the film company came to Krakow, Dagmara was working as a teacher.
2 She got a job doing translations for them.
3 There was a party at the hotel to celebrate Spielberg's birthday.
4 Spielberg's interpreter was late.
5 Dagmara was very nervous, so she drank a bottle of champagne to give herself courage.
6 Spielberg was very pleased with the way she did her job.

> **Making notes**
> When we make notes, we only write down key words, e.g. we write *film set every day* **NOT** ~~She had to go to the film set every day~~.

e ◆ **6.7** Now listen to three extracts from Part 2 of the interview. Complete the gaps with the key words.

1 I had to go to the *film* _____ _____ _____ and _____ Spielberg's _____ to the Polish _____, and also to the _____.
2 It was _____ _____, and I often felt as if I was a _____ _____.
3 The _____ was when we had to _____ a _____ _____ and _____ because Spielberg thought it _____ exactly _____.

f ◆ **6.8** You're now going to listen to the whole of Part 2. Read the questions. Then listen and write down some of the key words.
1 How many times were some scenes repeated? How did that make Dagmara feel?
2 Why did Spielberg start shouting at her? What happened after that?
3 In general, how did Spielberg treat her? What example does she give?
4 What scenes was she going to appear in as an extra? Why did she not appear in the final version of the film?
5 Did she ever work with Spielberg again?
6 What offer did Spielberg make to Dagmara? Does she regret not accepting it?

g Compare your key words with a partner. Then listen again and try to add more.

h Now, with a partner, answer the questions in **f**. Use your key words.

i Would you like to have done Dagmara's job? Do you think she made the right decision in the end?

6 SPEAKING

a Read the cinema interview. Think about your answers and reasons.

1 Can you think of a film you've seen which…?
- was incredibly funny
- made you feel good
- had a very sad ending
- you've seen several times
- sent you to sleep
- had a memorable soundtrack

2 Do you prefer…?
- seeing films at home or in the cinema
- seeing a English-speaking films
          b other foreign films
          c films from your country
- seeing foreign films dubbed or with subtitles

3 Tell me about a really good film you've seen in the last year.
- What kind of film is it?
- Is it based on a book or on a real event?
- Where and when is it set?
- Who stars in it? Who is it directed by?
- Does it have a good plot?
- Does it have a good soundtrack?
- Why do you like it?

b In pairs, interview each other. Ask for and give as much information as you can. Do you have similar tastes?

7 WRITING a film review

Ⓦ **Writing Bank 6** *p.125* Write a description of a film you would recommend.

6B In the picture

G modals of deduction: *might, can't, must*
V the body
P diphthongs

> She can't be his mother. → She is his mother. She looks very young for her age.

1 READING & SPEAKING

a Do you have a profile photo or photos on social media? Why did you choose them? How often do you change them? Show any that you can to a partner.

b Look at six types of profile photo described by a life coach. Are any of these similar to one you use? What do you think it means if you choose them?

1 A photo of you with your partner means…

2 A photo of you with your friends means…

3 Posing with animals or children means…

4 Looking down in your photo means…

5 Looking up in your photo means…

6 Changing your photo very often means…

c Now read the article and match the types of photo in **b** to their meanings A–F.

What your profile picture says about YOU

A life coach with a background in psychology has suggested that your profile picture might be saying more things about you than you realize. Coach Francesca, who is originally from Romania and now lives in London, has posted a series of popular video tips on social media. She explains why the photo you choose can reveal a lot of different things about your personality.

A _____ you want people to know you're outgoing

Extroverts often choose a picture of themselves in a group because this is where they feel safest. 'Extroverts tend to have colourful pictures where they're surrounded by many people,' Francesca says. The photo is often of them and their group of friends doing something exciting, or attending an event such as a festival or concert.

B _____ you're insecure

People who have a new profile picture every week tend to be indecisive and don't trust people easily. 'Constantly changing their profile picture can symbolize that the person doesn't have a strong identity,' says Francesca. Another reason for changing your profile picture often could be because someone has hurt you. Francesca recommends changing your profile picture just a few times a year, or if there's a major change in your life.

C _____ you could be relying too heavily on them

Francesca suggests that a profile photo of you as half of a couple means you see your partner as part of your own identity. You could have what psychologists call an 'anxious attachment' style, which means you worry that your partner will not reciprocate your feelings for them. There could be a deep-seated fear that they might leave you.

D _____ you empathize with others

Francesca says that having pictures with kids or animals shows that you have the ability to understand other people's feelings or take care of other people. The life coach suggests that people who choose this kind of profile picture might be subconsciously trying to appeal to potential partners. This is supported by research from the University of Jaén in Spain, which has shown that men are seen as less intimidating on dating apps when holding a small dog than when pictured alone.

E _____ you have a big ego

Social media was once a place for people to connect and share updates about their lives. However, many people have now become addicted to social media and are desperate to get attention. Rather than genuinely wanting to connect with others, they are using it to boost their own ego. So watch out for people who are looking down in their profile photo. 'Pictures looking down transmit a message of superiority and dominance,' says Francesca.

F _____ you want to attract a partner

Finally, Francesca suggests that looking up in your photos is a behaviour designed to appeal to a potential partner. So be careful with this one. 'Pictures looking up transmit a message of inferiority and submissiveness,' she says.

Coach Francesca's social media followers were fascinated by her analysis of profile pictures and even asked for more. 'I want more info,' commented a user. Another user posted that after watching her videos, they were going to change their profile picture immediately!

Adapted from @francescapsychology

d Read the article again. Which type of profile photo does Francesca say shows that...
1 you're not very good at making decisions
2 you might be giving out a dangerous message
3 you're afraid that you love somebody more than they love you
4 you may not realize that you want a partner
5 are not comfortable being on your own
6 you mainly want other people to be interested in you

e Talk to a partner.
If your profile photo type is included, do you agree with the interpretation? If not, what is your interpretation of your photo?
Can you think of any friends or family members whose photos fit with the interpretations in the article?

2 GRAMMAR modals of deduction

a 🔊 6.9 Listen to two people talking about a photo. Complete the sentences.

A I love your profile picture. How old are you in the photo?
B I ¹_____ be about five or six. Definitely not more than that.
A Where are you?
B Do you know, I can't remember. It ²_____ be the south of France. My grandmother had a house near Montpellier, so we sometimes spent the summer there.
A It ³_____ be the south of France – not in summer. You're wearing boots and a sweater! And it doesn't look like a Mediterranean beach.
B No, you're right. It ⁴_____ be Scotland, then. We sometimes went there.

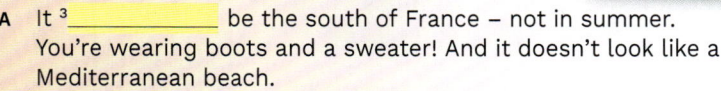

b Look at the highlighted modal verbs and answer the questions.
1 Which modal verbs mean *it's possible*? *might*, _____
2 Which modal verb means *it's very probable*? _____
3 Which modal verb means *it's impossible*? _____

c 🅖 **Grammar Bank** 6B *p.151*

d Look at the photos of four people. Make four deductions about each person, one with *must*, two with *might / could / may*, and one with *can't* + a phrase from the list. You can use the phrases more than once.
• **be** in his/her 20s / 40s / 50s / 80s
• **be** from Mexico / Asia / the UK
• **be** a millionaire / a space scientist / a model / a sports person / a professor
• **have** an Olympic medal / a fashion company / a grandchild / businesses in Africa / a doll named after him/her
• **be** good at skating / **present** a TV programme

He must be in his 20s.   *I think he could be in his 40s.*

e ▶ Video Watch and find out who the people are. Were your deductions correct? What else did you learn about them?

3 VOCABULARY the body

a Look at the photo. Can you name the parts of the body?

b 🅥 **Vocabulary Bank** The body *p.168*

c ▶ Video Watch the video. What are the people doing? What part of the body are they using?

4 PRONUNCIATION diphthongs

a Look at the five sound pictures of diphthongs. Say the sounds aloud. Why do you think the phonetic symbols have two parts?

1	2	3	4	5

b ▶ Video Watch and check.

c Write the words from the list in the correct columns.

bite eyes face hair mouth nose shoulders
smile stare taste throw toes

d 🔊 6.15 Listen and check. Then practise saying the phrases below.

f**ai**r h**ai**r   narr**ow** sh**ou**lders   a w**i**de m**ou**th
br**ow**n **eye**s   a R**o**man n**o**se   a r**ou**nd f**a**ce

5 READING & LISTENING

a Read the definition of *charisma*. Can you name any public figures who you think have charisma?

> **charisma** /kəˈrɪzmə/ *n.* the powerful personal quality that some people have which attracts and impresses other people

b Look at the photo of Colin Drury and Danish Sheikh. One is a journalist and one is a charisma coach. Who do you think is who? Why?

c Read the beginning of the article and check your answer to **b**. Then answer the questions.
1 What experience does Danish Sheikh have?
2 Is he successful?
3 What did he do yesterday? Why?
4 What problems does Colin Drury have?

d With a partner, tick (✓) any of the things in the list that you think people with charisma do.

People with charisma...
1 ☐ show other people what they are like
2 ☐ make other people feel important
3 ☐ talk a lot about themselves
4 ☐ never say anything about themselves
5 ☐ are self-confident
6 ☐ stand with their feet apart and arms wide
7 ☐ make eye contact, but don't stare
8 ☐ use a lot of hand gestures
9 ☐ speak very slowly
10 ☐ listen to people carefully

e 🔊 6.16 Listen to Colin talking about what he learns. Check your answers to **d**.

f Listen again. What does Colin say about...?
1 talking about yourself
2 remembering a past success
3 how to enter a room
4 what happens if you aren't really listening

g 🔊 6.17 At the end of the two days, Colin has a practical test. Listen and summarize.
1 In the pub, Colin has to...
2 Sheikh helps him by...
3 In the end, Colin thinks that charisma is about...

Colin Drury and Danish Sheikh

Can you learn how to be charismatic?

In the 21st century, *charisma* is the quality that people in all fields of life, from business to politics, would most like to have. But can you learn it? The man I have just met thinks so. His name is Danish Sheikh, and he is a charisma coach. He has worked with Microsoft, Yahoo, and the BBC, and he thinks he can turn anyone into George Clooney. He charges £150 an hour, and plenty of people are paying. And for two days, I'm going to be his student.

Yesterday, he followed me everywhere and watched how I behaved with people – in shops, in the hairdresser's, and in work meetings. His impressions of me are not good – for example, I can't make conversation, I have negative body language, and I don't smile enough. I also seem bored when I'm talking to people.

'But don't worry!' Sheikh says, cheerfully. 'We're going to fix all this.'

Adapted from The Guardian

h Look at these 'body' phrases from the listening. Can you demonstrate them?

| stand with your feet apart |
| have your chin up and your shoulders back |
| make eye contact   use hand gestures |
| cross your arms   shake hands   give a thumbs-up |

i Do you think it's possible to teach people to have charisma? Would you ever do a course like this? Why (not)?

6 LISTENING

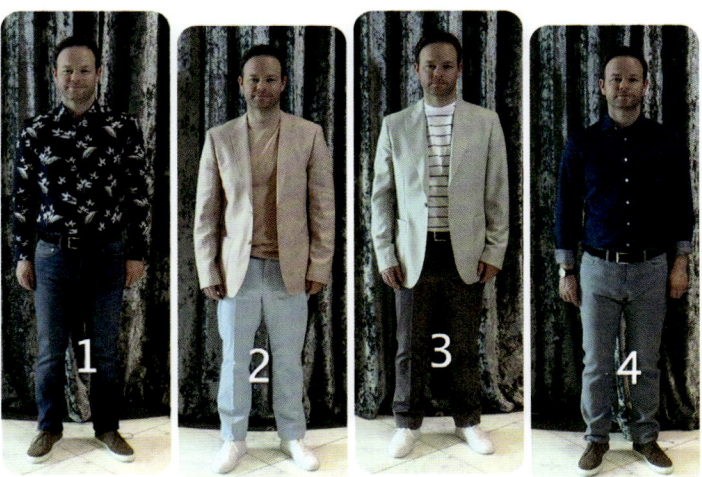

a Look at Sam wearing four different outfits. Which one do you think suits him best?

b ▶ Video Watch *A day with a personal stylist*. Which outfit does Sam like best? What did he think of the experience?

c Watch again. Tick (✓) three things in each group.

What Elin needs to find out about Sam
- what kind of lifestyle he has
- what kind of clothes he wore when he was younger
- where he usually shops for clothes
- what his partner thinks of his clothes
- how he feels about clothes in general

Things Elin thinks are important
- not buying cheap fashion that doesn't last
- checking what you already own before going shopping for clothes
- finding your own style
- having a pair of jeans that makes you feel good
- getting rid of clothes that you never wear

d Do you agree with Elin's tips? Why (not)?

5 & 6 Revise and Check

GRAMMAR

Circle a, b, or c.

1 Elliot served, but the ball ___ into the net.
 a went   b was going   c had gone
2 The athlete fell when she ___ towards the finishing line.
 a run   b was running   c had run
3 I didn't realize that you two ___ before.
 a didn't meet   b weren't meeting
 c hadn't met
4 **A** I can't find my glasses anywhere.
 B ___ them when you left home this morning?
 a Did you wear   b Were you wearing
 c Had you worn
5 ___ walk to work, or do you drive?
 a Do you use to   b Do you usually
 c Use you to
6 When I was a child, I ___ like vegetables.
 a don't used to   b didn't used to
 c didn't use to
7 ___ do any sport at university?
 a Did you use to   b Use you to
 c Did you used to
8 Lots of famous films ___ in San Francisco.
 a have shot   b have been shot
 c has been shot
9 He hates ___ about his private life.
 a asking   b being asking
 c being asked
10 Why ___ in New Zealand?
 a is the film being made
 b is the film making
 c is making the film
11 Some people believe that Shakespeare ___ all his plays.
 a didn't really write
 b wasn't really written
 c weren't really written
12 **A** I've just rung the doorbell, but there's no answer.
 B They ___ in the garden. Have a look.
 a can't be   b might be   c can be
13 I'm 29 and he's a bit older than me, so he ___ in his thirties now.
 a must be   b may be   c can't be
14 **A** Alina and Simon have broken up!
 B That ___ true! I saw them together just now.
 a mustn't be   b might be   c can't be
15 **A** Does your sister know Leo?
 B She ___ him. I'm not sure.
 a can't know   b may know
 c can know

VOCABULARY

a Write the parts of the body that you use to do these actions.
 1 smile _____   4 clap _____
 2 stare _____   5 bite _____
 3 smell _____

b Circle the correct word or phrase.
 1 Arsenal *won / beat* Chelsea 2–0.
 2 Can you book a tennis *course / court* on Friday?
 3 Sports players are very careful not to *get injured / get fit*.
 4 Real Madrid *scored / kicked* a goal just before half-time.
 5 I *do / go* swimming every morning during the week.

c Complete the words.
 1 Lucas is a very cl_____ friend. I've known him all my life.
 2 My wife and I have a lot in c_____.
 3 Gina and I lost t_____ after we both changed jobs.
 4 We g_____ to know each other very quickly.
 5 Louisa is getting married next month. Her f_____ is Italian.

d Write words beginning with *s* for the definitions.
 1 _____ the music of a film
 2 _____ the translation of the dialogue of a film on screen
 3 _____ _____ images often created by a computer
 4 _____ the most important actor in a film
 5 _____ a part of a film which happens in one place

e Complete the sentences with one word.
 1 I love working _____ at the gym. I go every evening.
 2 The player was sent _____ for insulting the referee.
 3 My sister and her boyfriend have broken _____.
 4 Did you know Amanda is going _____ with Erik's brother?
 5 The film is based _____ a famous novel.

PRONUNCIATION

a Practise the words and sounds.

Vowel sounds   **Consonant sounds**

b**ir**d   ph**o**ne   **e**gg   **ow**l   televi**s**ion   **z**ebra   **d**og   **t**ie

b 🅟 Sound Bank *p.174–5* Say more words for each sound.

c Which sound in **a** do the pink letters have in these words?
 1 book**ed**   3 eye**s**   5 w**or**ld
 2 cr**ow**d   4 sh**ou**lders

d Underline the stressed syllable.
 1 re|fe|ree   4 di|rec|tor
 2 re|view   5 co|lleague
 3 spec|ta|tors

Can you understand this text?

a Read the article once. What does the article say is the best exercise for all body types?

b Read the article again. Complete the gaps with A–G.
   A People with this body type have a wide choice of sports
   B For the same reason, it takes them longer to build muscle
   C They have broad shoulders and narrow hips, and their arms and legs are muscular
   D Everyone is a combination of types
   E If a person with this body type is very tall
   F It isn't easy for them to lose weight, but they quickly gain muscle
   G This body type is not typically agile or fast

Can you understand these people?

Philomena   Rachel   Aileen   Coleen   Miranda

▶ **Video** Watch and choose a, b, or c.

1 Philomena enjoys ___.
   a watching tennis   b doing gymnastics
   c watching diving

2 Rachel says that most people she knows who have been out with someone they met online ___.
   a are still with the other person
   b married the person they met
   c broke up with the person they met

3 Aileen kept a tissue with answers to the exam in ___.
   a her pocket   b the bathroom   c her backpack

4 Coleen ___.
   a prefers the *Lord of the Rings* films to the books
   b loves the books and the films
   c prefers the books to the films

5 Miranda chose a picture for her profile photo because ___.
   a she liked how she looked in it
   b it was taken in Las Vegas
   c it was taken on her wedding anniversary

Can you say this in English?

Tick (✓) the box if you can do these things.

Can you…?
1 ☐ tell an anecdote about something that happened to you using the past simple, past continuous, and past perfect
2 ☐ talk about three past and three present habits of yours
3 ☐ describe a film, saying where it was set, what it is based on, who it was directed by, and what you thought of it
4 ☐ make deductions about a photo on a friend's phone using *might be*, *must be*, and *can't be*

WHAT IS THE BEST SPORT FOR YOUR BODY TYPE?

You may have wanted to be a football superstar since you were a child, but this does not mean it is the best sport for you. Both your enjoyment of sport and whether you are actually good at it depends a lot on whether your choice of sport suits your body type. Here are some recommendations for the main body types:

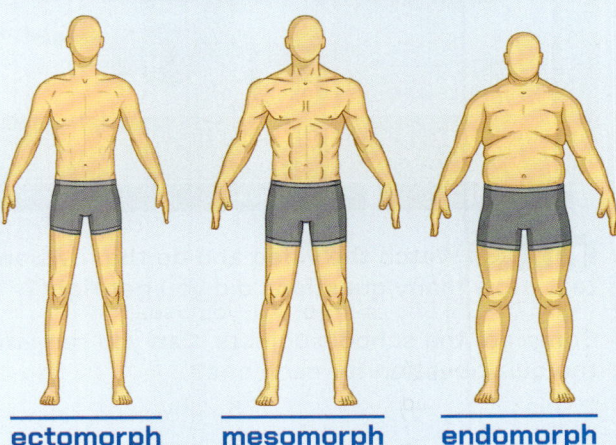

ectomorph   mesomorph   endomorph

Ectomorph body types are generally tall and slim with little body fat or muscle. Ectomorphs have narrow shoulders, chest, and hips, and thin arms and legs. They have difficulty putting on weight because of a fast metabolism. [1] ___. What suits ectomorphs is endurance sports. Running, swimming, and football are excellent choices for them. [2] ___, basketball is also a good sport for them.

A person with a **mesomorph** body type has the typical shape you imagine when you think of an athlete. [3] ___. Mesomorphs can naturally put on or lose weight and build muscle very easily. [4] ___, such as doing a triathlon (swimming, cycling, running), football, tennis, weightlifting, and other cardio activities.

Endomorphs generally have a higher percentage of body fat. [5] ___. They are often short, with a high waist, and well-developed upper arms and thighs. While an endomorph may not look very athletic, they can be very good at strength sports because of their larger mass. [6] ___, but sports like wrestling, discus-throwing, or weightlifting can work well.

It is important to note that in reality, no one is 100% endomorph or ectomorph. [7] ___. Other factors that affect athletic ability are diet and environment, and genetics also plays a key role. However, the most important thing is to choose a sport you enjoy, because the best exercise of all is the one that you will actually do!

Based on fitness websites

7A Term time

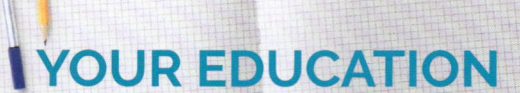

What will you do if you don't pass your exams? I'll probably retake them.

1 VOCABULARY education

a **Video** Watch the video and do the revision test. How many questions did you get right?

b Complete the school subjects. Can you remember the quiz question for each one?
1 his_____   5 phy_____
2 geo_____   6 liter_____
3 mat_____   7 bio_____
4 comp_____   8 chem_____

c  7.1 Listen and check. Under<u>line</u> the stressed syllable.

d **V Vocabulary Bank** Education *p.169*

2 PRONUNCIATION the letter u

> **The letter u**
> The letter *u* is usually pronounced /juː/, e.g. *uniform*,
> or /ʌ/, e.g. *lunch*, and sometimes /uː/, e.g. *blue*,
> or /ʊ/, e.g. *put*.

a Put the words from the list in the correct column.

f**u**ll l**u**nch m**u**sic p**u**pil p**u**t
res**u**lt r**u**de r**u**les st**u**dent
st**u**dy s**u**bject tr**u**e **u**niversity

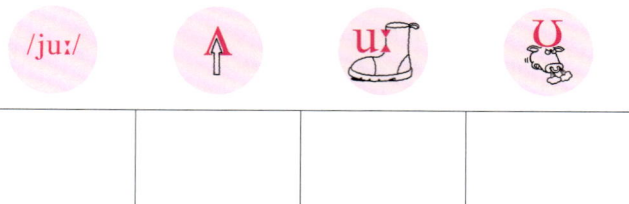

b 🔊 7.5 Listen and check. Practise saying the words.

c 🔊 7.6 Listen and write four questions or sentences.

3 SPEAKING

Interview a partner using the questionnaire. Ask for more information.

What kind of secondary school did (do) you go to?

YOUR EDUCATION

YOUR SCHOOL
- What kind of secondary school / you go to?
- / it a mixed school or single-sex?
- / you like it?
- How many students / there in each class?
  Do you think it / the right number?
- What time / your school day start and finish?

SUBJECTS AND HOMEWORK
- What subjects / you good and bad at?
- Which / your favourite subject?
- How often / you do PE or play sports?
- How much homework / you usually get? / you think it / too much?

RULES AND DISCIPLINE
- / you have to wear a uniform? / you like it? Why (not)?
- / your teachers too strict, or not strict enough? Why?
  What kind of punishments / they use?
- / pupils behave well, or / they misbehave?

G first conditional and future time clauses + *when*, *until*, etc.
V education
P the letter *u*

4 LISTENING

a Read the description of a BBC documentary *Back in time for school* and answer the questions.
1 Who is taking part in the programme?
2 What time period do the episodes cover?
3 What is the purpose of the documentary?
4 What do you think might be the most shocking things that the children discovered in the first programme?

Back in time for school

In a BBC documentary, 15 pupils and their teachers embark on an extraordinary time-travelling adventure. They travel through seven eras of British history; from a Victorian classroom in the 1890s through to the beginning of the digital revolution in the 1990s. Everything the students and teachers experience – from the lessons they learn, to the food they eat, technology, discipline, and playtime – is based on historical data and school records from the past. They discover just how much life at school has changed over the past 100 years.

Episode 1: 1890s–1910s
In this first programme, the pupils discover what it was like for the lucky 4% of children from ordinary families who went to school in this period, when education was still mainly for the rich. Lunch is fish pie with a rice pudding. Today's children aren't very enthusiastic, but Victorian schoolchildren would have been grateful for a meal like this. Rules are strict, and one of the pupils is punished by having his left hand tied to the desk. Children are separated into classes for girls and boys: the boys learn Latin, to prepare them for a profession, but the girls are taught how to be housewives. They learn to make beds, clean, and how to put up wallpaper. Towards the end of this period, people are afraid that a war is coming, so the boys are also taught how to fight.

b In which decade do you think these things first happened?

1920s–30s   1940s–50s   1960s   1970s   1980s   1990s

1 _____ Girls learn typewriting and boys learn bricklaying.
2 _____ The government gives all children a free bottle of milk.
3 _____ Female teachers have to leave if they get married.
4 _____ The internet is used in schools.
5 _____ Computers are used in schools.
6 _____ Boys and girls are taught together for all subjects.

c 🔊 7.7 Now listen to a description of the other episodes from the programme, and check your ideas in **b**.

> **Glossary**
> **the 11 plus** an exam that all children used to take when they were 11 to decide which type of secondary school they should go to
> **Grammar School** a secondary school for academic children who passed the 11 plus
> **Secondary Modern** a vocational school for less academic children who failed the 11 plus
> **Comprehensive School** a secondary school for children of all abilities

d Listen again and answer the questions.

1920s–30s
1 What is Esperanto? What do the teachers use to help them learn it?
2 What is cod liver oil and why do the children have to take it? What else do they do to improve their health?

1940s–50s
3 What was the 'revolution' in education?
4 In what way are girls and boys being taught differently?

1960s
5 What kind of school do the children try out?
6 What subjects do boys and girls still do separately? What subject do they do together?

1970s
7 What examples of new subjects are mentioned?
8 What fashions are the children not allowed to follow at school?

1980s
9 How are school meals different from before?
10 What two examples of PE are mentioned?

1990s
11 What kind of things do the children do in their free time at school?
12 Why will education never be the same again?

e What do you think education was like when your parents were at school? What was the same and what was different from now? What has changed in schools in your country in the 21st century?

69

5 GRAMMAR first conditional and future time clauses + *when*, *until*, etc.

a In pairs, answer the questions.
1 When was the last time you did an exam? Did you pass or fail?
2 What's the next exam you are going to do? How do you feel about it?
3 What do you usually do the night before an exam?
4 How do you usually feel just before you do an exam?
5 Have you ever failed an important exam you thought you had passed (or vice versa)?

b ▶Video Olivia is waiting for her A level results. A journalist interviews her at home. Watch Part 1. Then answer the questions.
1 What's the top grade you can get at A level?
2 Does Olivia think she's passed?
3 What does she want to do if she gets good results?
4 When and where will she get her exam results?
5 How will she celebrate if she gets good results?
6 What will she do if she doesn't get the results that she needs?

c ▶Video Watch Part 2. What grades did Olivia get? What's she going to do?

d ▶Video Can you remember what Olivia said? Try to complete the sentences. Then watch some extracts and check.
1 They won't give me a place **unless** _____ at least two A*s and an A.
2 **As soon as** _____ tomorrow, I'll go to school and pick them up.
3 I don't want to plan any celebrations **until** _____ the results.
4 **If** I don't get the grades I need, my parents _____ me.
5 **When** _____ a bit more positive, I'll decide what to do.

e ⓖ **Grammar Bank** 7A *p.152*

f Ask and answer with a partner. Make full sentences.
What will you do…?
- as soon as you get home
- if you don't do well in your next exam or test
- when this course finishes
- if it rains at the weekend

6 READING & SPEAKING

The UK student site

Is it really worth going to uni?

a In pairs, answer the questions that match your situation.

Are you at university now?
What are you studying? Are you enjoying it? Is there anything you don't like? What are you planning to do when you graduate?

Did you go to university?
Yes What did you study? Did you enjoy it? Was there anything you didn't enjoy?
No Are you happy you didn't go? What are you doing now?

Would you like to go to university?
Yes What would you like to study? Why? Do you think you'll enjoy it?
No Why not? What would you like to do instead?

b Look at the question on a UK student website. What do you think *Is it really worth…?* means?

c Now read the comments and mark them ✓ (= yes, it's worth it), ✗ (= no, it isn't worth it), or **S** (= it's sometimes worth it).

d Which of the comments do you think are true about university education in your country?

Comments

1 It depends what you want to do. Some degrees are worth it, like medicine or dentistry. But I think media studies, and things like that, are a waste of time.

2 Uni gives you the time and space to find out what you really want to do in life. And it has a lot of social benefits, like friends, clubs – that sort of thing.

3 There are so many better alternatives out there, in my opinion. I got a place at uni to do accountancy, but I chose to do an apprenticeship. All my friends are now at uni and in debt. I'm 20 and I'm earning money and learning on the job.

4 Since the Covid-19 pandemic, a lot more teaching at uni is online or recorded lectures. I don't think it's good value if you don't see your tutors face to face very often. You could just study from home. I don't think I would choose to go to uni now.

5 It still amazes me how everyone thinks that uni is the only solution to their future. Trust me, it isn't.

6 I'm a software engineer at a global tech company. A degree is preferred, but not essential. The recruitment team always say if they have two people, and one is self-taught and has experience, and the other has just finished uni with no experience, they'll choose the first. But often they ask for a degree AND experience.

e Look at the photos of Archie, who went to university, and Emily-Fleur, who didn't. Do you think either of them regrets their choice?

Archie Hooper, 23, studied drama in London.

Emily-Fleur Sizmur didn't go to university and runs her own business.

f **Communication** University or not? **A** *p.110* **B** *p.115* Ask and answer about Archie and Emily-Fleur.

g In your opinion, who made a better decision about university, Emily-Fleur or Archie? Why?

7 SPEAKING

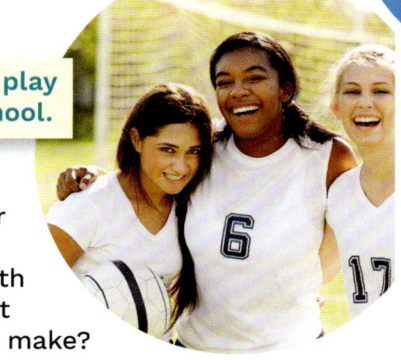

All children should play a team sport at school.

a 🔊 **7.10** Listen to someone giving their opinion. Does she agree or disagree with the statement? What four points does she make?

b 🔊 **7.11** Listen to some extracts from **a**. Complete the gaps in the information box.

> **Organizing and presenting your opinions**
>
> The ¹_____ I've chosen is...
>
> I { ²_____ agree / partly agree / disagree } for the following reasons:
>
> ³_____ of all, I think that...
>
> My second ⁴_____ is that...
>
> ⁵_____ important point is that...
>
> ⁶_____,...

c In small groups, each choose a different statement from the list. Decide if you agree or disagree. Write down at least three reasons and put them in order, from most to least important.

School
- School doesn't prepare students for life. They should be taught practical things, like childcare, and how to cook healthy food.
- Physical education should be optional.
- Primary pupils shouldn't get any homework, and secondary students not more than one hour a night during the week.
- Schools should spend most of the time on maths, science, and computing, and less on arts subjects like history and literature.

University
- University courses are too long. They should be a maximum of two years.
- University students shouldn't be allowed to have jobs during term-time.
- Students should choose to study a subject they love, not necessarily one that will get them a good job.
- University students should live independently, not with their parents.

d Explain to the rest of your group what you think about your statement. The others in the group should listen. At the end, they can vote for whether they agree or disagree with you, and say why.

7B House or home?

I like living with my parents.   *I don't. If I could afford it, I'd move out.*

G second conditional, choosing between conditionals
V houses
P sentence stress, the letter c

1 READING & SPEAKING

a With a partner, look at the photos and answer the questions.
1 Where do you think these young people are living? Which do you think is the most comfortable place to live? Why?
2 Which place would you prefer to live in? Why?
3 Where do you live? How comfortable is it? Who do you live with? Do you get on well? Do you argue about anything? What?

b Look at the title of the article. With a partner, think of one advantage and one disadvantage of living with your parents when you're an adult.

c Read the article. Were your ideas in the list?

Things you know if you still live with your parents

In the UK, 28% of adults aged 20–34 are living at home with their parents. This has gone up by 15% in the last ten years. Many have left home and then moved back again because of high living costs. So, what are the pros and cons?

The downside

- It doesn't [1]_____ how old you are, you'll always be a child to them. They'll tell you to put a coat on every time you leave the house.
- It's really [2]_____ when you meet new people to admit you're still sleeping in your childhood bedroom.
- You have to [3]_____ them know all your movements and text them to say you're going to be home late.
- 99% of the time after a night out, your parents will be [4]_____ , waiting for you – even if it's 4.00 a.m. Every day of your life, you [5]_____ ,'You treat this house like a hotel.'
- You become the household IT technician. If anything goes [6]_____ in the house to do with phones, broadband, or TV, you're called to the rescue.

But on the other hand...

- At weekends, you wake up with the smell of bacon and eggs.
- The fridge and cupboards always have something in them, and generally a lot better than you could [7]_____ .
- There's nothing better than home-cooked food, and you've [8]_____ that you'll never be able to cook as well as your parents.
- You've also realized that at home, there's a magical laundry powder that [9]_____ all the stains from your washing and makes it super clean.
- You had no idea how much [10]_____ cost. In fact, you didn't even know until recently that you had to pay for water!

So, despite how much you complain about still living with your parents, you know perfectly well that they've allowed you to save money, you have somewhere (nice) to live for far less than the cost of renting elsewhere, and they fill your stomach with good food. And for that, you're eternally grateful.

Adapted from Metro

72

d Read the article again and choose the correct word to complete the gaps.
1 matter / mind
2 embarrassing / embarrassed
3 leave / let
4 wake / awake
5 hear / listen
6 bad / wrong
7 afford / pay
8 realized / known
9 removes / retires
10 notes / bills

e Cover the text and, in pairs, try to remember all the pros and cons of living with your parents.

f Talk to a partner.
- What percentage of young people aged 20–34 do you think live with their parents in your country?
- Are the pros and cons similar in your country?
- Which two advantages and two disadvantages do you think are the most important?
- How do you think parents feel about having their adult children living at home?

2 GRAMMAR second conditional, choosing between conditionals

a Read some comments posted in response to the article in **1**. Do they want to leave their parents' home? Why (not)?

> **Vivienne@Montreal, Canada**
> I know there's a good side, but all I want is somewhere that's my own, where I can do what I want, where I can have my own furniture and pictures, where no one can tell me what to do. If I had the money, I'd move out immediately.

> **Marco@Naples, Italy**
> I'm perfectly happy living with my parents. If I lived on my own, I'd have to pay rent and do the housework and the cooking. Here, somebody else cooks and cleans, I have a nice room… Why would I want to leave? Even if I could afford it, I wouldn't move out. Not until I get married…

> **Andrea@Melbourne, Australia**
> It isn't that my parents aren't good to me – they are. If they weren't, I wouldn't live with them. But I'm 29 and I just don't feel independent.

> **Carlos@Valencia, Spain**
> I'd love to move out. I get on well with my parents, but I think I'd get on with them even better if I didn't live at home. My mum drives me mad – it isn't her fault, but she does. And I'd really like to have a dog, but my mum is allergic to them.

b Now answer the questions with a partner.
1 In the highlighted phrases, what tense is the verb after *if*?
2 What form is the other verb?
3 Do the phrases refer to a) a situation that will probably happen soon, or b) a situation they are imagining?

c **G** **Grammar Bank** 7B *p.153*

d **C** **Communication** Guess the sentence **A** *p.110* **B** *p.115* Practise first and second conditionals.

3 PRONUNCIATION & SPEAKING
sentence stress

a 🔊 **7.13** Listen and repeat the sentences. Copy the rhythm.
1 If I **lived** on my **own**, I'd **have** to **pay rent**.
2 If we **get** a **mortgage**, we'll **buy** the **house**.
3 Would you **leave home** if you **got** a **job**?
4 I **won't move out** if I **can't afford** it.
5 If it were **my flat**, I'd be **happy** to **do** the **cleaning**.

b Choose six sentence beginnings and complete them so they are true for you.

If I…
- could live anywhere in my town or city, I'd…
- have some free time this weekend, I'll…
- won a 'dream holiday' in a competition, I…
- could choose any car I liked, I…
- get a new phone this year, I…
- could choose my ideal job, I…
- don't have time to do the homework tonight, I…
- was asked to work abroad for a year, I…
- couldn't use the internet for a week, I…
- feel like going out tonight, I…

c Work with a partner. **A** say your first sentence. Try to get the correct rhythm. **B** ask for more information. Then **B** say your first sentence.

> *If I could live anywhere in my city, I'd live in the old part.*

> *Why the old part?*

73

4 VOCABULARY houses

a ▶ Video Watch the video. What rooms did Andrea, Beata, and Anna show you? Try to remember four things in each room.

b V Vocabulary Bank Houses *p.170*

c With a partner, decide what the difference is between…
1 *the outskirts* and *a suburb*
2 *a village* and *a town*
3 *a roof* and *a ceiling*
4 *a balcony* and *a terrace*
5 *a chimney* and *a fireplace*
6 *the ground floor* and *the first floor*
7 *wood* and *wooden*

5 PRONUNCIATION the letter c

a Practise saying the words in groups 1–5.
1 **c**arpet **c**astle lo**c**ation **c**osy **c**ountry bal**c**ony **c**ooker **c**upboard **c**ushion **c**urtains
2 **c**ity **c**inema de**c**ide **c**entre entran**ce** **c**eiling terra**ce** **cy**cle agen**cy** **i**cy
3 spa**c**ious spe**c**ial musi**c**ian
4 o**cca**sion a**cco**mmodation a**ccu**se
5 a**cce**nt su**cce**ss a**cci**dent

b Complete the pronunciation rules with /s/, /ʃ/, /k/, or /ks/.
1 c before *a*, *o*, or *u* is pronounced _____.
2 c before *i*, *e*, or *y* is pronounced _____.
3 *ci* before a vowel is pronounced _____.
4 *cc* before *a*, *o*, or *u* is pronounced _____.
5 *cc* before *e* or *i* is pronounced _____.

c 🔊 7.17 Now listen to the words in **a** and check your answers to **b**.

6 READING & LISTENING

a Read about the two people in the photos. Did you know any of this information? Have you ever heard any of their music?

George Frideric Handel (1685–1759) was a German-British composer, well known for his operas, oratorios and anthems. His famous oratorio 'Messiah', and orchestral pieces 'Water Music' and 'Music for the Royal Fireworks' are still immensely popular, and his coronation anthem 'Zadok the Priest' has been performed at every British Coronation since 1727.

Fun fact Handel had a terrible temper – he once threatened to throw an opera singer out of the window!

James (Jimi) Hendrix (1942–1970) was an American guitarist, singer, and songwriter. He is widely regarded as one of the most influential electric guitarists in the history of popular music, and one of the most celebrated musicians of the 20th century. Hendrix had three UK top ten hits ('Hey Joe', 'Purple Haze', and 'The Wind Cries Mary'), and in 1968 his album Electric Ladyland reached number one in the US.

Fun fact Some people believe that there are so many green parakeets in London because Hendrix released two in Carnaby Street in the 1960s.

b Look at some information about a London museum. What is surprising about 23–25 Brook Street?

Handel Hendrix House

Buy your tickets now

Two successful and innovative musicians left their countries and came to live in London, the city where music was happening. One came in the early 18th century, when London was the centre for opera, and one came in the swinging 1960s, when the Beatles and the Rolling Stones were revolutionizing pop music. Where did they choose to live? In the same building, 23–25 Brook Street…

Handel House
The history of Handel's house
Read more >

Hendrix Flat
Find out more about Hendrix's flat
Read more >

c ▶ **Video** Look at photos 1–8 from the Handel Hendrix House. Whose house do you think they are in, Handel's (**GFH**) or Hendrix's (**JH**)? Watch *Handel Hendrix House* and check.

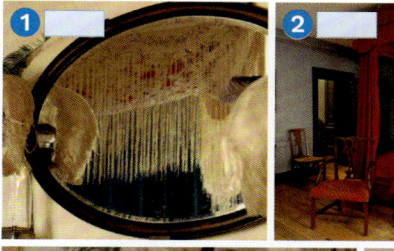

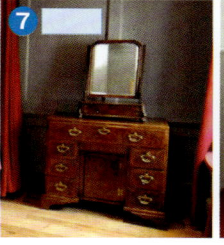

d Now look at some facts from the video. Can you remember who each extract is about?

1. ____ However, after becoming a British citizen five years later, he decided to continue renting the house.
2. ____ He moved in briefly in July, before returning to the United States for an extensive tour.
3. ____ There was a basement containing the kitchens, and on the ground floor, there was a room at the front for receiving visitors.
4. ____ The second floor contained the bedroom at the front, with a dressing room at the back where he kept his clothes.
5. ____ In the largest room, he kept his instruments (a harpsichord and a little house organ), and he occasionally rehearsed there.
6. ____ He bought curtains and cushions from the nearby John Lewis department store, as well as ornaments from Portobello Road market and elsewhere.
7. ____ In January the following year, he gave a series of press and media interviews and photo shoots in the flat.
8. ____ Over the years, his flat was used as an office, until it was taken over in 2000 by the Handel House Trust.
9. ____ He was buried in Westminster Abbey, and more than 3,000 people attended his funeral.
10. ____ He died in London at the age of 27, but in a hotel, not in the Brook Street flat.

e Match the words and phrases in the list to definitions 1–5.

move in   move to   owner   settle   upper

1. _____ *n* the person to whom sth belongs
2. _____ *v* start living in a place
3. _____ *v* make a place your permanent home
4. _____ *adj* located above sth, e.g. the ~ floor
5. _____ *v* change where you live from one place to another

f Have you ever visited a house where a famous person lived? Where was it? What was it like?

7 SPEAKING & WRITING
describing a house or flat

a Think for a few minutes about what your dream home would be like and make brief notes. Use **Vocabulary Bank Houses** *p.170* to help you.

- Where would it be?
- What kind of house or flat would it be?
- How many rooms would it have?
- What special features would it have?
- What would the decoration be like?

b In groups, describe your dream homes. Give as much detail as possible. Whose do you like best?

c Ⓦ **Writing Bank 7** *p.126* Write a description of your house or flat.

75

EPISODE 4 PICTURES OF YOU

Together again?

Practical English | making suggestions

1 TALKING IN THE PARK

a **Video** Watch *Talking in the park*. What kind of conversation do Ben and Izzy have?
   a uncomfortable and tense
   b polite and friendly
   c relaxed and friendly

b Watch again. Then choose the correct answer.
   1 Ben finished his course last *week / month*.
   2 Ben's tutor Andre *has / hasn't* helped him with his show.
   3 Izzy *is / isn't* surprised about Andre.
   4 Ben thinks Andre was a *good / bad* teacher.
   5 Ben *has / hasn't* forgotten who Max is.
   6 Izzy *has / hasn't* changed her mind about Max.
   7 Izzy *tells / doesn't tell* Ben why she wanted to talk.

2 MAKING SUGGESTIONS

a **Video** Watch *Making suggestions*. Then number the places 1–5 in the order they talk about them. Where do they decide to go in the end? Why?
   ☐ The Red Lion   ☐ Les Amis
   ☐ Pomodora   ☐ The Nag's Head
   ☐ a coffee shop

b **Video** Look at some extracts from the conversation. Try to remember the missing words. Then watch and check.

| Izzy | Where ¹_____ we go for that drink? |
| Ben | Well, there's a really nice coffee shop up the road. We ²_____ go there. |

| Ben | Why ³_____ we go to a pub? |
| Izzy | ⁴_____ idea. ⁵_____ about The Nag's Head? |

| Ben | Or ⁶_____ about The Red Lion? |
| Izzy | It's always too busy in there. |

| Ben | What about ⁷_____ to Les Amis? |
| Izzy | That's a great ⁸_____. |

| Izzy | So ⁹_____ we go there? |
| Ben | ¹⁰_____ not? |

c **Video** Watch and repeat the highlighted phrases and sentences in **b**. Copy the rhythm and intonation.

76

> **Verb forms: infinitive or gerund?**
>
> Remember to use the infinitive (without *to*) after *Shall we...?*, *We could...*, *Let's...*, and *Why don't we...?*, e.g. *Shall we go there? Why don't we go to a pub?*
>
> Remember to use the gerund (*-ing*) after *What about...?* and *How about...?*, e.g. *What about going to Les Amis?*
>
> You can also use a noun after *What / How about...?*, e.g. *How about The Red Lion?*

d Practise the extracts in **b** with a partner. Then change roles.

e Work in small groups. Make suggestions and try to agree on...
- somewhere to have a drink after class.
- a film to see on Saturday night.
- how to celebrate the end of term.

3 A GREAT OPPORTUNITY

a ▶ Video Look at the photos and answer the questions. Then watch *A great opportunity* and check your answers.
1 What do you think Ben and Izzy are talking about?
2 What do you think Carla's just seen?

b Watch again. Then answer the questions.
1 What happened when Max went jogging with Izzy and Ben?
2 What does Izzy say about Ben's photos?
3 What business advice does Izzy give Ben?
4 How does Carla feel at the end of the scene? Why?

4 SOCIAL ENGLISH

a Match a phrase from **A** to a response in **B**.

A	B
1 I finished my course last month. And I passed my exams.	How could I forget?
2 So, what did you want to talk to me about?	I'll tell you over a drink.
3 Do you remember when Max came jogging with us in the park?	Well done!
4 I wanted to ask you something about work.	Yes, it has. I'm looking forward to working with you.
5 Well, it's been really nice seeing you again.	Sure, go ahead.

b ▶ Video Watch and check.

c Practise the phrases and responses in pairs. Then change roles.

> **WHAT DO YOU THINK?**
>
> In pairs, talk about Carla. Does she think Izzy is interested in Ben again? Does she think Ben is interested in Izzy? What would you do now if you were Carla? What do you think is going to happen in the last episode?

8A The right job for you

G choosing between gerunds and infinitives
V work
P word stress

What would you like to do after university? ▸ I'd like to be an accountant. I enjoy working with numbers.

1 VOCABULARY work

a Look at the picture of Clare at work. With a partner, make guesses about her job.
  1 What do you think Clare does?
  2 Who do you think the woman in the black suit is?
  3 Do you think Clare likes her job?

b ▶ Video Watch the video and check your answers to **a**. Then number sentences A–I in the correct order (1–9). Watch again and check.
  A ☐ She decided to **set up** an online business selling cupcakes.
  B ☐ Clare **worked for** a marketing company.
  C ☐ She was **unemployed** and had to **look for a job**.
  D ☐ One day, they had an argument and Clare **resigned**.
  E ☐ Her business is **doing very well**. Clare is a success!
  F ☐ She **applied for** a lot of jobs and sent in CVs.
  G ☐ She had a **good salary**, but she didn't like **her boss**.
  H ☐ She had some interviews, but she didn't **get the jobs**.
  I ☐ She had to work very long hours and **do overtime**.

c Watch the video again without the sound. Say the sentences for each picture.

d V **Vocabulary Bank** Work *p.171*

Words with different meanings
Sometimes the same word can have two completely different meanings, e.g.
She has a **degree** in economics.
(= a university qualification)
It was only four **degrees** this morning.
(= temperature)

e With a partner, explain the difference in meaning between the pairs of sentences.
  1 a He's **running** a business.
     b He's **running** a marathon.
  2 a Marion **was fired** last week.
     b When the man **fired** the gun, everyone screamed.
  3 a I **work** in a shop.
     b My laptop **doesn't work**.
  4 a There's a **market** for this product.
     b There's a **market** where you can buy vegetables.
  5 a Steve has set up a **company**.
     b Steve is very good **company**.

2 PRONUNCIATION & SPEAKING word stress

a Under<u>line</u> the stressed syllable in each word. Use the phonetics to help you.
  1 a|pply /əˈplaɪ/
  2 sa|la|ry /ˈsæləri/
  3 re|dun|dant /rɪˈdʌndənt/
  4 ex|pe|ri|ence /ɪkˈspɪəriəns/
  5 o|ver|time /ˈəʊvətaɪm/
  6 per|ma|nent /ˈpɜːmənənt/
  7 qua|li|fi|ca|tions /ˌkwɒlɪfɪˈkeɪʃnz/
  8 re|sign /rɪˈzaɪn/
  9 re|spon|si|ble /rɪˈspɒnsəbl/
  10 tem|po|ra|ry /ˈtemprəri/

b 🔊 8.4 Listen and check. Practise saying the words.

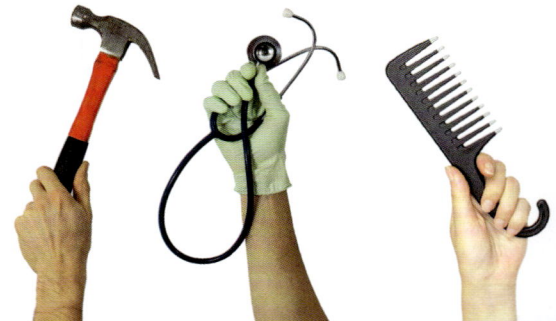

c Think of someone you know who has a job. Prepare answers to the questions below.
- What does he / she do?
- What qualifications does he / she have?
- Is his / her job...?
  – full time or part time
  – temporary or permanent
- Where does he / she work (in an office, at home, etc.)?
- What hours does he / she work?
- Does he / she have to do overtime?
- Does he / she get a good salary?
- Does he / she like the job? Why (not)?
- Would you like to do his / her job? Why (not)?

d Work in pairs. **A** interview **B** about his or her person's job. Ask more questions if you can. Then swap.

I'm going to tell you about my cousin. Her name's Corinne.

What does she do?

3 GRAMMAR
choosing between gerunds and infinitives

a Complete the questionnaire by putting the verbs in the correct form: the gerund (e.g. *working*) or *to* + infinitive (e.g. *to work*).

Match your personality to the job

1	I'd like <u>to work</u> as part of a team.	work
2	I enjoy _____ people with their problems.	help
3	I don't mind _____ a very large salary.	not earn
4	I'm good at _____ to people.	listen
5	I'm good at _____ quick decisions.	make
6	_____ risks doesn't worry me.	take
7	I'm happy _____ by myself.	work
8	I'm not afraid of _____ large amounts of money.	manage
9	I'm good at _____ myself.	express
10	I always try _____ my instincts.	follow
11	It's important for me _____ creative.	be
12	I enjoy _____.	improvise
13	_____ complex calculations is not difficult for me.	do
14	I enjoy _____ logical problems.	solve
15	I find it easy _____ theoretical principles.	understand
16	I am able _____ space and distance.	calculate

b Read the questionnaire and tick (✓) **ONLY** the sentences that you strongly agree with. Discuss your answers with a partner.

c **Communication** Match your personality to the job *p.118* Find out the results. Do you agree?

d Look at the sentences in the questionnaire. Complete the rules with the gerund or *to* + infinitive.
1 After some verbs, e.g. *enjoy* and *don't mind*, use _____.
2 After some verbs, e.g. *would like*, use _____.
3 After adjectives, use _____.
4 After prepositions, use _____.
5 As the subject of a phrase or sentence, use _____.

e **Grammar Bank** 8A *p.154*

f Write something for **FIVE** of the things in the circles.

- something you're **planning to do** in the summer
- a country you'**d like to visit** in the future
- somebody you **wouldn't like to go** on holiday with
- a job you'**d love to do**
- a job you **hate doing** in the house
- somebody you find very **easy to talk to**
- something you're **afraid of doing**
- a sport, activity, or hobby you **love doing**
- something you **enjoy doing** on Sunday mornings
- something you **must do** or **buy** urgently

g Work in groups. Tell the others about what you have written and answer any questions they have.

I'd love to be an architect.   *Why?*

Because I think it would be great to...

4 WRITING a covering email

Writing Bank 8 *p.128* Write an email to send with your CV to apply for a job.

5 READING & SPEAKING

a Read the first part of an article about the TV programme *Dragons' Den*. Answer the questions.
1. Who are the 'Dragons'?
2. Where do the contestants meet them?
3. How does the programme work?
4. Is there a similar TV programme in your country?

b Look at the photos and read about three products that were presented on the show. Answer the questions and say why.
Which product do you think…?
1. the Dragons invested in and has been successful
2. the Dragons didn't invest in and has been a failure
3. the Dragons didn't invest in, but has been very successful

In the Dragons' Den

From left to right: Steven Bartlett, Peter Jones, Deborah Meaden, Touker Suleyman, Sara Davies

Dragons' Den is a UK TV series which has been on TV every year since the original show in 2005, with similar versions in many different countries. In the UK programme, contestants present their ideas for a product or service to five very successful business people. These people are nicknamed 'the Dragons', and the intimidating room where they meet the contestants is called 'the Den'. The Dragons, who are multi-millionaires, are prepared to invest money in any business that they believe might be a success. In return, they take a share in the profits. The contestants are usually entrepreneurs, product designers, or people with a new idea for a product or a service. They have three minutes to make their pitch, then the Dragons ask them questions about it and its possible market. Finally, the Dragons say if they are prepared to invest or not. If they are not convinced by the presentation, they say the dreaded words, 'I'm out'. So far, the highest amount the Dragons have ever offered on the programme is £250,000, and the highest percentage of a business contestants have given away is 79%.

Glossary
den the hidden home of some types of wild animal
entrepreneur a person who makes money by starting or running businesses
make a pitch present something you're trying to sell

Oppo ice cream

Brothers Charlie and Harry Thuillier came up with the idea of a low-calorie ice cream when they were travelling in Brazil. Charlie worked on over 1,000 recipes before coming up with a product they thought worked – an ice cream that tasted delicious, but had fewer calories than an apple. They asked the Dragons for £60,000 in exchange for a 7% share of the business.

Wonderbly

A group of four dads from East London, Asi, Tal, David, and Pedro, asked the Dragons for £100,000 in exchange for 4% of their company. Their product was a personalized book where the child's name appears as the main character in the story. It is called *The Little Boy / Girl Who Lost His / Her Name*, and tells of a child who has lost their name and goes on an adventure to find it.

Eggxactly

James Seddon, an entrepreneur and egg enthusiast, asked the Dragons for £75,000 investment in his new invention, an egg cooker which can boil an egg quickly and easily without using water. He used to find it hard to make the perfect boiled egg for his daughter. His machine uses a microprocessor to calculate the exact time the eggs need to be cooked 'eggxactly' as you like them.

c **Communication** Dragons' Den **A** *p.111* **B** *p.116* **C** *p.118*
Work in groups of three. Find out what happened.

d Which (if any) of the three products would you be interested / definitely not interested in buying? Why? Do you think they are, or could be, successful in your country? Why (not)?

6 LISTENING

a Look at the photo of two more *Dragons' Den* contestants and their product. Do you think they were successful?

Jake and Joe asked for £60,000 in exchange for 20% of their online photo-framing business Frame Again.

b 🔊 8.8 Listen to Part 1 of an interview with Joe about his experience. Mark the sentences **T** (true) or **F** (false).
1 Joe and Jake applied to be on *Dragons' Den* together.
2 They prepared their pitch very quickly.
3 The show was filmed in Manchester.
4 They didn't do any preparation the night before.
5 They only slept for a few hours the night before the programme.
6 They were the third contestants on that programme.
7 Other contestants waited for up to 12 hours for their turn.
8 They met one of the Dragons while they were waiting to go on.

c Listen again. Correct the **F** sentences.

d 🔊 8.9 Listen to Part 2. What was different about Joe and Jake's experience compared to the other contestants'?

e Listen again and make notes. What does Joe say about…?
1 smiling at Deborah Meaden
2 Jake's first words
3 'I'm out.'
4 Peter's appearance
5 Jessops
6 the job offer

f 🔊 8.10 Listen to the end of the interview. What did Joe and Jake decide to do? Why? Did they think it was the right decision?

7 SPEAKING

a ▶ Video Watch *A product presentation*. Would you buy this new product? Why (not)?

b Watch the video again. Number the questions 1–5 in the order they answer them.
A ☐ How much will it cost?
B ☐ What is the product for? Give a detailed description.
C ☐ Who are you? What's the name of your product?
D ☐ Do you have an advertising slogan for the product?
E ☐ Who is the product for?

c ▶ Video Now watch some extracts from the video in **a**. Then complete the gaps in the information box.

> **Presenting a product**
> 1 Hello / Good morning. I'm Max, and _____ is Jasmine.
> 2 We're here to tell you about our new _____.
> 3 The _____ of our new product is…
> 4 We think (*Forever Fresh*) is going to be very _____ because…
> 5 The _____ is very reasonable.
> 6 And our _____ is…

d Work with a partner. Imagine you are going to appear on *Dragons' Den*. Choose one of the products below, or invent your own, and think about your answers to the questions in **b**.

an app   a chair   a dessert   a drink   a gadget
a lamp   a pen   a phone   a sandwich

e You are going to present your product to the class together. Spend a few minutes preparing your presentation. Take turns to give the information. Use the language from the information box.

f You also have money to invest in one of the products your classmates present. Listen to their presentations and decide which one to vote for.

8B Service with a smile?

G reported speech: sentences and questions
V making nouns from verbs
P the letters *ai* and *air*

She said that she was going to complain.   *Did they give her a refund?*

1 READING & SPEAKING

a Look at some questions and comments. Who do you think people might say them to: a taxi driver, a doctor, a hairdresser, or a personal trainer? Mark them **TD**, **D**, **H**, or **PT**. Write **A** if you think it could be to all of them.

1. ☐ Could you turn the radio down, please?
2. ☐ I'd like to try something a bit different today.
3. ☐ How many do I have to do?
4. ☐ Is there anything I can take for it?
5. ☐ Not too short, please.
6. ☐ Terrible weather, isn't it?
7. ☐ What do you think it is?
8. ☐ What's the traffic like?
9. ☐ Sorry, I can't do any more.
10. ☐ I had a terrible argument with my partner last night.

b Compare with a partner. Do you agree?

c Read the article and complete the headings with the four jobs in **a**.

d Read the article again. What did or do these people do? Write **S** (Sacha), **D** (Dorothy), **L** (Luke), or **R** (Rachel).

1. ☐ They listened and praised someone for doing the right thing.
2. ☐ They listened and shared a similar experience.
3. ☐ They often hear people saying exactly the same thing.
4. ☐ They sometimes ask a lot of questions, but on other occasions they just listen.

'They treat me like a therapist'

Four people who work with the public talk about the things strangers tell them.

Sacha, _____, 50

Most conversations I have are very simple: How's your day been? How's the weather? How's the traffic? That sort of thing. But occasionally I'll have an interaction that stays with me. Once a young woman in her late 20s got in. When I asked how her day had been, she started crying. She told me that she had been quite ill, and was finding it hard to cope. I told her that it was my first day back at work, because my wife had had the same illness. I pulled over and we both just sat and cried together. It's not unusual for cabbies to have very honest conversations, because people know they are not going to see us again. Passengers treat me like a temporary psychotherapist at times. They have told me about problems in their marriages, failing business relationships, anxiety. I keep driving and keep listening. Some conversations can get quite embarrassing!

Dorothy, _____, 28

I work some of the time in a geriatric ward and, when I'm doing my rounds, I often hear people having funny conversations. One said she'd like to take the doctor home with her, and another said she didn't like the nurse's face. There's a detective element to the conversations I have with my patients – I'm always trying to get to the root of their current health problems and what they need. I always introduce myself to everyone in the room; it's important to break down any barriers and create a friendly atmosphere. I treat everything, from the most minor to the most serious issues. When relatives lose someone, it is never easy. Sometimes it is not just words that are needed. Relatives need you to listen. After all, you were with their loved one in their final moments.

Luke, _____, 27

Conversations are the best part of my job, because actually it can be quite boring. The main topic is love or relationships. The most special conversation I've had with a client took place very recently. A Somali woman came in to try out some styles for her wedding; she's marrying a man who is half-English and half-French. She wanted two styles, with an evening one that paid homage to her Somali culture. I had spent weeks researching the styles and when I held up the mirror so she could see the final look, she burst into tears. She told me not one member of her family was going to attend because they didn't approve. This hairstyle was her way of incorporating Somali culture into her wedding, so that if her family saw her wedding photographs, they would see that she is still proud of who she is. I told her that she was brave and strong and right for standing up for her belief in love.

Rachel, _____, 26

I often have emotional conversations with my clients because I build a rapport with them. I give every person lots of time and attention. We often talk about problems with dating. One client told me a story about realizing her partner had views she strongly disagreed with. In the end, she left him. I heard the whole story while she was lifting weights. There's one conversation that I overhear every day. 'Bro, you are looking hench' one will say to the other. And the other person will always reply with, 'I'm just trying to be like you, bro.' If you've never heard that conversation in the gym, then you haven't been going enough.

Glossary
bro *n, informal* brother, a friendly way of addressing a man
hench *adj, informal* muscular

Adapted from The Guardian

e Find words or phrases in the article for definitions 1–8.

Sacha
1 _____ deal with a difficult situation
2 _____ _____ stopped the car at the side of the road

Dorothy
3 _____ _____ _____ _____ _____ find out the main cause of a problem
4 _____ not important or serious

Luke
5 _____ _____ test or use sth in order to see how good it is
6 _____ _____ _____ started to cry

Rachel
7 _____ a connection or relationship
8 _____ raising sth to a higher position

f Do you normally chat to taxi drivers, hairdressers, etc.? If yes, what about? If not, why not?

2 GRAMMAR reported speech

a Look at three examples of reported speech from the article. Complete the direct speech.
1 When I asked how her day had been, she started crying.
  When I asked her, 'How _____ _____ _____?', she started crying.
2 She told me not one member of her family was going to attend because they didn't approve.
  She told me, 'Not one member of my family _____ _____ _____ attend because they _____.'
3 One said she'd like to take the doctor home with her.
  One said, 'I _____ _____ _____ take the doctor home with me.'

b 🅖 **Grammar Bank** 8B *p.155*

c ▶ **Video** Watch the video. Complete the sentences on the screen using reported speech.

3 LISTENING

a Have you ever had a problem with luggage when you were travelling, e.g. on a train or flight? What happened?

b 🔊 8.13 You're going to listen to a story about bad customer service. First, listen to six extracts and complete the gaps with the verbs in the list.

claim   complained   contacted   dropped
offered   produced   reported   throwing

1 They're _____ guitars out there!
2 They immediately _____ to United Airlines.
3 For nine months, he tried to _____ compensation.
4 Dave wrote a song about his experience and _____ a music video to go with it.
5 United Airlines _____ Dave and _____ him a payment.
6 The BBC _____ that United Airlines' share price had _____ by 10%.

c 🔊 8.14 Now listen to the whole story. Answer the questions.
1 Why did Dave Carroll write a song?
2 Why did it have such a dramatic effect?

d Try to put the events in the correct order 1–10. Then listen again and check.
- [1] Dave and his band flew from Halifax to Chicago.
- [ ] He wrote a song about his experience.
- [ ] United Airlines contacted him and offered him money.
- [ ] They got their connecting flight to Omaha, Nebraska.
- [ ] Dave discovered that his guitar was damaged.
- [ ] He complained again to United Airlines by phone and email, but they didn't help him.
- [ ] He did a lot of media interviews.
- [ ] The baggage handlers were throwing their guitars, so they complained to airline staff.
- [ ] He put a video of the song on YouTube.
- [10] United Airlines lost a lot of money.

e Have you ever experienced very good or very bad customer service? What happened?

4 VOCABULARY
making nouns from verbs

a Look at some nouns from the guitar story. What verbs do they come from?

compensation   complaint   payment

b 🅥 **Vocabulary Bank** Word building *p.172* Do Part 1.

c ▶ Video Watch the video. Make a noun for each clip using one of the verbs on the screen.
1 serve – *service*

5 PRONUNCIATION
the letters *ai* and *air*

a 🔊 8.17 Listen and under<u>line</u> the stressed syllable. Then write the words in the correct column according to the pronunciation of *ai* and *air*.

airline   barg**ai**n   cert**ai**n   cl**ai**m   compl**ai**n   cont**ai**n
em**ai**l   expl**ai**n   p**ai**d   rep**air**   w**ai**ter

b 🔊 8.18 Listen and check. Then answer the questions, according to the pronunciation of the pink letters.
1 How is *ai* usually pronounced a) when it's stressed, b) when it's unstressed? Which word is an exception?
2 How is *air* usually pronounced?
3 Is *said* pronounced /seɪd/ or /sed/?

6 READING

Going the extra mile

In the age of social media, a story about a good (or bad) customer service experience is not limited to you and your friends. The best stories can go viral on social networks very quickly, bringing good or bad publicity to companies overnight. Here are five heart-warming true stories that reached millions of people because of the power of the internet.

A Nordstrom
One day, a member of the security staff in a Nordstrom department store noticed a woman crawling around on her hands and knees in the clothes department. She said she was looking for a diamond that had fallen out of her wedding ring while she was trying on clothes earlier that day. The man got down on the floor and searched with her. Then he asked a group of cleaners to help, and they searched, too. Finally, they looked through _____!

B Le Creuset
Anna Kafkalias was delighted to find a Le Creuset casserole worth £270 on sale in a charity shop for £20. Unfortunately, it had no lid. She decided to contact Le Creuset to ask if she could buy a lid separately. The customer service agent said that they had some ex-display items and would be happy to send her one for free. 'She even asked _____.'

C Ritz-Carlton Hotels
Chris Hurn's family spent their holiday at the Ritz-Carlton Hotel in Florida. Unfortunately, when they got home, they realized that they had left Chris's young son's favourite toy, Joshie the giraffe, at the hotel. The child was very upset, so Chris told him that Joshie was staying at the hotel for a bit of extra holiday. That evening, the hotel phoned to say that they had found Joshie. Chris thanked them and explained that he'd told his son that Joshie was having an extra holiday. Two days later, a parcel arrived. In it was Joshie, a present of a Frisbee and a football, and a photograph of _____.

D Trader Joe's
At Christmas a few years ago, in Pennsylvania, USA, it snowed so hard that an 89-year-old man couldn't leave his home. His daughter was worried that he didn't have enough food. She called several stores and asked if they would deliver food to her father's home, but they all said no. Eventually, she spoke to someone at a store called Trader Joe's. They also told her that they didn't deliver – normally. But because she was so worried, they said that they would make an exception. The employee then wished her a Merry Christmas. Half an hour later, the food arrived at her father's house, with _____!

E Apple
A man bought the latest iPad online, but when his wife saw it, she thought it was too expensive, so he immediately sent it back to Apple. He put a Post-it note on the screen that said, 'Wife said no'. Apple employees thought this was very funny, and the story reached two senior managers, who decided to do something about it. They refunded his money, but they also sent the iPad back to him with another Post-it note saying, '_____'.

a Read the introduction to the article. Why is good customer service more important than it used to be?

b Read the five stories. In pairs, try to guess how the last sentence of each story ends.

c **Communication** Going the extra mile *p.118* Read and check. Were you correct?

d Read the stories again. In which stories…?
1 ☐ ☐ does someone get what they wanted to buy without paying
2 ☐ ☐ does someone get something in the post
3 ☐ ☐ is the problem solved on the same day

e Which example A–E do you think…?
  • is the funniest
  • cost the company most money
  • took the company most time
  • was the most difficult to organize
  • is the best customer service

7 LISTENING & SPEAKING

a What do you think are the top five things that people complain about in hotels?

b ▶ Video Watch *How to complain* Part 1 and check your answers to **a**.

c ▶ Video Now watch Part 2. Phil, a hotel guest, complains in three situations. What does he do wrong each time? How does he do it better the second time?

d **Communication** I want to speak to the manager **A** *p.111* **B** *p.116* Role-play two conversations.

e Have you ever complained about something in a hotel, restaurant, or shop? What happened?

7&8 Revise and Check

GRAMMAR

Circle a, b, or c.
1 We'll miss the train if we ___.
   a don't hurry
   b won't hurry
   c didn't hurry
2 If you help me with the washing-up, ___ in five minutes.
   a we'll finish
   b we finish
   c we finished
3 I won't get into university unless ___ good grades.
   a I'll get   b I get   c I don't get
4 If we moved to a bigger house, we ___ a dog.
   a can have   b could have   c will have
5 I'd be sad if my brother and his wife ___.
   a break up   b 'll break up   c broke up
6 If I had a job, I ___ live with my parents.
   a won't   b wouldn't   c didn't
7 If I won a lot of money, ___ a big house.
   a I'd buy   b I'll buy   c I buy
8 Samuel's really good at ___ problems.
   a solve   b solving   c to solve
9 ___ clothes online saves a lot of time.
   a Buying   b To buy   c Buy
10 I wouldn't ___ that car if I were you.
    a get   b getting   c to get
11 It's really important ___ the receipt.
    a keep   b to keep   c keeping
12 He said he ___ to his lawyer tomorrow.
    a will speak   b spoke   c would speak
13 I asked Helena if ___ coming to the party.
    a she is   b she was   c was she
14 The little girl ___ that she was lost.
    a told   b said us   c told us
15 Felicity asked me where ___.
    a did I work
    b I was work
    c I worked

VOCABULARY

a Complete with one word.
1 The UK school year has three _____.
2 Children under five can go to _____ school.
3 UK high schools are called _____ schools.
4 Children who _____ very badly at school may be expelled.
5 A school where you study, eat, and sleep is called a _____ school.

b Circle the correct word.
1 We live in a residential area *in / on* the outskirts of Cardiff.
2 The *roof / ceiling* in our flat is very low, so don't hit your head!
3 Close the garden *gate / door* or the dog might get out.
4 Our flat is *in / on* the fifth floor of a large block of flats.
5 On the shelf above the *chimney / fireplace* there are some photos.

c Complete the words.
1 I did a lot of ov_____ last week – two hours extra every day.
2 He works night sh_____ at the local factory.
3 It's only a t_____ job, from March to September.
4 I'd like to s_____ up a small business, making children's clothes.
5 Ralph loves being s_____-_____ – it means he's his own boss.

d Complete the sentences with a noun formed from the **bold** word.
1 I don't like shopping in supermarkets because there is too much _____. **choose**
2 My flatmates and I have an _____ about who does what in the house. **agree**
3 I'm sure the new company will be a _____. **succeed**
4 I made a _____ about the service in the hotel. **complain**
5 We went on a _____ to support the unemployed. **demonstrate**
6 The new staff restaurant is a great _____ on the old one. **improve**
7 If you want to get a job, you need good _____. **qualify**
8 My sister has been working as a _____ for the EU. **translate**
9 Some _____ say that drinking coffee may be good for us. **science**
10 I want an _____ for what happened yesterday. **explain**

PRONUNCIATION

a Practise the words and sounds.

Vowel sounds: boot, bull, chair, train
Consonant sounds: key, snake, shower, nose

b Sound Bank p.174–5 Say more words for each sound.
c Which sound in **a** do the pink letters have in these words?
   1 c*ei*ling   3 rep*ai*r   5 sp*ac*ious
   2 em*ai*l   4 r*oo*f

d Underline the stressed syllable.
   1 se|con|dary   3 de|li|ve|ry   5 a|chieve|ment
   2 un|em|ployed   4 a|pply

Can you **understand this text?**

a Read the article once. Choose the best title.
1 It's good to...
2 Look, but don't...
3 Pay less if you don't...

b Read the article again. Complete the gaps with the best word or phrase for the context.
1 a break   b create   c obey
2 a value   b weight   c cost
3 a able   b interested   c prepared
4 a choosing between   b depending on
   c thinking of
5 a less   b longer   c shorter
6 a encourage b tell   c don't allow
7 a buying   b finding   c losing
8 a colleagues b shoppers   c sales assistants

Can you **understand these people?**

Philomena   Adina   Daniel   Scott   Coleen

▶ **Video** Watch and choose a, b, or c.
1 Philomena's maths teachers ___.
   a made her want to become a teacher herself
   b were very inspiring
   c weren't as good as her history teacher
2 Adina is happy to buy ___ online.
   a anything   b most things   c food and clothes
3 Daniel remembers being annoyed with a waiter who ___.
   a didn't want to serve his table
   b complained about the tip
   c wasn't polite
4 Scott currently ___.
   a only has a small garden   b doesn't have a garden
   c has a lot of plants in his garden
5 At the start of her career, Coleen thought that a good salary was ___ an enjoyable job.
   a more important than   b less important than
   c as important as

Can you **say this in English?**

Tick (✓) the box if you can do these things.
Can you...?
1 ☐ describe the schools you went to (or have been to) and say what you liked or didn't like about them
2 ☐ describe your ideal holiday house
3 ☐ say a) what you will do if you don't pass your English exam at the end of the course, b) what you would do if you won a lot of money
4 ☐ report three questions that somebody has asked you today and say what you answered

_____ TOUCH!

IF YOU want to save money when shopping, ¹_____ the simple rule that you've probably shouted at the kids 100 times: don't touch anything! Touching anything, from a banana to a Ferrari, makes your brain automatically place more ²_____ on an item.

This has been revealed in a study from Ohio and Illinois state universities, which investigated how much people were ³_____ to pay for an item before and after touching it. The item was a cheap coffee mug, but just a few seconds of contact made people want to pay more for it than those who had looked but not touched.

The study, published in the journal *Judgment and Decision-Making*, tested 144 people and examined how much they were prepared to pay in an auction for the mug, ⁴_____ how long they had held it. The ⁵_____ people held the mug, the more they were prepared to pay, with those holding it for ten seconds valuing it at $2.44 and those who held it for 30 seconds valuing it at $3.91.

Some kinds of stores have been using these tactics for years; for example, car showrooms ⁶_____ customers to test drive new cars and pet shops give people animals to hold. But Waleed Muhanna, the author of the study, was surprised how quickly people felt that, once they had touched something, it was theirs. 'People become attached and are prepared to pay more to avoid ⁷_____ the object,' he said. He hopes that understanding how quickly they can get attached to something may help ⁸_____ to make better decisions about what to buy.

Adapted from The Times

9A I was so lucky!

G third conditional
V making adjectives and adverbs
P sentence rhythm, weak pronunciation of *have*

You were really lucky! | Yes, if my plane hadn't been delayed, I would have missed it.

1 LISTENING

a Read the questions. Say what you would do and why.
   What would you do if…?
   1 you were lost in a city where you didn't speak the language, and your phone had run out of battery
   2 you arrived in a foreign town late at night, and the hostel you had booked into was closed
   3 you fell over in the street and hurt yourself, and you saw a group of teenage boys coming towards you
   4 you arrived at the airport with very little time before your flight, and there was a huge check-in queue

b Read the beginning of an article from Solo Traveler website about being helped by a stranger. Answer the questions.
   1 What was the difficult situation that she was in?
   2 What did the stranger do? Why was it especially kind?

Home   Start   How-to Tips   Trips/Deals   Stats

Strangers helping strangers

 By Tracey Nesbitt

On my very first solo trip, I got completely lost. I was standing on a street corner, in a city where I did not speak the language, trying to read a map and crying. I was terrified that I would miss my train home. When a stranger approached me and put his hand on my arm, I nearly jumped out of my skin. In fact, he was asking if I was lost. He then spoke to me in English and asked whether I needed help. I said that I was trying to find the train station and needed to get there in a hurry. He told me that he was on his way there himself and would show me the way. He walked with me to the entrance of the station. When I turned to thank him, he had already gone, walking back in the direction from which we had just come. I then realized that he had not been going to catch a train at all. He had just taken me there out of kindness.

I have never forgotten that experience and I was interested in hearing more stories like mine, so I asked the Solo Traveler Facebook group, 'What is your favourite story of a kindness received from a stranger while traveling solo?' and people from around the world sent me some really heart-warming stories.

c 🔊 9.1 Look at photos A–F and listen to Tracey tell the stories of three more people who were helped by strangers. Match two photos to each story.

d Listen again and check why the following are mentioned.
   Story 1 Katya
   1 10 p.m.
   2 a room in a hostel
   3 a bar owner and his wife
   4 two in the morning
   5 a small hotel

   Story 2 Gerry
   1 tripped on the kerb
   2 bleeding a lot
   3 13 or 14 years old
   4 some tissues
   5 a school nurse

   Story 3 Jenn
   1 London and then the US
   2 several hundred people
   3 'What am I going to do?'
   4 a flight to Brazil
   5 a much shorter line

   Glossary
   line *n* American English for *queue*. Stand in line = verb
   sidewalk *n* American English for *pavement*

e Now in groups of three, each retell one of the stories using the photos and the notes above. Help each other to remember the details of the three stories.

f Have you ever helped a stranger, or been helped by a stranger? What happened?

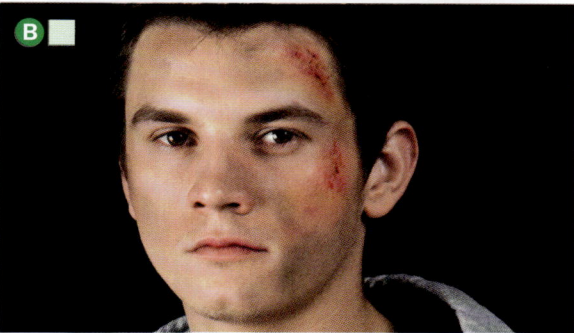

2 GRAMMAR third conditional

a Match the sentence halves about the four stories in **1**.
1 If the stranger hadn't been able to speak English to Tracey, ☐
2 If Katya's hostel had been open, ☐
3 If the boys hadn't helped Gerry, ☐
4 If the man hadn't found Jenn the right queue, ☐

A he wouldn't have been treated so quickly.
B she wouldn't have needed a hotel.
C she would have missed her flight.
D he might not have been able to help.

b Do the sentences in **a**...?
a describe how the stories really ended
b imagine what might have happened

c **G** Grammar Bank 9A *p.156*

d ▶ Video Watch the video once. Then watch again and make five third conditional sentences about Keith's bad day. Use the verbs on the screen.
If he hadn't got up late,...

3 PRONUNCIATION sentence rhythm, weak pronunciation of *have*

a 🔊 9.3 Listen and repeat the third conditional sentences in three stages. Copy the rhythm. How is *have* pronounced after *would*?
1 If I'd **known** you were **ill**,
I would have **come** to **see** you.

If I'd **known** you were **ill**, I would have **come** to **see** you.

2 If the **weather** had been **better**,
we would have **stayed longer**.
If the **weather** had been **better**, we would have **stayed longer**.

3 If I **hadn't stopped** to get **petrol**,
I **wouldn't** have been **late**.
If I **hadn't stopped** to get **petrol**, I **wouldn't** have been **late**.

4 We would have **missed** our **flight**
if it **hadn't** been **delayed**.
We would have **missed** our **flight** if it **hadn't** been **delayed**.

b 🔊 9.4 Listen and write five third conditional sentences.

c **C** Communication Guess the conditional A *p.111* B *p.116*
Practise third conditionals.

89

4 READING & SPEAKING

a Do you consider yourself in general to be a lucky person? Why (not)?

> **Topic sentences**
> In a text, paragraphs usually begin with a *topic sentence*. This sentence tells you what the paragraph is going to be about.

b You are going to read an article about luck. Read topic sentences A–E. Then read the article and match the topic sentences to paragraphs 1–5. Use the highlighted words and phrases to help you.

A But is it possible to use these techniques to win the lottery?

B A few years ago, I led a large research project about luck.

C Eventually, we uncovered four key psychological principles.

D In a second phase of the project, I wanted to discover whether it was possible to change people's luck.

E The results revealed that luck is not a magical ability, or the result of random chance.

c Read the article again. Choose a, b, or c.
1 In his first research project into luck, the author asked the volunteers to _____.
   a record what happened to them every day
   b answer questions about their jobs
   c live together for a few months
2 In one experiment, the unlucky people _____.
   a didn't count the photographs correctly
   b didn't notice something important in the newspaper
   c were not able to finish the task
3 The researchers concluded that lucky people are generally _____.
   a optimistic
   b hard-working
   c ambitious
4 In a second phase of the project, Wiseman asked his volunteers to _____.
   a change their jobs
   b change their attitude
   c change their lifestyle
5 Wiseman believes that _____.
   a being lucky in your personal life is more important than being lucky at work
   b winning the lottery is as important as being lucky in your personal life
   c winning the lottery is less important than being lucky in your personal life

How to improve your luck and win the lottery twice (possibly)

Richard Wiseman

A British couple have just won £1m in the EuroMillions lottery for a remarkable second time. The chances of this happening are more than 283 billion to one. They are clearly incredibly lucky – but is there anything we can all do to increase the chances of being lucky ourselves?

1 ☐ I studied the lives of more than 400 people who considered themselves either very lucky or very unlucky. I asked everyone to keep diaries, complete personality tests, and take part in experiments.

2 ☐ Nor are people born lucky or unlucky. Instead, lucky and unlucky people create much of their good and bad luck by the way they think and behave. For example, in one experiment, we asked our volunteers to look through a newspaper and count the number of photographs in it. However, we didn't tell them that we had placed two opportunities in the newspaper. The first was a half-page advert clearly stating, 'STOP COUNTING. THERE ARE 43 PHOTOGRAPHS IN THIS NEWSPAPER.' A second advert later on said, 'TELL THE EXPERIMENTER YOU'VE SEEN THIS AND WIN £150.' The lucky people quickly spotted

90

these opportunities, partly because they tended to be very relaxed. In contrast, the unlucky people focused anxiously on the task of counting the photos and so tended not to see the advertisements. Without realizing it, both groups had created their own good and bad luck.

3 ☐
- Lucky people create and notice opportunities by developing a relaxed attitude to life and being open to change.
- Lucky people tend to listen to their intuition and act quickly. Unlucky people tend to analyse situations too much, and are afraid to act.
- Lucky people are confident that the future will be positive, and this motivates them to try, even when they have little chance of success. Unlucky people are sure that they will fail, and so they often give up before they have begun.
- Lucky people keep going, even when they are likely to fail, and they learn from their mistakes. Unlucky people get depressed by the smallest problem, and think that the problems are their fault, even when they aren't.

4 ☐ I asked a group of 200 volunteers to use the four key principles and to think and behave like a lucky person. The results were remarkable. In a few months, about two-thirds of the group became happier, healthier, and more successful in their careers.

5 ☐ Unfortunately not. Lotteries are purely chance events, and nothing can really influence your chances of success. However, the good news is that being lucky in your personal life and career is far more important than winning the lottery.

Adapted from The Guardian

d Ask and answer the questions with a partner.
1 Do you agree with Richard Wiseman that people are not born lucky or unlucky, but can learn to make their own luck?
2 Can you remember a time when you were either very lucky or very unlucky? What happened?
3 Do you know anyone who you think is particularly lucky or unlucky? Why?
4 Think of a time when you were successful at something. Do you think it was because you worked hard at it, or because you were lucky and in the right place at the right time?

5 VOCABULARY making adjectives and adverbs

> A few years ago, I led a large research project about **luck**. I studied the lives of more than 400 people who considered themselves either very **lucky** or very **unlucky**.

a Look at the **bold** words in the sentences above. Which is a noun and which are adjectives? Using the word *luck*, can you make...?
1 a positive adverb   2 a negative adverb

b **V** Vocabulary Bank Word building *p.172* Do Part 2.

c Read the rules for the sentence game.

The sentence game

1 You must write correct sentences with the exact number of words given (contractions count as one word).
2 The sentences must make sense.
3 You must include a form of the given word (e.g. if the word is *luck*, you can use *lucky*, *luckily*, *unlucky*, etc.).

d Work in teams of three or four. Play the sentence game. You have five minutes to write the following sentences.

1 *fortune* (11 words)
2 *comfort* (9 words)
3 *luck* (7 words)
4 *care* (6 words)
5 *patience* (12 words)

e Your teacher will tell you if your sentences are correct. The team with the most correct sentences is the winner.

9B Power cut

G quantifiers
V electronic devices
P linking, *ough* and *augh*

You look a bit stressed! — *Yes, I have too much work and not enough time!*

1 VOCABULARY electronic devices

a How many devices do you have with screens? Which one do you use the most?

b Match the words and photos.
- an adaptor /əˈdæptə/
- a charger /ˈtʃɑːdʒə/
- a keyboard /ˈkiːbɔːd/
- a memory stick /ˈmeməri stɪk/
- a (wireless) mouse /maʊs/
- a plug /plʌg/
- a printer /ˈprɪntə/
- a remote control /rɪˈməʊt kənˈtrəʊl/
- a router /ˈruːtə/
- a socket /ˈsɒkɪt/
- a speaker /ˈspiːkə/
- a switch /swɪtʃ/
- a USB-C cable /juːesbiːˈsiː ˈkeɪbl/
- a voice assistant /ˈvɔɪs əˈsɪstənt/

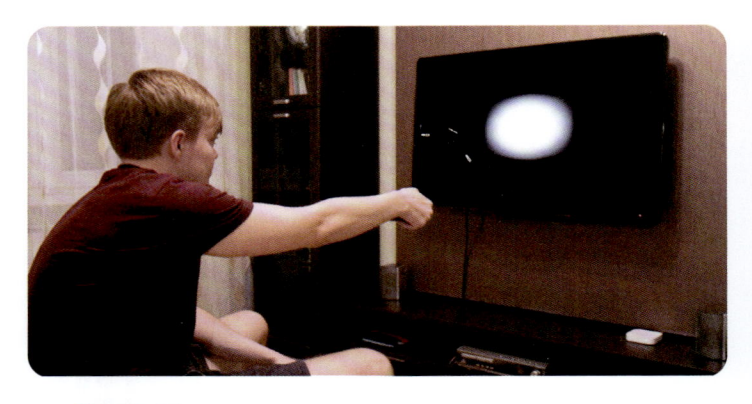

c ◉ 9.7 Listen and check. Then cover the words and test each other.

d ▶ Video Watch the video. Match clips 1–10 to sentences A–J.
- A ☐ I turned down the heating.
- B ☐ I switched on my laptop.
- C ☐ I turned up the volume.
- D ☐ I plugged in my charger.
- E ☐ I switched off the TV.
- F ☐ I unplugged the router.
- G ☐ I installed some software.
- H ☐ I updated an app.
- I ☐ I set the alarm for 7.00.
- J ☐ I deleted a photo.

92

2 PRONUNCIATION linking

a 🔊 9.8 Listen and repeat A–E. Try to link the words.
- A I **turned it down**.
- B I **switched it on**.
- C I **turned it up**.
- D I **plugged it in**.
- E I **switched it off**.

> **Separable phrasal verbs**
> Remember that many phrasal verbs are separable, i.e. the object can go between the verb and particle, e.g. *switch the TV on*, or after the particle, e.g. *switch on the TV*. However, if the object is a pronoun, it must go between the verb and particle, e.g. *switch it on* NOT *switch on it*.

b Answer the questions with a partner. Give reasons.
1. Do you normally switch off your computer when you stop using it? Why (not)?
2. Do you ever unplug electronic devices at night to save energy? What about when you go on holiday?
3. What time of year do you tend to turn your heating on / off?
4. Do you normally listen to music with headphones or with a speaker? Why?
5. In your house, do you usually agree about what the temperature should be, or is someone always turning the heating or air conditioning up and down? What about with the volume on the TV?

"WHO TURNED UP THE THERMOSTAT?"

3 LISTENING & SPEAKING

a Imagine there was a power cut in your house. What would you find it most frustrating not to be able to do?

b 🔊 9.9 Listen to Chris Stokel-Walker, a journalist from *The Times*, describing his experiment of living for a day with no power. What part of the day do you think he found the most difficult? On the whole, would you say it was a positive or a negative experience for him?

c Listen again. What things couldn't Chris do during his day without power? Make notes for each of these times.
1. 7 a.m. – 9 a.m.
2. 9 a.m. – midday
3. midday – 2 p.m.
4. 2 p.m. – 6 p.m.
5. 6 p.m. onwards

d Read some of the expressions Chris uses. What do the **bold** verb phrases mean?
1. I read the news on my tablet and the battery life **drops from 65% to 55%** in a few minutes.
2. Skype calls really **drain the power**.
3. I **close down** unnecessary programs and turn the brightness of my screen down to its lowest level.
4. Finally, my **laptop battery dies** just after lunch.
5. Thankfully, I can continue to **work in the cloud** on my phone.
6. Two and a half years ago, he decided to **live off-grid**.

e Discuss the questions.
1. Are power cuts frequent where you live? What causes them?
2. Think of a time when you've been without power at home. What did you find difficult? Was there anything you liked about not having power?
3. Do you ever suffer from 'battery anxiety'? How low does the battery need to go for you to start worrying?
4. What do you think about people like Chris's friend Joel, who live off-grid? Is it good to live without technology?

4 GRAMMAR quantifiers

a With a partner, read sentences 1–6 and think about what the missing words could be. Don't write them in yet.
1 I used to have _____ _____ of different gadgets, but now I use my phone for almost everything.
2 I'd like to have a better computer, but I don't have _____ _____ to buy one right now.
3 I spend _____ _____ time online. I think I need to take a break.
4 I have a lot of friends on social media, but only _____ _____ of them are close friends.
5 I never watch TV or films on my phone, because the screen isn't _____ _____.
6 I like Apple products, but I can't afford them – I think they're _____ _____.

b ◉ 9.10 Now listen and complete the sentences in a. Did you guess correctly?

c Ⓖ Grammar Bank 9B p.157

d Talk to a partner. Are the sentences in a true for you? Say why (not).

5 PRONUNCIATION ough and augh

> ough and augh
> Be careful with the letters ough and augh. There are several different pronunciations. Try to remember how to pronounce the most common words which have this combination of letters.

a Write the words from the list in the correct column.

although bought brought caught cough daughter
enough laugh thought through tough

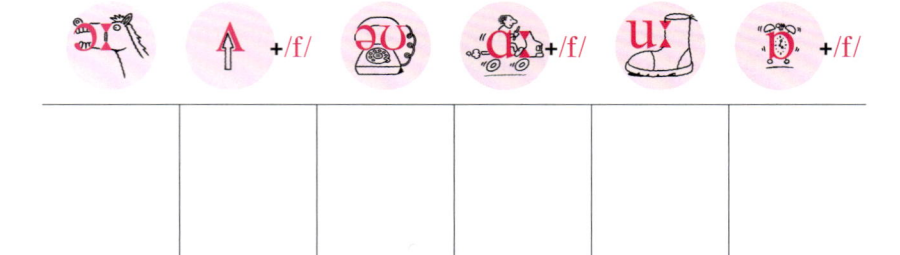

b ▶ Video Watch and check. Then watch again and repeat the sounds and words. Which is the most common sound?

c ◉ 9.15 Listen to sentences 1–5. Practise saying them.
1 I bought a new iPhone, although I thought it was very expensive.
2 My daughter's caught a bad cold.
3 We've been through some tough times.
4 I didn't laugh! It was a cough.
5 You haven't brought enough wine!

6 READING & SPEAKING

a Work with a partner and answer the questions. Who has a more organized digital life?
• Approximately how many emails do you have in your inbox? Do you organize them into folders?
• How often do you add new apps on your phone or delete old ones?
• How many photos do you have on your phone? Are they organized into albums? How quickly could you find a photo you wanted to show someone?
• How many friends do you have on social media? How many of them are real friends? Do you ever unfollow your friends?
• How many people in your 'contacts' have you not contacted in the last year?
• How many different passwords do you have? How do you remember them?
• Do you accept cookies when you visit new websites? Why (not)? How often do you unsubscribe from marketing emails?
• What do you do with your old digital devices, e.g. old phones, tablets, etc.?

b Look at the title of the article and the headings. Tick (✓) the areas of your digital life that you think you need to tidy up.

c Read the article and complete the gaps with a verb from the list.

answer   click   find   forget   free up
keep   recycle   update

d Search the text. Find six words with the prefix un- to complete the extracts.

Tip 1 Why should you have hundreds of un_____ or un_____ emails?

Tip 2 Un_____ software or apps that you don't use.

Tip 4 You can 'un_____' friends without them knowing…

Tip 7 If you get un_____ emails from companies and organizations, don't just delete them – un_____.

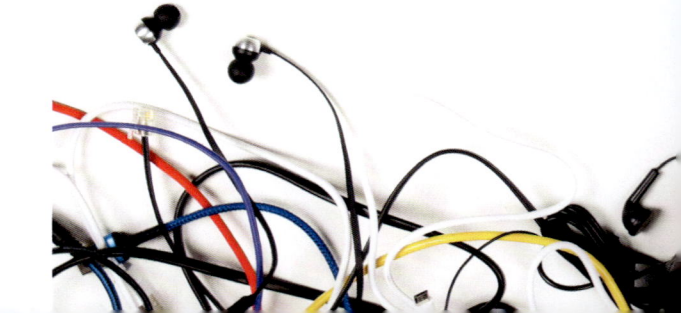

8 ways to tidy up your digital life

A clean, tidy room makes you feel better about your home. In the same way, a tidy phone, tablet, or computer makes you feel better about your digital life. So if your digital life is a mess, try these tips – the benefits are huge.

1 Inbox messages
Most people have too many emails in their inbox. You don't have hundreds of unopened or unanswered letters in your house, so why should you have hundreds of unopened or unanswered emails? If you can _____ an email in less than two minutes, do it right away. If it will take longer, don't leave it in your inbox – move it into a 'work in progress' folder and reply later.

2 Old software or apps
Uninstall software or apps that you don't use. This will _____ a lot more space on your hard drive or phone.

3 Photos
You wouldn't put bad photos in a physical photo album, so don't keep bad photographs (or videos) on your phone – just delete them. Having poor-quality photos just makes it more difficult to _____ a good photo when you need one.

4 Friends
Having too many friends on social media makes it more difficult to _____ in touch with the ones you really care about. You can 'unfollow' friends without them knowing, so you won't hurt their feelings.

5 Contact information
_____ contact information regularly and delete contacts you no longer need. Most people don't do this often enough.

6 Passwords
Use a password manager app, like 1Password. This gives you as many different passwords as you need and remembers them for you. You'll never _____ a password again.

7 Email marketing
If you get unwanted emails from companies and organizations, don't just delete them – unsubscribe. It should only take a few seconds. Just _____ on the 'unsubscribe' link at the bottom of the email.

8 Old devices
If you've been using technology for any length of time, you probably have a collection of things that you no longer use – memory sticks, USB cables, chargers, old phones, and tablets. If you can't give them to somebody who would use them, _____ old devices properly.

Adapted from Becoming Minimalist website

e Complete the sentences with *un-* and the words from the list.

clear   comfortable   do   follow
helpful   known   lock   read

1 Why do you have over 100 _____ emails?
2 If you want to _____ what you've done, press Ctrl+Z.
3 I had to _____ her as she was posting some really annoying things.
4 I can't _____ my phone – I've forgotten the password.
5 The IT Support person was very _____. I still can't print anything.
6 I didn't answer the phone, because it said 'caller _____'.
7 I can't set up the new router – the instructions are really _____.
8 I hate earbuds – I find them really _____.

f Which of the tips in the article would be most useful for you? Choose your top three. Then discuss your choices in small groups and say why.

7 WRITING
a 'for and against' essay

W Writing Bank 9 *p.129* Write an essay about the advantages and disadvantages of smartphones.

Ben's big show

EPISODE 5 PICTURES OF YOU

Practical English | asking indirect questions

1 PAMELA'S ADVICE

a **Video** Look at the photos. What do you think Izzy is thinking? What advice does Pamela give her? Watch *Pamela's advice* and check.

b Watch again. Then answer the questions.
1 What does Izzy say about…?
   a Ben's photos
   b the meal with Ben
   c the hug
2 What does Pamela say about…?
   a Izzy using Ben's photos
   b Izzy and Ben's break-up

2 ASKING INDIRECT QUESTIONS

a **Video** Watch *Asking indirect questions*. Then answer the questions.
1 Do they still feel something for each other?
2 Do they both want the same things in the future?
3 Do they want to get back together?

b **Video** Complete the extracts from the conversation with the phrases in the list. Then watch again and check.

Can you tell me…   I'd like to know…
could you tell me…   I wonder…   Do you know…

Izzy	So, ¹_____ what you think of Izzy?
Ben	I think she's an awesome person. She's smart. She's funny.
Izzy	But you broke up, didn't you? ²_____ if you think you should get back together.
Ben	Well, I think it's complicated…
Ben	³_____ if you want kids?
Izzy	I don't know. It's not really something I think about.
Izzy	But I still feel something for you.
Ben	⁴_____ if we'll always feel something for each other.
Ben	The truth is I'm interested in someone else.
Izzy	⁵_____ who it is?

American and British English

smart /smart/ = *intelligent* in American English
smart /smaːt/ = *well-dressed* in British English

c Watch and repeat the highlighted phrases and sentences in **b**. Copy the rhythm and intonation.

d Practise the extracts in **b** with a partner. Then change roles.

Indirect questions

We often put *Can / Could you tell me....?, Do you know...?, I'd like to know..., I wonder...* to make questions less direct or more polite. When we do this, the direct question becomes a normal positive sentence.

Compare:

What do you think of Izzy?
Could you tell me **what you think** of Izzy?

Do you want kids?
Do you know **if** (or **whether**) **you want** kids?

e Make indirect questions by using the beginnings given.

1 'Where's the station?'
   Excuse me. Can you tell me _____?

2 'What do you think?'
   I'd like to know _____.

3 'Is Jack coming tonight?'
   I wonder _____.

4 'What's the time?'
   Do you know _____?

5 'What time does the show start?'
   Could you tell me _____?

f ⓒ **Communication** Asking politely for information
   A *p.112* **B** *p.117* Practise indirect questions.

3 A HAPPY ENDING?

a ▶ Video Watch *A happy ending?* Then number the photos 1–5.

b Watch again. In pairs, use the photos in the correct order to tell each other what you remember from each scene.

4 SOCIAL ENGLISH

a Match a phrase from **A** to a response in **B**.

A	B
1 So I went to Ben's exhibition.	☐ I, um...Yes, actually, I do.
2 Hey, bro!	☐ Emma! It's great to see you!
3 You look exhausted.	☐ Oh, just an old friend.
4 Do you think this is good enough?	☐ Did you? What did you think of his photos?
5 By the way, who was the photographer?	☐ Yeah. There's just been a lot going on this week.

b ▶ Video Watch and check.

c Practise the phrases and responses in pairs. Then change roles.

WHAT DO YOU THINK?

In pairs, talk about *Pictures of you*. Did you like the ending? What was the best part of the story for you? What do you think might happen if there were a Season 4? Would you recommend *Pictures of you* to a friend? Why?

10A Idols and icons

G relative clauses: defining and non-defining
V compound nouns
P word stress

Who is she? She's the author who wrote To Kill a Mockingbird.

1 READING & LISTENING

a Read the introduction to an article and look at the photos. Do you recognize any of the people?

The year our heroes died

It is traditional to celebrate the achievements of famous and influential people when they die. However, one year of the 21st century stands out – 2016. In that year, an unusually high number of iconic people died. They were from all walks of life and had achieved many different things, but they were all heroes in their own way.

b Now read about one of the people in the photo. Who do you think it is?

_____ was born in south London in 1947. He was good at singing, and studied art, music, and design at college. He began his career by singing in many different bands, but he was ambitious and talented, and it was soon clear that he should go solo. At the same time, he studied theatre, including mime, and started an arts club. Then, in July 1969, he had his first big hit, when his song about an astronaut coincided with the Apollo 11 moon landing.

During the 70s, he went on stage as a science-fiction character – an intergalactic rockstar visiting a doomed planet Earth. He had unusual eyes, the result of a fight at school when he was 15, which made him seem a little unearthly, and his incredible costumes and performances made him as popular as the Beatles. However, there were professional pressures and problems with drugs. He became extremely thin, and his marriage, which had initially been happy, ended during this period.

By the 1980s, he had changed direction again. A talented actor, he appeared in *The Elephant Man* on Broadway, and in several films, e.g. *The Hunger* alongside Catherine Deneuve and the Second World War drama *Merry Christmas, Mr Lawrence*. He reinvented his musical style and had many huge international hits and concert tours as a global rockstar.

In April 1992, he married the Somalian model Iman and bought a home in New York. These changes in his life inspired him to create new music. Six weeks after the 9/11 attacks in 2001, he performed alongside iconic musicians Paul McCartney, Jon Bon Jovi, Billy Joel, the Who, and Elton John in a big benefit concert.

He had an uncomfortable relationship with fame. At the beginning of his career, he saw it as a way of getting creative freedom, but in later years he hated it. After a heart attack in 2003, he took himself almost entirely out of the public eye. He wanted to move back to London, but he felt more anonymous in New York.

He worked with enormous energy, right up to his death, aged 69, on 10 January 2016. He was still filming the music video for his single, *Lazarus*, shortly before he died. Francis Whately, who produced several films about him, said, 'There was nothing he wasn't willing to learn about… He was incredibly polite, well informed, utterly charming. But I would question anyone who said they really knew him. I don't think anyone knew him.'

c Read the article again. In which decade did he…?

1960s 1970s 1980s
1990s 2000s 2010s

1 create a new performing persona
2 do a lot of acting
3 get divorced
4 become much more private after a sudden illness
5 have his first big hit
6 make his last record
7 remarry
8 sing at a charity concert
9 hurt one eye

2 GRAMMAR relative clauses

a Read five more facts about the people in **1**. Complete the relative clauses with *who*, *whose*, *which*, or *where*. Do you know who the facts are about?
1. After leaving school, he went to Chelsea College of Art, _____ he studied graphic design.
2. He was stalked for a long time by a man _____ was dressed as a giant pink rabbit, and kept appearing at his concerts!
3. His father, _____ name was also Cassius Clay, was a sign and billboard painter.
4. Singer James Blunt, _____ lived with her while recording his first album, called her 'his American mother'.
5. The Al Janoub football stadium in Qatar, _____ was still under construction when she died, was where the 2022 World Cup final was held.

b **Grammar Bank** 10A *p.158*

c In pairs, look at the photos in **1** again.
- **A** Say a sentence about one of the people beginning *He / She is the actor / writer*, etc. *who / that / whose...*
- **B** Identify the person and add more information about him / her if you can.

Then change roles.

3 SPEAKING

a Look at the questions. How many can you answer?

What do you call...?
1. a person who appears in crowd scenes in films
2. the place with black and white stripes where you cross the road
3. the part of the body you use to taste
4. the thing which covers the top of a house
5. a man who a woman is going to marry

b **Communication** Relative clauses quiz **A** *p.112* **B** *p.117* Write and ask quiz questions.

4 WRITING a biography

Writing Bank 10 *p.130* Write a biography of an interesting or successful person.

d **Video** Watch *The year our heroes died*. Complete the names and occupations of four more people who died in 2016.
1. Alan _____, _____
2. Zaha _____, _____
3. Muhammad _____, _____
4. Carrie _____, _____

e Watch again. Then in groups, try to remember as many facts as you can about each person.

f Make a presentation to the other groups about one of the people. Were there any facts that your group left out?

g Do you particularly admire any of these people? Think of a famous person who you admire. What is it about them that makes you admire them?

5 LISTENING

a 🔊 **10.3** Look at four famous examples of British design which featured on stamps. Do you have, or have you seen, any of these things? In which decade do you think they were created? Listen and check.

b 🔊 **10.4** Now listen to an audio guide for an exhibition about British design. Make notes about the following things.

1 **The red phone box**
- the Post Office
- Liverpool Cathedral and Tate Modern
- red, silver, and blue
- the Royal Academy of Arts in Piccadilly
- libraries and art galleries

2 **The Anglepoise™ lamp**
- suspension systems for cars
- Carwardine's company going bankrupt
- the human arm
- the Anglepoise model 1227
- hospital theatres and military aeroplanes

> **Glossary**
> a spring

3 **The Penguin book covers**
- Allen Lane and a railway platform in 1935
- his secretary
- Edward Young and London Zoo
- Agatha Christie and Ernest Hemingway
- orange, blue, and green covers

4 **The miniskirt**
- the Beatles and the first man on the moon
- 'Bazaar' in the King's Road
- Mary Quant's school uniform
- tap dancers and the Mini
- Coco Chanel

c Compare your answers with a partner. Then listen again and add more information.

d Cover the notes and look at the design icons. What facts can you remember about them?

e Which of the four do you think has the most attractive design? What would you consider to be examples of iconic design in your country?

British Design Classics

The red phone box, designed by Giles Gilbert Scott

The Anglepoise lamp, designed by George Carwardine

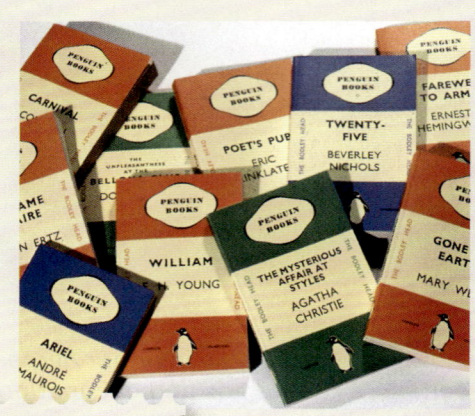

The Penguin book covers, designed by Edward Young

The miniskirt, designed by Mary Quant

6 SPEAKING

a Write the names of people, things, or places in as many of the rectangles as you can.

- a famous dead person (who) you admire
- an everyday object (that) you own that you think has a beautiful design 
- a famous living person (that) you admire
- an object (which) you would like to own whose design you love
- an iconic landmark (that) you really like
- a book cover or a film poster (that) you think has a great design
- a company whose design you love

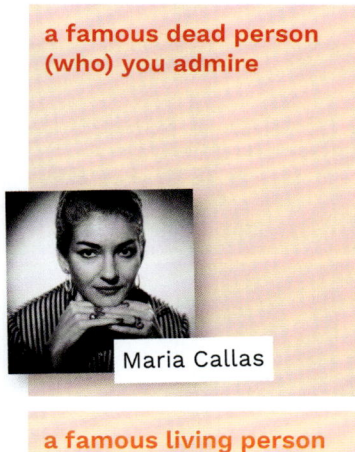

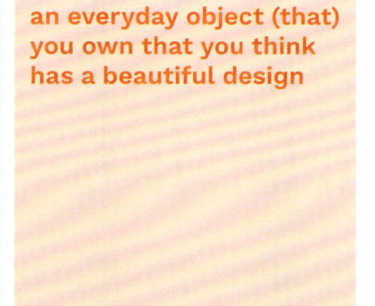

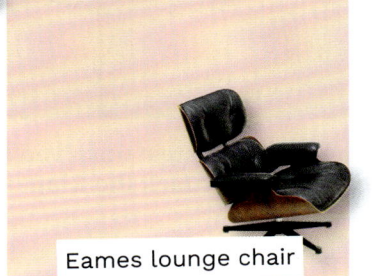

Maria Callas

a blue and white mug

Yotam Ottolenghi, chef

Eames lounge chair

Hindu temple, north London

Marimekko

Klara and the Sun

b In groups, talk about your people, things, and places. Explain why you admire them.

7 VOCABULARY & PRONUNCIATION
compound nouns; word stress

a Match a noun from column **A** to a noun from column **B** to make compound nouns.

A	B
paper	manufacturer
book	street
fashion	box
car	cover
desk	designer
tourist	back
phone	attraction
shopping	lamp

b ◆ 10.5 Listen and check. Which one is written as one word? Is the first or second noun usually stressed? Practise saying the compound nouns in **a** with the correct stress.

c In pairs, try to answer all the questions in **three minutes** with compound nouns from Files 1–10.

Compound nouns race

1. What do you call part of a road that only bicycles can use?
2. What do you call the busy time of day when many people are going to work or going home?
3. What do you call a building where people play, e.g. basketball or volleyball?
4. What do you need to book if you want to play tennis with someone?
5. What do you call a long line of cars that can't move?
6. What should you put on when you get into a car?
7. What do you call the person who is in charge of a school?
8. What do you call the music in a film?
9. What kind of books or films are about the future, often outer space?
10. What gadget can you ask to switch on the radio for you?
11. If you are in a lift and you press G, where do you want to go?
12. What do you call a school which is paid for by the government?

10B And the murderer is...

G question tags
V crime
P intonation in question tags

You were a detective with Scotland Yard, weren't you? ▶ **Yes, I was.**

1 VOCABULARY & READING crime

a Have you heard of Jack the Ripper? Do you know anything about him?

b Match the words in the list to definitions 1–9.

detectives /dɪˈtektɪvz/   evidence /ˈevɪdəns/
murder /ˈmɜːdə/   murderer /ˈmɜːdərə/
prove /pruːv/   solve /sɒlv/   suspects /ˈsʌspekts/
victims /ˈvɪktɪmz/   witnesses /ˈwɪtnəsɪz/

1 _____ *n* police officers who investigate crimes
2 _____ *n* people who see something which has happened and then tell others (e.g. the police) about it
3 _____ *n* people who are hurt or killed by somebody in a crime
4 _____ *n* a person who kills another person deliberately
5 _____ *n* the crime of killing a person illegally and deliberately
6 _____ *n* the facts, signs, etc. which tell you who committed a crime
7 _____ *n* people who are thought to be guilty of a crime
8 _____ (a mystery) *v* to find the correct answer to why something happened
9 _____ (sth) *v* to use facts and evidence to show something is true

c ◉ **10.6** Listen and check. Practise saying the words.

d Read the article about an unsolved crime and complete the gaps with words from **b**.

e Read the article again and find the answer to these questions.
1 Where and when did the murders take place?
2 How many murders were there?
3 How long did the murders go on for?
4 What kind of people have been suspects?

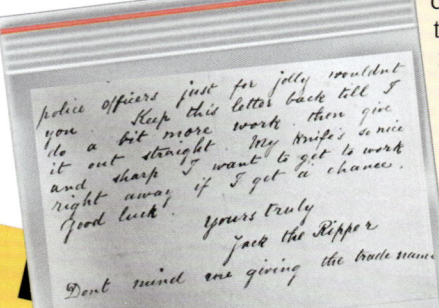

THE GREATEST UNSOLVED CRIME

One of the greatest unsolved ¹*murder* mysteries of all time is that of Jack the Ripper.

In the autumn of 1888, a brutal ²_____ walked the dark, foggy streets of Whitechapel, in east London, terrorizing the inhabitants of the city. The ³_____ were all women and the police seemed powerless to stop the murders. There were no ⁴_____ to the crimes, so the police had no idea what the murderer looked like. Panic and fear among Londoners was increased by a letter sent to Scotland Yard by the murderer. In the letter, he made fun of the police's attempts to catch him and promised to kill again. It finished, 'Yours truly, Jack the Ripper'. This was the first of many letters sent to the police. The murders continued – five in total. But in November, they suddenly stopped, three months after they had first begun.

Jack the Ripper was never caught, and for more than a century, historians, writers, and ⁵_____ have examined the ⁶_____, and tried to discover and ⁷_____ his identity. Hundreds of articles and books have been written and many films made about the murders. But the question, 'Who was Jack the Ripper?' has remained unanswered. There have been plenty of ⁸_____, including a doctor, a businessman, a painter, a sailor, a singer, and even a member of the royal family, and all sorts of people over the years have tried to ⁹_____ this real-life murder mystery.

2 LISTENING

a 🔊 **10.7** Listen to Part 1 of an interview with a retired police inspector, who is an expert on Jack the Ripper. Who is Jan Bondeson's suspect? Write 1 in the box and complete his occupation.

1 Jan Bondeson   2 Bruce Robinson   3 Patricia Cornwell

Walter Sickert, a _____

Hendrik de Jong, a _____

Michael Maybrick, a _____

Glossary
the Freemasons a secret society whose members help each other and communicate using secret signs
Isle of Wight an island off the south coast of England
DNA the chemical in the cells of animals and plants that carries genetic information

b Listen again and make notes about Jan Bondeson's theory in the chart.

	1 Jan	2 Bruce	3 Patricia
what evidence there is			
what Inspector Morton thinks			

c 🔊 **10.8, 10.9** Repeat for Part 2 (Bruce Robinson's theory) and Part 3 (Patricia Cornwell's theory).

d Which of the three suspects do you think is the most / least credible? Do you know of any famous unsolved crimes in your country?

3 GRAMMAR question tags

a Look at four questions from the interview and complete the gaps.
1 'You were a detective with Scotland Yard, _____ _____?'
2 'It's incredible, _____ _____?'
3 'But he was never arrested, _____ _____?'
4 'But you don't think she's right, _____ _____?'

b 🔊 **10.10** Listen and check. Now make the direct questions for 1–4. What's the difference between the two types of question?

c Ⓖ **Grammar Bank** 10B *p.159*

4 PRONUNCIATION & SPEAKING
intonation in question tags

a 🔊 **10.12** Listen and complete the conversation between a policeman and a suspect.

> **P** Your surname's Jones, [1]_____?
> **S** Yes, it is.
> **P** And you're 27, [2]_____?
> **S** Yes, that's right.
> **P** You weren't at home last night at 8.00, [3]_____?
> **S** No, I wasn't. I was at the theatre.
> **P** But you don't have any witnesses, [4]_____?
> **S** Yes, I do. My wife was with me.
> **P** Your wife wasn't with you, [5]_____?
> **S** How do you know?
> **P** Because she was with me. At the police station. We arrested her yesterday.

b 🔊 **10.13** Listen and repeat the statements and question tags. Copy the rhythm and intonation.

c Ⓒ **Communication** Just checking A *p.112* B *p.117* Role-play a police interview.

d Which TV detective series or murder mystery films are popular in your country at the moment? Do you enjoy watching these kinds of programmes?

5 READING & LISTENING

a Do you enjoy reading detective stories? If so, do you have a favourite author?

b 🔊 10.14 Read and listen to Part 1 of a detective story set in 1890s London. Match the names in the list to characters and places 1–6.

Coburg Square   Dr Watson   Fleet Street
Jabez Wilson   Sherlock Holmes   Vincent

1 _____, the narrator
2 _____, a detective
3 _____, a shopkeeper
4 _____, the shopkeeper's new assistant
5 _____, the location of the shop
6 _____, the location of the office of the Red-headed League

c Read again and answer the questions with a partner.
1 What kind of person can work for the Red-headed League, according to the advert?
2 What is unusual about the work?

Why do you think…?
- Mr Wilson had to 'be in the office the whole time'
- the office closed after eight weeks

d 🔊 10.15 Now listen to Part 2. Number the events 1–6 in the order they happened.
☐ Holmes examined Jabez Wilson's house.
☐ Holmes spoke to Vincent.
☐ Holmes closed his eyes and thought about the problem.
☐ Holmes and Watson explored what was in the street behind the square.
☐ Holmes and Watson travelled to Coburg Square.
☐ Holmes looked at the other houses in the square.

Why do you think Holmes…?
- hit the pavement with his stick
- looked at the knees of Vincent's trousers
- looked at the expensive buildings in the street behind the square

What do you think…?
- Holmes is going to do at 10 o'clock tonight
- the serious crime might be

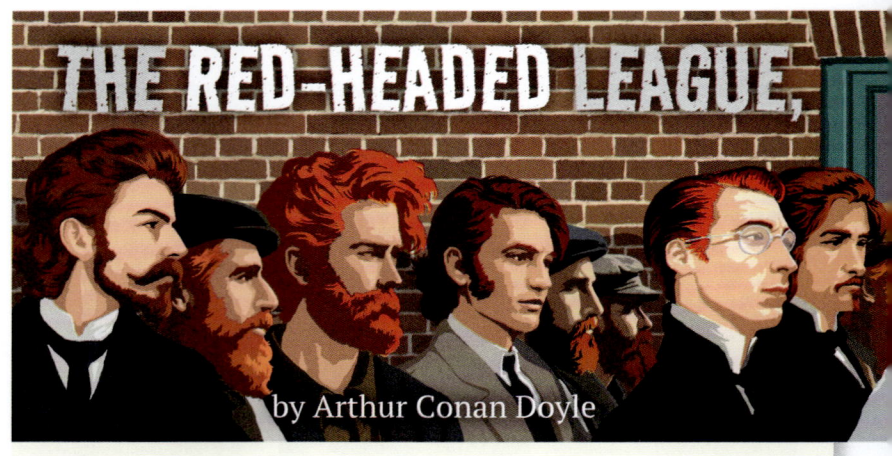

THE RED-HEADED LEAGUE,
by Arthur Conan Doyle

PART 1

When I arrived at Baker Street one morning, Mr Sherlock Holmes was in conversation with a gentleman with fiery red hair.

'Ah, Watson!' he said, 'This is Mr Jabez Wilson, with a very strange story. Please start again, Sir.'

05 'Well Mr Holmes, I live above a small shop near the City, in Coburg Square. It is not doing very well just now. About a month before this story begins, I employed a new assistant, but I can only afford him because he comes for half pay. It's strange, because Vincent is very clever. He could earn more money somewhere, but he says he wants to
10 learn the job. His one fault perhaps is that he spends too much time in the cellar, developing his photographs.

Eight weeks ago, Vincent came into the shop with a newspaper in his hand. "Mr Wilson, I wish that I had red hair," he said. "There's a job for The Red-Headed League. The salary is a couple of hundred pounds a
15 year." And he showed me an advertisement. It said:

THE RED-HEADED LEAGUE: Vacancy. All red-headed men above the age of 21 may apply. Salary £4 a week* for light work. Apply in person on Monday at 11 o'clock at our office in Fleet Street.

"The League was founded by an American millionaire," said Vincent.
20 "He was red-headed, and when he died, he left his fortune to men like him. With your red hair, you would surely get the job, Mr Wilson."

I very much needed the money, so on Monday we shut the shop and went to the address. It was a fantastic sight. Fleet Street was crowded with red-headed men, though not many had such a vivid colour as my own.
25 Vincent pushed me through the crowd and we soon found ourselves in the manager's office. He was a small man with hair even redder than mine. He admired my hair greatly, although he pulled it hard to check it was real!

"Congratulations, the job is yours," said the manager. "The hours are 10.00 to 2.00 and the pay is £4 a week. The work is to copy out the
30 Encyclopaedia Britannica. You must be in the office the whole time. If you leave, you will lose the job. When can you start?"

Vincent quickly offered to look after the shop in the mornings, and I went home, very pleased with my good fortune.

The next day, I started work. The manager paid me £4 every week. He
35 checked on me regularly at the beginning, but I never left the office and after a time, he stopped coming. Eight weeks passed, then suddenly, it all came to an end. This morning I went to work as usual, but the office was locked and there was a notice on the door. It said: "The Red-Headed League is dissolved."

40 I didn't know what to do. Nobody in Fleet Street had heard of The Red-Headed League. Then I thought of you, so I came here.'

'Mr Wilson,' said Holmes, 'I will take your case and give you an answer in a couple of days.'

Glossary
cellar an underground room often used for storing things
the City London's financial and business centre

* a high salary in the 1890s

PART 3

I went to Baker Street at 10.00 that evening. As I entered, I heard the sound of voices. Holmes was with a police officer I knew from Scotland Yard, and another man with a thin face, who Holmes introduced as Mr
05 Merryweather, Director of the City Bank.

We all drove into the City. Holmes didn't say much during the long drive. We reached the same main street we had been in that morning and followed Mr Merryweather down a small path between two
10 buildings. We went through a side door, along a small corridor to a big iron door, then down some steps and through another iron door into a dark passage. Mr Merryweather lit a lantern and eventually we found ourselves in a cellar full of huge boxes.

15 'We must be quiet,' Holmes said. 'We have at least an hour to wait, for they won't act until Mr Wilson is in bed. We are, Watson, in the cellar of the City Bank. Some robbers are very interested in this cellar at present.'

20 'It is our French gold,' whispered Mr Merryweather, pointing at the huge boxes. 'It's an unusually large amount to keep in one building. We borrowed it some months ago from the Bank of France.'

'We can't risk the robbers seeing our light, Mr
25 Merryweather,' observed Holmes. 'We must cover that lantern and sit in the dark. I will stand behind this box and you three behind those. When I flash a light, go for them. If they fire, Watson, shoot. They only have one way out, and that is back through the house behind the
30 bank, in Coburg Square.'

'Wilson's shop!' I exclaimed.

'And I have an inspector and two more men there,' said the police officer.

'So now we must be silent and wait,' whispered Holmes.
35 He covered the lantern and left us in absolute darkness.

e 🔊 **10.16** Read and listen to Part 3. Answer the questions.
1. Who is Mr Merryweather?
2. Where are they waiting?
3. Who are they waiting for?

How do you think the story is going to end?

f 🔊 **10.17** Listen to Part 4 and check. Were you right?

g With a partner, can you remember how Holmes explained these things?
1. The Red-Headed League was set up to make Mr Wilson…
2. Vincent agreed to work for Mr Wilson for half pay because he needed to…
3. Holmes hit the pavement in front of the shop with his stick to check…
4. Holmes looked at the knees of Vincent's trousers because he wanted to see if…
5. He looked at the expensive buildings in the street behind the square to discover…
6. The office of The Red-Headed League closed after eight weeks because…
7. Holmes enjoys solving cases because…

6 LISTENING

a ▶ **Video** Watch *Queens of crime*. Who do you think had a more interesting life? Who do you think had a happier life?

b Complete the chart with notes on what you remember about the two writers' lives and books.

	Ruth Rendell	Agatha Christie
her life • born • parents • marriages • other things		
her books • first novel • detectives • pseudonyms • approach to crime writing		

c Compare your notes with a partner. Then watch again. Are there any facts that you both missed?

d Have you read any books by Ruth Rendell or Agatha Christie? Did you like them? Are there any other crime novelists whose books you enjoy?

105

9 & 10 Revise and Check

GRAMMAR

Circle a, b, or c.
1 If you ___ on time, we wouldn't have missed the start of the film.
   a arrived
   b 'd arrived
   c would have arrived
2 What ___ if that man hadn't helped you?
   a you would do
   b you would have done
   c would you have done
3 If she ___ me that she was arriving this morning, I would have gone to the airport to pick her up.
   a told   b would tell   c had told
4 I would have finished the exam if I ___ about another ten minutes.
   a would have had
   b had had
   c would have
5 I'm afraid there's ___ time left.
   a no   b none   c any
6 There are ___ good programmes on tonight. I don't know what to watch.
   a a lot of   b a lot   c plenty
7 Is there ___ in the car for me, too?
   a room enough
   b enough room
   c too much room
8 Most people have ___ close friends.
   a very little
   b very few
   c not much
9 Is he the man ___ you met at the party?
   a –   b whose   c which
10 Is that the woman ___ husband is a famous writer?
   a who   b that   c whose
11 *The Starry Night*, ___ was painted in 1889, is by Vincent van Gogh.
   a which   b what   c that
12 I'm very fond of Suzana, ___ I used to share a flat with at university.
   a who   b –   c that
13 They're very rich, ___?
   a are they   b aren't they   c isn't it
14 Your brother's been to New Zealand, ___?
   a wasn't he   b isn't he   c hasn't he
15 You won't be late, ___?
   a will you   b won't you   c are you

VOCABULARY

a Complete the sentences with a word formed from the **bold** word.
1 I left home late, but _____ I got to work on time. **luck**
2 He's _____ with his work. It's always full of mistakes. **care**
3 This sofa is really _____. It's much too hard. **comfort**
4 I love this jacket, but _____ it's too expensive. **fortunate**
5 Don't be so _____! The bus will be here soon. **patience**

b Complete with a verb.
1 It was too hot in the room, so I _____ the heating down.
2 I need to _____ my alarm for 5.30, as I have an early flight.
3 It's a good idea to _____ your computer during a storm.
4 Could you _____ up the volume? I can't hear very well.
5 If you're not watching the TV, please _____ it off.

c Complete the words from the definitions.
1 you use this to change the TV channel   r_____ c_____
2 you use this on a computer to write   k_____
3 you use this to convert a European plug to a British one   a_____
4 it's the place on the wall where you plug things in   s_____
5 you use this to move the cursor on a computer   m_____

d Complete the compound nouns.
1 b_____ cover   4 t_____ attraction
2 fashion d_____   5 phone b_____
3 desk l_____

e Complete the words.
1 The d_____ was convinced that the man's alibi was false.
2 I'm sure he's guilty, but I can't pr_____ it.
3 Jack the Ripper's v_____ were all women.
4 They are sure they will be able to s_____ the mystery.
5 Walter Sickert is a s_____ in the Jack the Ripper case.

PRONUNCIATION

a Practise the words and sounds.

Vowel sounds   **Consonant sounds**

up   horse   clock   tourist   flower   witch   yacht   vase

b ▶ Sound Bank p.174–5 Say more words for each sound.

c Which sound in **a** do the pink letters have in these words?
1 c**au**ght   3 en**ou**gh   5 t**ou**gh
2 c**ou**gh   4 sol**v**e

d Underline the stressed syllable.
1 com|for|ta|ble   3 ca|ble   5 e|vi|dence
2 a|dap|tor   4 wit|ness

106

Can you understand this text?

a Read the article once. Complete headings 1–4.
b Read the article again. Mark the sentences **T** (true), **F** (false), or **DS** (doesn't say).
  1 The London Dungeon is both funny and frightening.
  2 The Dungeon isn't very popular.
  3 You're not allowed to talk to the actors.
  4 You can spend as long as you like at the Dungeon.
  5 The characters and stories are all historically accurate.
  6 The Dungeon is suitable for very young children.
  7 Tickets for children under 16 cost half the adult price.
  8 Booking online is cheaper than paying on the day.

Can you understand these people?

1 Sean **2** Adrian **3** Nick **4** Emma **5** Coleen

▶ **Video** Watch and choose a, b, or c.
  1 Sean helped a little girl who had ___.
     a left her toy panda on a train
     b dropped her toy panda in the station
     c lost her toy panda in the car park
  2 Because of Google maps, Adrian no longer ___.
     a uses his car's satnav   b plans his route in advance
     c buys maps
  3 Nick's favourite detective is ___.
     a a female detective in *The Killing*
     b a male detective in *The Bridge*
     c a female detective in *The Bridge*
  4 Emma is going to buy a dress by Maggie Sottero ___.
     a because she's getting married
     b although they're very expensive
     c because she saw some in a magazine
  5 Coleen considers she has been lucky ___.
     a because she has never had a car accident
     b on many occasions
     c because she recently survived a car accident

Can you say this in English?

Tick (✓) the box if you can do these things.
  Can you…?
  1 ☐ complete these three sentences:
        If you'd told me about the party earlier,…
        I would have bought those shoes if…
        I wouldn't have been so angry if…
  2 ☐ describe something that you do too much and something that you don't do enough
  3 ☐ describe a person that you admire, saying who they are, what you know about them, and why you admire them
  4 ☐ check five things you think you know about somebody using question tags

THE LONDON DUNGEON

1 _____ IS THE LONDON DUNGEON?

The London Dungeon brings together amazing actors, special effects, stage performances, scenes, and rides in a truly unique and exciting experience that you see, hear, touch, smell, and feel. It's dark, atmospheric, hilarious, and sometimes a bit scary.

2 _____ DOES IT WORK?

We've been entertaining audiences at The London Dungeon for over 40 years and it's one of the capital's 'must-see' attractions. We take you on a 90-minute journey through 1,000 years of London's unpleasant past. You and your companions walk through the Dungeon, moving from show to show, guided by our professional actors.

The shows are based on real London history and legends, without the boring bits! You'll get up close and personal with scary characters including Jack the Ripper and the infamous barber of Fleet Street, Sweeney Todd.

It's a theatrical experience. That means authentic sets and theatrical storytelling. On your journey, you'll pass through foggy East London streets and houses, and the horrific torture chamber. Believe us, it's better than a sightseeing trip or boring museum tour of London.

3 _____ 'S IT FOR?

The London Dungeon is scary fun for everyone except very young guests and very sensitive adults! Our recommended age is 12 years old and above, and guests who are under 16 years of age must be accompanied by an adult over 18 years of age.

4 _____ AHEAD!

The London Dungeon is particularly brilliant for people who can plan ahead and book online! Not only will you save money, you won't have to wait on the day. We get busy, so make things easy on yourself and book in advance.

Adapted from The London Dungeon website

Communication

PE1 How fantastic! Student A

a Read your sentences 1–9 to **B**. **B** must react with a phrase, e.g. *You're kidding, Oh no!*, etc.
1 My hobby is collecting old English tea cups.
2 I spilled some coffee on my laptop last night and now it doesn't work.
3 I'm going to New York next week.
4 My cat can open the kitchen door.
5 Someone stole my bike yesterday.
6 My grandmother was a Member of Parliament.
7 I won €2,000 in the lottery yesterday!
8 My uncle is 104.
9 My parents met when they were only 15.

b Listen to **B**'s sentences and react with a phrase.

c Tell **B** some real (or invented) news about you for **B** to react. React to **B**'s news.

2A Money Q&A Student A

a Ask **B** your first question. Ask for more information if you can.

> What do you spend your money on apart from food, rent, etc.?

> I go out a lot at weekends and…

b Then answer **B**'s first question. Continue with questions 2–7. If you don't want to answer, say, *I'm sorry, I'd rather not talk about that.*
1 What do you spend your money on apart from food, rent, etc.?
2 What kind of things do you normally buy online? Why don't you buy them in a shop?
3 Have you bought anything nice this week?
4 What's the most expensive thing you've ever bought? Was it worth it?
5 Is there anything you'd love to buy, but can't afford at the moment?
6 Did you get pocket money when you were a child? If yes, did you use to save it or spend it?
7 Do you know someone who has raised money for charity? Which one?

2B Are you hungry? Student A

a Ask **B** your questions. He / She must respond with the phrase in brackets.

> 1 Is the water cold? (Yes, it's **freezing**.)
> 2 Was the film funny? (Yes, it was **hilarious**.)
> 3 Were you tired after the exam? (Yes, I was **exhausted**.)
> 4 Was the flat dirty? (Yes, it was **filthy**.)
> 5 Is your suitcase big? (Yes, it's **huge**.)
> 6 Were you surprised that she passed her test? (Yes, I was **amazed**.)
> 7 Are you sure that he's coming? (Yes, I'm **positive**.)

b Respond to **B**'s questions. Say *Yes, it's… / I'm…*, etc. + the strong form of the adjective which **B** used in the question. Remember to stress the strong adjective.

> Is the soup hot?

> Yes, it's boiling.

c Repeat the exercise. Try to respond as quickly as possible. Use *absolutely* or *really*.

3A I'm a tourist – can you help me? Student A

a Imagine you are an English-speaking tourist in your town / city (or the nearest big town). **B** lives in the town. You are planning to **get around using public transport**. Ask **B** questions 1–5. Get as much information from **B** as you can.

> 1 What kind of public transport is there?
> 2 What's the best way for me to get around the city?
> 3 Can I hire a bike or e-scooter? Are there any cycle lanes?
> 4 Is it easy to find taxis? How expensive are they?
> 5 What's the best way to get to the airport from the town centre? How long does it take?

b Then change roles. **B** is an English-speaking tourist in your town / city, and has **hired a car**. Answer **B**'s questions and give as much information as you can.

5A Fair play Student A

a Read your story and underline any verbs in the past continuous or past perfect.

A Kenyan runner called Abel Mutai was competing in a cross-country race in Spain in 2012. He was winning the race easily, but he stopped running about ten metres before the finishing line. He thought he'd won the race. The crowd were shouting at him – they were telling him to carry on, but he didn't understand them because he didn't speak any Spanish. A Spanish runner, Iván Fernández, was second in the race behind Mutai and he slowed down and told Mutai to keep running. Mutai started running again and crossed the line first. 'I did what I had to do,' said Fernández. 'He was the rightful winner.'

b Cover your story and tell it to B using the verb prompts in the list in the correct tenses.
- Abel Mutai   compete   cross-country race
- win easily   stop running   think win
- the crowd shout   tell him to carry on
- Mutai not understand   not speak Spanish
- Iván Fernández   be second
- slow down   tell Mutai keep running
- Mutai start running   cross the line first

A Kenyan runner called Abel Mutai was competing in a cross-country race in Spain. He…

c Now listen to B's story.

5B How we met Student A

a Read the story and answer the questions.
1 How did they meet?
2 How did their relationship develop?
3 What happened in the end?
4 What makes their relationship work?

b Now tell B about Savannah and Michael.

c Listen to B's story about Nick and Tess.

Savannah and Michael

When Savannah broke up with her ex, she left her job in London and went to live in Barcelona, where she got a job teaching English. She loved the lifestyle, and quickly found a new group of friends. She also used dating apps to meet new people. Soon, she noticed Mike's profile. He was Australian, and was also living in Barcelona. After a lot of messaging, they met in person for brunch. Instead of a short meal, the date lasted eight hours!

The relationship developed very quickly. Savannah invited Mike to England for Christmas, but after the holiday, when they returned to Barcelona, Mike's visa was running out and he had to go back to Australia. They thought it would be too hard to continue their relationship, so they split up at the end of January. But very soon, the couple realized they didn't want to be apart. Savannah travelled to Australia in the summer and Michael visited London at Christmas. They used to talk on the phone every day, and Mike sent Savannah lots of romantic letters; once, in the month before Valentine's Day, he sent 40 cards with all the different things he loved about her.

Finally, Savannah moved to Sydney and they got engaged in 2020. Unfortunately, then she became seriously ill, but Michael looked after her and when she recovered, they got married in a small ceremony at the local registry office.

Savannah says, 'Mike is the most positive person I've ever met.' Mike says, 'Savannah never thinks about herself. We definitely made the right choice to be together.'

Adapted from The Guardian

7A University or not? Student A

a Read about Archie.

Archie Hooper, 23, studied drama in London.

I loved my three years at university. I had some lectures and classes, but most of the time I was free to plan my own time. My friends and I studied plays, wrote essays and shared ideas, and we also did quite a lot of acting in our spare time. It was a great three years and at the end of it I decided I wanted to be an actor.

After graduating, I moved to Leeds with my girlfriend because she had a job offer with a good starting salary. My plan was to work as a waiter or a shop assistant to pay the rent and bills, and look for a real job at the same time. I've applied for at least 60 acting jobs, but unfortunately, I haven't been successful. I realize now that my university course didn't have enough practical experience and in fact there are more opportunities back in London than here in Leeds.

Right now, I'm working for a delivery company, which isn't much fun, but I'm confident that I will find something better soon. It's difficult at the moment, but I'm only 23 and there's plenty of time. I'm very happy I studied drama. It helped me decide who I want to be.

b Ask **B** your questions about Emily-Fleur.

When did Emily-Fleur leave school?   *When she was...*

Questions about Emily-Fleur
1 When did Emily-Fleur leave school?
2 Why didn't she go to university?
3 Where did she get her idea for her business?
4 What was the first wedding she photographed?
5 How did she get more bookings?
6 When did she buy her equipment?
7 Why does she think it was good to start a business young?
8 Why doesn't she envy her friends at university?

c Now answer **B**'s questions about Archie.

7B Guess the sentence
Student A

a Look at sentences 1–6 and think of the missing verb phrase (+ = positive, – = negative). **Don't write anything yet!**

1 I'd cook dinner every day if I _____ earlier from work. +
2 If we _____ this summer, maybe we can afford to get a new car. –
3 I think you _____ more if you see it in 3D. +
4 I'd see my grandparents more often if they _____. +
5 I _____ the fish if I were you. It isn't usually very good here. –
6 I _____ if the water was a bit warmer. +

b Read sentence 1 to **B**. If it isn't right, try again until **B** tells you, 'That's right'. Then write it in. Continue with 2–6.

c Now listen to **B** say sentence 7. If it's the same as your sentence 7 below, say, 'That's right'. If not, say 'Try again', until **B** gets it right. Continue with 8–12.

7 I'll **never be able to** buy a house unless my parents help me.
8 If I met my ex in the street, I **wouldn't say hello** to him.
9 If it **wasn't so late**, I'd stay a bit longer.
10 The flight **will be more comfortable** if we go in business class.
11 I wouldn't mind the winter so much if it **didn't get dark** so early.
12 If I had more money, I**'d buy a house** with a beautiful garden.

8A Dragons' Den Student A

Read about Oppo. Think about the questions below. Then tell your group.
- Did any of the Dragons like the product?
- Did they decide to invest?
- Was the product successful in the end?

Oppo ice cream

The Dragons were not impressed by the brothers, as they said they weren't dressed appropriately – they were wearing suits, which the Dragons thought was too formal if they were promoting ice cream! However, they thought the ice cream actually tasted great. In the end, they decided not to invest, mainly because one of them, Deborah Meaden, had previously invested in an ice cream company which had failed. But now they probably regret their decision. After going on the show, Oppo ice cream tripled its value, and today their ice cream is sold in 6,000 stores across 13 countries. They even have some celebrity investors, such as tennis player Andy Murray and entrepreneur Richard Branson.

8B I want to speak to the manager Student A

Look at the situations and spend a few minutes preparing what you are going to say. Then role-play the conversations.

1 **You're a customer.** You bought something in a clothes shop in the sales yesterday (decide what) and there's a problem (decide what).
Go back to the shop. **B** is the shop assistant. You'd like to change it for another identical one. If you can't, you'd like a refund.
You start.

Excuse me. I bought…

2 **You're the manager of a restaurant.** Your normal chef is off this week and you have a temporary chef who is not very good. One of the waiters has had a problem with a customer, who would like to speak to you. **B** is the customer. When customers complain, you usually offer them a free drink or a coffee. If it's absolutely necessary, you might give a 10% discount on their bill, but you would prefer not to.
B will start.

9A Guess the conditional
Student A

a Look at sentences 1–6 and think of the missing verb phrase ([+] = positive, [−] = negative). **Don't write anything yet!**

1 We _____ the hotel if we hadn't used satnav. [−]
2 If I _____ that it was your birthday, I would have bought you something. [+]
3 If I _____ about the concert earlier, I would have been able to get a ticket. [+]
4 The burglar wouldn't have got in if you _____ the window open. [−]
5 If our best player hadn't been sent off, we _____ the match. [+]
6 I wouldn't have recognized her if you _____ me who she was. [−]

b Read sentence 1 to **B**. If it isn't right, try again until **B** tells you, 'That's right'. Then write it in. Continue with 2–6.

c Now listen to **B** say sentence 7. If it's the same as your sentence 7 below, say, 'That's right'. If not, say, 'Try again' until **B** gets it right. Continue with 8–12.

7 If we hadn't taken a taxi, we **would have missed** the train.
8 If I hadn't gone to the party that night, I **wouldn't have met** my partner.
9 If I'd known that programme was on last night, I **would have watched** it.
10 If I**'d listened** to my friends, I would never have married James.
11 I **would have gone out** with you last night if I hadn't had to work late.
12 I **wouldn't have been** so angry if you had told me the truth right from the start.

PE5 Asking politely for information
Student A

a You are a tourist in **B**'s town. You are going to stop **B** in the street. You want to ask questions 1–5 and you want to be very polite. Rewrite 2–5 as indirect questions.

1 Do shops open on Sundays?
Could you tell me *if shops open on Sundays*?

2 Is there a post office near here?
Do you know _____?

3 What time do banks close here?
Could you tell me _____?

4 Where's the railway station?
Do you know _____?

5 Does the number 21 bus go to the city centre?
Can you tell me _____?

b Ask **B** your indirect questions 1–5. Always begin *Excuse me*.

c Now **B** is a tourist in your town. **B** stops you in the street and asks you some questions. Answer politely with the necessary information.

10A Relative clauses quiz Student A

a Complete the questions with a relative clause to describe the **bold** words. Start the clause with *who*, *which*, *that*, or *where*, or no relative pronoun when there is a new subject.

1 **a pedestrian** What do you call somebody…?
2 **a loan** What do you call some money…?
3 **fans** What do you call people…?
4 **a boarding school** What do you call a place…?
5 **a coach** What do you call the person…?
6 **traffic lights** What do you call the things…?
7 **golf course** What do you call the place…?
8 **selfish** What do you call somebody…?
9 **a router** What do you call the thing…?

b Ask **B** your question 1.

c Now answer **B**'s question 1.

d Continue with 2–9.

10B Just checking Student A

a You are a police inspector. **B** is a suspect in a crime. Ask **B** the questions below, but don't **write anything down**. Try to remember **B**'s answers.

- What's your name?
- Where do you live?
- How old are you?
- Where were you born?
- Are you married?
- What do you do?
- What car do you drive?
- How long have you lived in this town?
- What did you do last night?
- Where were you at 7.00 this morning?

b Now check the information with **B** using a question tag.

Your name's Ivan Horváth, isn't it?

You live in Bratislava, don't you?

c Change roles. Now you are the suspect and **B** is the police inspector. Answer **B**'s questions. You can invent the information if you want to.

d **B** will now check the information he / she has. Say, 'Yes, that's right', or 'No, that's wrong' and correct the wrong information.

PE1 How fantastic! Student B

a Listen to **A**'s sentences and react with a phrase, e.g. *You're kidding, Oh no!* etc.

b Read your sentences 1–9 for **A** to react.
   1 I failed my driving test yesterday.
   2 My grandfather has just run a marathon at the age of 90.
   3 I've been given a grant to study for a year in the USA.
   4 My hobby is collecting film posters.
   5 I've seen the film *The Lord of the Rings* 50 times.
   6 I lost my phone today and I don't know where it is.
   7 I'm going to be on a TV reality show next month.
   8 My sister knows the guitarist in Coldplay.
   9 My dog is 26 years old.

c Tell **A** some real (or invented) news about you for **A** to react. React to **A**'s news.

2A Money Q&A Student B

a Answer **A**'s first question. If you don't want to answer, say, *I'm sorry, I'd rather not talk about that.*

> *What do you spend your money on apart from food, rent, etc.?*
> *I go out a lot at weekends and...*

b Then ask **A** your first question. Ask for more information if you can. Continue with questions 2–7.
   1 How much do you spend on food and drink each week?
   2 Are you good at finding bargains in the sales?
   3 Do you ever pay for things with cash or do you always pay with a card or your phone? Are there any shops near you that only accept contactless payment?
   4 Do you spend much money on travelling? What was the last trip you went on? Was it expensive?
   5 Do you ever give money to charity?
   6 Have you ever lent money to anyone? Why (not)? Have you ever borrowed money from your parents? What for?
   7 Is the cost of living going up in your country? What kinds of things are getting more expensive?

2B Are you hungry? Student B

a Respond to **A**'s questions. Say *Yes, it's... / it was...*, etc. + the strong form of the adjective which **A** used in the question. Remember to stress the strong adjective.

> *Is the water cold?*   *Yes, it's freezing.*

b Ask **A** your questions. He / She must respond with the phrase in brackets.
   1 Is the soup hot? (Yes, it's **boiling**.)
   2 Are you afraid of snakes? (Yes, I'm **terrified**.)
   3 Was the teacher angry? (Yes, he / she was **furious**.)
   4 Is the bedroom small? (Yes, it's **tiny**.)
   5 Are the children hungry? (Yes, they're **starving**.)
   6 Is the book interesting? (Yes, it's **fascinating**.)
   7 Was she happy with the present? (Yes, she was **delighted**.)

c Repeat the exercise. Try to respond as quickly as possible. Use *absolutely* or *really*.

3A I'm a tourist – can you help me? Student B

a Think of the town / city where you are, or the nearest big town. **A** is a foreign tourist who is planning to **get around using public transport**. You live in the town. Answer **A**'s questions and give as much information as you can.

b Then change roles. You are an English-speaking tourist in your town / city. **A** lives in the town. You have **hired a car**. Ask **A** questions 1–5. Get as much information from **A** as you can.
   1 What time is the rush hour in this town?
   2 Where are there often traffic jams?
   3 What's the speed limit? Are there speed cameras anywhere?
   4 What will happen if I park somewhere illegal?
   5 Where's the nearest tourist attraction outside the city? How long does it take to drive there?

5A Fair play Student B

a Read your story and underline any verbs in the past continuous or past perfect.

In the Rio Olympics in 2016, athlete Nikki Hamblin from New Zealand was running in a heat for a place in the final of the 5,000 m. During the race, Hamblin tripped and knocked into another competitor, American Abbey D'Agostino, and they both fell to the ground. D'Agostino got up and helped Hamblin to get up too, but then it became clear that D'Agostino had hurt her foot. When Hamblin realized what had happened, she ran next to D'Agostino, and they helped each other to the finish line. Both runners qualified for the final, but D'Agostino couldn't run because of her injury. However, they both received a Fair Play award from the International Olympic Committee.

Glossary
heat one of several races before the final in a competition; the winners go through to the final

b Now listen to **A**'s story.

c Cover your story and tell it to **A** using the verb prompts in the list in the correct tenses.
- Rio Olympics   Nikki Hamblin   run in heat   5,000 m
- trip   knock into D'Agostino   both fall
- D'Agostino get up   help Hamblin   hurt her foot
- Hamblin realize   run next to   help each other   finish line
- qualify for the final   D'Agostino not can run   both receive award

In the Rio Olympics, a New Zealand athlete called Nikki Hamblin was running in a heat of the 5,000 m. During the race...

5B How we met Student B

a Read the story and answer the questions.
1. How did they meet?
2. How did their relationship develop?
3. What happened in the end?
4. What makes their relationship work?

b Listen to **A**'s story about Savannah and Michael.

c Now tell **A** about Nick and Tess.

Nick and Tess

Nick was living in Bristol when his mother died. It was a really bad time. One day he decided to go to Bordeaux, in France, where there was a Euro 2016 match that he really wanted to see. He couldn't get a ticket, but there were big screens around the city. Tess, a French student, was working at the event. She was giving free footballs to children. Nick saw her and thought she was beautiful. He asked her for a football. She told him to come back at the end of the day and she kept a football especially for him. He asked her out for dinner.

On their first date, they got on really well, but they didn't kiss at the end of the night. The next day, they met again for coffee before Nick travelled home, but there was still no kiss. Tess was disappointed because she liked him. She knew which flight he was catching, so she decided to go to the airport to say a last goodbye. Nick was checking in when she arrived. When he saw Tess, he was amazed. They had their first kiss at the airport.

Over the next few weeks, Nick made two more trips to France. Then Tess moved to London and she and Nick saw each other regularly. The following year, they decided to live together, and they moved to Liverpool, as it was cheaper than London. Their wedding was delayed because of Covid, but they plan to marry soon, in Bordeaux.

Nick says, 'What I love most about Tess is her positivity.' Tess says, 'Nick is so interesting. There's nothing we can't talk about.'

Adapted from The Guardian

7A University or not? Student B

a Read about Emily-Fleur.

Emily-Fleur Sizmur, 17, runs her own photography business.

I left school at 16. I've never been very interested in school or academic achievement. I still don't know my GCSE results – a friend went to school to pick them up for me, but I've never opened the envelope!

When I left school, I was ready to start a business. Three of my sisters were getting married and I saw a gap in the market for wedding photographers in our area. I'd always loved taking photos and I saw an opportunity to make money doing something I liked. One of my science teachers was getting married and I asked her if I could take some pictures. She agreed and I put up my photos on social media the following day. Within a week, I had bookings for two more weddings. When I'd done six weddings, I spent £3,000 on better equipment.

I don't think my age was a disadvantage, in fact, I think starting out young has been a huge help. People are more prepared to give someone young a chance. If I was 30 and starting out in this business with no experience, I think it would be much more difficult. A lot of my friends are going to university soon, but I don't envy them. They'll have to get out into the real world one day and I'm already here.

Glossary
GCSEs national exams taken by English and Welsh schoolchildren at the age of 16

b Answer A's questions about Emily-Fleur.

c Now ask A your questions about Archie.

What did Archie study at university? — *He studied...*

Questions about Archie
1 How long did Archie spend at university?
2 What did he do on a typical day?
3 What did he do after he graduated?
4 What did he plan to do in Leeds?
5 How many jobs has he applied for?
6 What's he doing at the moment?
7 Is he enjoying life?
8 Does he regret studying drama?

7B Guess the sentence
Student B

a Look at sentences 7–12 and think of the missing verb phrase (+ = positive, – = negative). **Don't write anything yet!**

7 I'll _____ buy a house unless my parents help me. –
8 If I met my ex in the street, I _____ to him. –
9 If it _____, I'd stay a bit longer. –
10 The flight _____ if we go in business class. +
11 I wouldn't mind the winter so much if it _____ so early. –
12 If I had more money, I _____ with a beautiful garden. +

b Listen to **A** say sentence 1. If it's the same as your sentence 1 below, say, 'That's right'. If not, say 'Try again', until **A** gets it right. Continue with 2–6.

1 I'd cook dinner every day if I **got home** earlier from work.
2 If we **don't go on holiday** this summer, maybe we can afford to get a new car.
3 I think you**'ll enjoy the film** more if you see it in 3D.
4 I'd see my grandparents more often if they **lived nearer**.
5 I **wouldn't have** the fish if I were you. It isn't usually very good here.
6 I**'d go swimming** if the water was a bit warmer.

c Now read sentence 7 to **A**. If it isn't right, try again until **A** tells you, 'That's right'. Then write it in. Continue with 8–12.

8A Dragons' Den Student B

Read about **Wonderbly**. Think about the questions below. Then tell your group.
- Did any of the Dragons like the product?
- Did they decide to invest?
- Was the product successful in the end?

Wonderbly

During the pitch, the Dragons were impressed by how quickly the business had grown. But one of the Dragons, a father himself, was so convinced that it was a good idea that he invested all the money they were asking for in exchange for just 5% of the company. It was a clever decision. Wonderbly has now sold over eight million books in countries all over the world, and *The Little Boy / Girl Who Lost His / Her Name* has been translated into many different languages. Another popular book is called *The Birthday Thief*, which uses the child's birth date as the focus of the story.

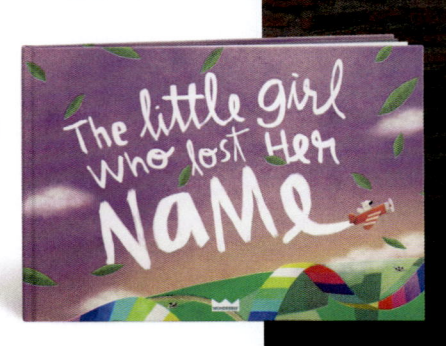

8B I want to speak to the manager Student B

Look at the situations and spend a few minutes preparing what you are going to say. Then role-play the conversations.

1 **You're a shop assistant in a clothes shop. A** is a customer and is going to come to you with a problem with something he / she bought in the sales yesterday. You can't change it for an identical one because there are no more in his / her size. Try to persuade **A** to change it for something else, because you don't usually give refunds during the sales.

   A will start.

2 **You're a customer in a restaurant.** You have just finished your meal and you didn't enjoy it at all (decide what was wrong with it). You complained to the waiter, but the waiter didn't solve the problem. You have asked the waiter to call the manager. **A** is the manager. Try to get at least a 50% discount on your meal.

   You start.

   Good evening. Are you the manager?

9A Guess the conditional Student B

a Look at sentences 7–12 and think of the missing verb phrase ([+] = positive, [−] = negative). **Don't write anything yet!**

7 If we hadn't taken a taxi, we _____ the train. [+]

8 If I hadn't gone to the party that night, I _____ my partner. [−]

9 If I'd known that programme was on last night, I _____ it. [+]

10 If I _____ to my friends, I would never have married James. [+]

11 I _____ with you last night if I hadn't had to work late. [+]

12 I _____ so angry if you had told me the truth right from the start. [−]

b Listen to **A** say sentence 1. If it's the same as your sentence 1 below, say 'That's right'. If not, say 'Try again' until **A** gets it right. Continue with 2–6.

1 We **wouldn't have found** the hotel if we hadn't used satnav.
2 If I **had remembered** that it was your birthday, I would have bought you something.
3 If I**'d known** about the concert earlier, I would have been able to get a ticket.
4 The burglar wouldn't have got in if you **hadn't left** the window open.
5 If our best player hadn't been sent off, we **would have won** the match.
6 I wouldn't have recognized her if you **hadn't told** me who she was.

c Now read sentence 7 to **A**. If it isn't right, try again until **A** tells you 'That's right'. Then write it in. Continue with 8–12.

PE5 Asking politely for information
Student B

a You are a tourist in **A**'s town. You are going to stop **A** in the street. You want to ask questions 1–5 and you want to be very polite. Rewrite 2–5 as indirect questions.

1. Do shops close at lunchtime?
   Could you tell me <u>if shops close at lunchtime</u> ?
2. Is there a cash machine near here?
   Do you know _____?
3. Where's the nearest chemist's?
   Can you tell me _____?
4. What time do buses stop running at night?
   Do you know _____?
5. Do banks open on Saturday mornings?
   Could you tell me _____?

b **A** is a tourist in your town. **A** stops you in the street and asks you some questions. Answer politely with the necessary information.

c Now ask **A** your indirect questions 1–5. Always begin *Excuse me*.

10A Relative clauses quiz Student B

a Complete the questions with a relative clause to describe the **bold** words. Start the clause with *who*, *which*, *that*, or *where*, or no relative pronoun when there is a new subject.

1. **shy** What do you call somebody...?
2. **a remote control** What do you call the thing...?
3. **a referee** What do you call the person...?
4. **a cycle lane** What do you call the place...?
5. **a biopic** What do you call a film...?
6. **knee** What do you call the part of the body...?
7. **a nursery school** What do you call the place...?
8. **a colleague** What do you call a person...?
9. **a scooter** What do you call a thing...?

b Answer **A**'s question 1.

c Now ask **A** your question 1.

d Continue with 2–9.

10B Just checking Student B

a You are a suspect in a crime. **A** is a police inspector. Answer **A**'s questions. You can invent the information if you want to.

b **A** will now check the information he / she has. Say, 'Yes, that's right', or 'No, that's wrong' and correct the wrong information.

c Change roles. Now you are a police inspector and **A** is a suspect. Ask **A** the questions below, but **don't write anything down**. Try to remember **A**'s answers.

- What's your name?
- Where do you live?
- How old are you?
- Where were you born?
- Are you married?
- What do you do?
- What car do you drive?
- How long have you lived in this town?
- What did you do last night?
- Where were you at 7.00 this morning?

d Now check the information with **A** using a question tag.

Your name's John Hatton, isn't it?

You live in New York, don't you?

PE3 Could you do me a favour? Students A+B

a Look at the verb phrases below. Choose two things you would like somebody to do for you. Think about any details, e.g. how many children you have, how much money you need, etc.
- **look after** (your children, your dog for the weekend, your flat while you're away, etc.)
- **lend you** (some money, their car, etc.)
- **give you** a lift (home, to the town centre, etc.)
- **help you** (with a problem, with your homework, to paint your flat, to choose some new clothes, etc.)

b Ask as many other students as possible. Be polite (*Could you do me a big favour? Would you mind...? Do you think you could...?*) and explain why you want the favour. How many people agree to help you?

8A Match your personality to the job Students A+B

In which group(s) do you have most ticks (✓)? Read the appropriate paragraph to find out which jobs would suit you. Would you like to do any of them?

If you have most ticks in 1–4, the best job for you would be in the 'caring professions'. If you are good at science, you could consider a career in medicine, for example, becoming a doctor or nurse. Alternatively, teaching or social work are areas which would suit your personality.

If you have most ticks in 5–8, you should consider a job involving numbers, for example, becoming an accountant, or working in the stock market. The world of business would also probably appeal to you, especially sales or marketing.

If you have most ticks in 9–12, you need a creative job. Depending on your specific talents, you might enjoy a job in the world of music, art, or literature. Areas that would suit you include publishing, journalism, graphic design, fashion, or the music industry.

If you have most ticks in 13–16, you have an analytical mind. You would suit a job in computer science or engineering. You also have good spatial sense, which would make architecture and related jobs another possibility.

8B Going the extra mile Students A+B

A Nordstrom
Finally, they looked through **all the dirt in their vacuum cleaners and found the woman's diamond**!

B Le Creuset
'She even asked **what colour I wanted, and I received it within a week**.'

C Ritz-Carlton Hotels
In it was Joshie, a present of a Frisbee and a football, and a photograph of **Joshie by the hotel pool**.

D Trader Joe's
Half an hour later, the food arrived at her father's house, with **a note saying that it was free**!

E Apple
They refunded his money, but they also sent the iPad back to him with another Post-it note saying, **'Apple said yes'**.

8A Dragons' Den Student C

Read about **Eggxactly**. Think about the questions below. Then tell your group.
- Did any of the Dragons like the product?
- Did they decide to invest?
- Was the product successful in the end?

Eggxactly

A few minutes after starting his pitch, everything went wrong for James. He tried to demonstrate how his gadget could make a boiled egg quickly and easily, but at the end of the cooking time, the egg was still raw! James promised that he had tested the product and that it worked, but when the Dragons asked him why this one was faulty, he answered, 'I haven't got a clue'. In spite of the disastrous pitch, two of the Dragons agreed to invest all the money for 20% of the company each. However, later, they changed their minds and the deal fell through. Eggxactly received 2,000 pre-orders, but although you can still find their website online, the product is no longer available.

Writing Bank

6 A film review

Classic films you must see

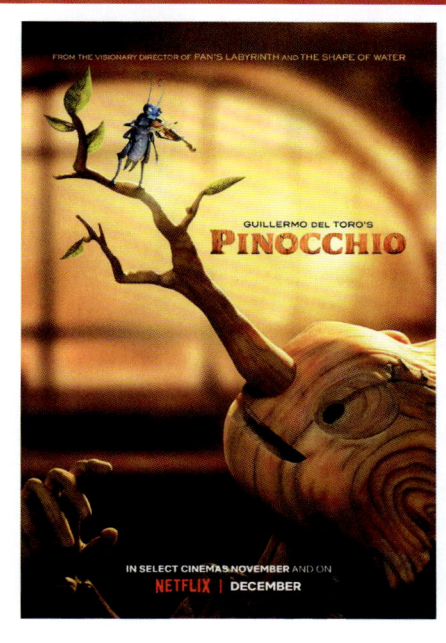

Guillermo del Toro's Pinocchio (2022)

1. This version of *Pinocchio* was directed by Guillermo del Toro and Mark Gustafson. It's an animated film, and is based on the Italian novel *The Adventures of Pinocchio* by Carlo Collodi. It stars Gregory Mann as the voice of Pinocchio, together with Ewan McGregor, Finn Wolfhard, and Cate Blanchett. *Guillermo del Toro's Pinocchio* won an Oscar for Best Animated Feature in 2023.

2. Del Toro's version of *Pinocchio* is set in Italy. However, in the film, the action takes place in a real historical moment: the period when Mussolini was becoming popular. It was filmed in studios in Mexico and the USA.

3. The story is about a man called Geppetto who makes a puppet out of wood. Geppetto is lonely because his son, Carlo, has died. The puppet, Pinocchio, comes to life, but, unlike Carlo, he's very naughty and he doesn't listen to Geppetto – for example, he doesn't go to school when he should. Pinocchio can't die and although he is run over by a lorry, he soon comes back to life again. Pinocchio leaves home and joins first the circus, and then the army. All this time, Geppetto is looking for him, but then Geppetto is swallowed by a sea monster and lives in its stomach. In the end, Pinocchio saves Geppetto, but the ending isn't completely happy.

4. I strongly recommend *Guillermo del Toro's Pinocchio*. It's beautifully made, and it has an important message: you don't have to be perfect for people to love you. There are many different versions of Pinocchio, but for me, this is the best.

a Read the review. What is the message of the film?

b Read the review again. Match paragraphs 1–4 to the topics in the list. What tense do we use to talk about the plot of a book or film?

- [ ] the plot:
- [ ] recommendation:
- [ ] general information:
- [ ] setting:

Making a paragraph plan
When we are writing a text, we organize similar information into three or four groups. We use these groups to write paragraphs. Before we start writing, it's useful to make a paragraph plan.

c Read the information box. Then match the things in the list to the topics in **b**.

the type of film   the director   what the story is about
the stars   the ending   reasons you like it
any prizes it won
when and where the story takes place
where it was filmed

d Look at the highlighted phrases in the review. Then complete the sentences about some more classic films.
1. *Napoleon* _____ Ridley Scott.
2. The action in *Star Wars: The Force Awakens* _____ a galaxy far, far away.
3. *Sully*, with Tom Hanks, _____ a true story about a pilot called Chesley Sullenberger.
4. *The Imitation Game* _____ Benedict Cumberbatch as scientist Alan Turing.
5. *The Great Gatsby* _____ New York in the 1920s.
6. A classic ghost story, *The Sixth Sense* _____ a boy who can see dead people.
7. Most of Spielberg's *West Side Story* _____ locations in New York City.
8. _____ *Oppenheimer*. It's a brilliant film.

e Plan a review of a film that you would recommend. Plan four paragraphs. Make notes on the topics in **c**.

f Write your review. Use your notes in **e**, the paragraph plan in **b**, and some of the highlighted phrases.

g Check your review for mistakes in spelling, grammar, and punctuation.

← p.61

7 Describing a house or flat

a The website HomeRent.com is for people who want to rent out their homes for holidays. Read two posts from the website. Would you like to rent either of these places? Why (not)?

b Read the posts again and answer the questions for both homes.

Paragraph 1
1 Where exactly is it?

Paragraph 2
2 How many rooms are there, and what are they like?
3 Is there any outdoor space?

Paragraph 3
4 What's the neighbourhood like?
5 How far is it from places of interest?
6 What public transport is there?

Paragraph 4
7 Who is it most suitable for?
8 Are there any house rules?

HomeRent.com

Fabulous one-bedroom flat in Florence

1 This flat is **perfectly situated** in Florence with a stunning view of the Palazzo Vecchio and Piazza della Signoria. It is **on the second floor** of a lovely old building.

2 This attractive flat has a spacious double bedroom, a sunny living room, a fully equipped kitchen with a dining area, and a large bathroom with shower. There is a flat-screen TV in the living room and there is also wi-fi and air conditioning.

3 **The neighbourhood**, San Giovanni district, is in the centre of the city. The area is mainly pedestrian, and the Uffizi Gallery, Piazza della Repubblica, and Piazza del Duomo are all very near. It's **a 15-minute walk from** Firenze Santa Maria Novella railway station.

4 The flat is **ideal for** a couple who would like to go sightseeing in this beautiful city. It is a no-smoking house and **no pets are allowed**.

126

Add your home   Log in   ≡

🔍 Search

Beach villa in Kusadasi, Türkiye

beautiful

1. Kusadasi is a ~~nice~~ holiday resort on the west coast of Türkiye, 80 km south of Izmir.

2. The house has three double bedrooms, a living room, a *nice* kitchen, and two bathrooms. All the rooms have air conditioning, and the bedrooms have their own balconies. There is a *nice* terrace with a table and chairs, so you can eat outside. There are *nice* views of the beach and the mountains. There is a communal area with a *nice* garden and a swimming pool.

3. The house is walking distance from several *nice* beaches, where you can do a lot of different water sports. It's also a short drive from the mountains, so you can go hiking. There are regular buses to both the beaches and the mountains.

4. This house is *nice* for a family with children, or for three couples. It is not suitable for pets.

Using adjectives to persuade the reader

When we describe something we want to rent out or sell, we use positive adjectives to make it attractive to the reader.

This **wonderful** cottage has a **cosy** living room. Enjoy **relaxing** summer evenings on the **huge** terrace.

c Read the information box. Then read about the flat in Florence again. Underline the adjectives that help to 'sell' the flat? What do they mean?

d Now read about the villa in Türkiye again. Improve the description by replacing the adjective *nice* with a positive adjective from the description of the flat. Often there is more than one possibility.

e Imagine you want to rent out your home to tourists. Plan a description for a website. Plan four paragraphs. Make notes on the questions in **b**.

f Now write your description. Use your notes in **e** and the advice in the information box. Include some of the highlighted phrases, which are typical in a description of this kind.

g Check your description for mistakes in spelling, grammar, and punctuation.

⬅ p.75

8 A covering email

a Read the job advertisement and answer the questions.
1 How many job areas are they recruiting for?
2 Which three job requirements are mentioned?
3 What do you need to do to apply?

b Now read the covering email. In which area is Ricardo applying for a job?

c Read the covering email again. Circle the appropriate phrase in 1–8. Is the language formal or informal? Why?

> **Including relevant information**
> When we apply for a job, we send a CV (*curriculum vitae*) describing our qualifications, skills, and experience, and a covering email explaining why we would be suitable for the role. To plan the covering email, we refer to the advertisement and identify the main job requirements. Then, in the email, we include information about ourselves that connects with these requirements.

d Read the information box. Which information in the email matches the job requirements?

e Choose a job from the advert. Plan a covering email (to send with your CV) to apply for the job. Make notes on the information you can include that connects with the job requirements in the advert.

f Now write your covering email. Use your notes in e and write in a formal style. Include some of the highlighted phrases, which are typical in an email of this kind.

g Check your covering email for mistakes in spelling, grammar, and punctuation.

→ p.79

We are looking for hard-working, enthusiastic, and energetic people to work at the next World Athletics Championships.

There are vacancies in the following areas:
- Administration
- Hospitality and catering
- Translation and language services
- Medical support

All applicants must have appropriate training and experience, and a B1 level of English is a minimum requirement.

Send your CV and a covering email (in English) to: **recruitment@wac.com**

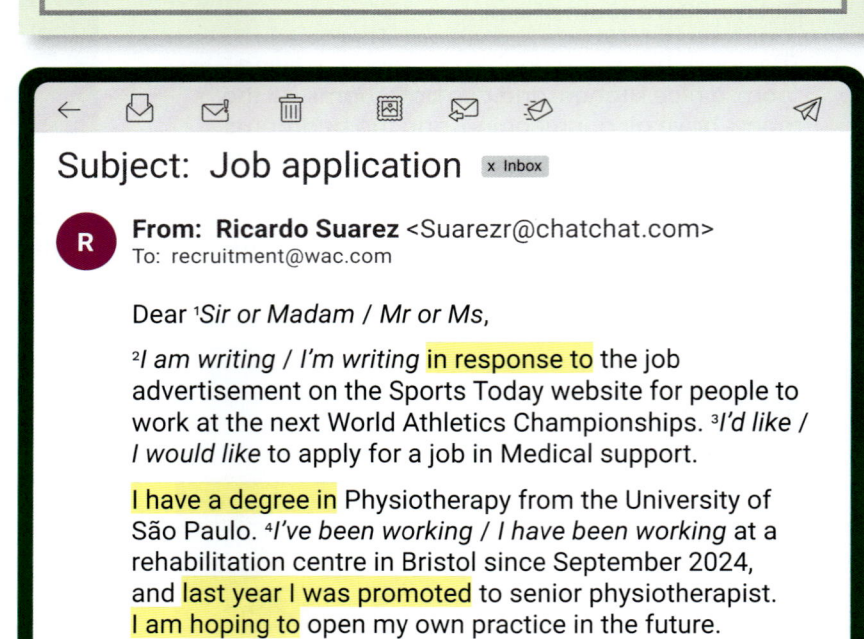

Subject: Job application x Inbox

From: Ricardo Suarez <Suarezr@chatchat.com>
To: recruitment@wac.com

Dear ¹*Sir or Madam / Mr or Ms*,

²*I am writing / I'm writing* in response to the job advertisement on the Sports Today website for people to work at the next World Athletics Championships. ³*I'd like / I would like* to apply for a job in Medical support.

I have a degree in Physiotherapy from the University of São Paulo. ⁴*I've been working / I have been working* at a rehabilitation centre in Bristol since September 2024, and last year I was promoted to senior physiotherapist. I am hoping to open my own practice in the future.

⁵*About / Regarding* my level of English, I passed the B2 exam two years ago. I am currently attending classes and I hope to take the C1 exam in June this year.

⁶*I'm sending you / I attach* my CV for your reference.

⁷*Hope to hear from you soon! / I look forward to hearing from you.*

⁸*Yours sincerely, / Yours faithfully,*

Ricardo Suarez

9 A 'for and against' essay

a Look at the title and read the essay. Is the writer generally for or against Wikipedia?

b Cover the text and try to remember...
  1 three good things about Wikipedia.
  2 three bad things about it.

Wikipedia, for and against

1 Wikipedia is an online encyclopaedia. It has become the main source of information for millions of people every day and is a wonderful resource. However, it has both advantages and disadvantages.

2 On the one hand, Wikipedia has information about more or less everything and the information is easy to find. Secondly, Wikipedia usually gives a good basic introduction to a topic. It also gives links and references to other sources, so it is easy to find out more if you want to.

3 On the other hand, there are also disadvantages. For example, the information on Wikipedia is sometimes inaccurate, which is a problem if it is your only source of information. In addition, you don't know who has written the articles. It may be an expert, but it may be an amateur, and sometimes there is a personal or political bias as well.

4 In conclusion, if you are looking for information, Wikipedia is a useful tool, although you can't always rely on it. It is an excellent place to start, but it shouldn't be your only source – it is important to get your information from other more reliable places, too.

c Read the essay again. Match paragraphs 1–4 to the sections in the list.
  ☐ advantages
  ☐ the writer's opinion
  ☐ introduction: what Wikipedia is
  ☐ disadvantages

> **Adding and contrasting information**
> When we want to **add** information, we can use *also, in addition, as well,* and *too*.
> When we want to **contrast** information, we can use *however, although, but,* and *on the one hand / on the other hand*.

d Read the information box. Then circle the correct options.
  1 Electric cars are still very expensive, *although / as well* prices are coming down.
  2 Desktops have a larger memory than laptops. They *however / also* usually last longer.
  3 Many students like taking notes on a tablet, *on the one hand / but* others prefer a pen and paper.
  4 There's no paper in the printer, and it's run out of ink, *too / however*.
  5 You can use the app to check your bank account. *In addition / Although*, you can use it to send and receive money.
  6 Earbuds are more convenient than headphones. *As well / On the other hand*, the sound quality isn't always as good.
  7 It's very easy to pay contactless for everything. *However / Also*, this can cause problems for people who don't have a bank card.

e Read the beginning of another 'for and against' essay. Then make notes in the chart with your ideas.

Smartphones – for and against
Nowadays, a phone isn't just for phone calls. Most people have a smartphone, with many different apps and constant access to social media…

Advantages	Disadvantages

f Plan your essay. Plan four paragraphs. Use the sections in **c**. Complete the introduction and decide your own opinion.

g Now write your essay. Use your notes in **f** and the language in the information box. Include some of the highlighted phrases, which are typical in an essay of this kind.

h Check your essay for mistakes in spelling, grammar, and punctuation.

← p.95

10 A biography

a Do you know anything about Umberto Eco? What book is he most famous for?

b Read the biography and check. Then complete it with non-defining relative clauses A–E.

A who was a German art teacher
B which sold 15 million copies
C which produced a variety of cultural programmes
D where he became friends with artists, painters, musicians, and writers
E which is a murder mystery

Umberto Eco
(1932–2016)

1 Umberto Eco was born in Italy in 1932. He was a novelist, critic, and academic. When he was young, he loved reading everything from comics to classic novels. His father, who was an accountant, wanted Umberto to be a lawyer, but he decided to study philosophy and literature at the University of Turin.

2 After he graduated, he worked for Radiotelevisione Italiana, ¹___. During this time, he started to write novels.

3 In September 1962, he married Renate Ramge, ²___. They had a son and a daughter. They lived in an apartment in Milan, ³___. In the 1970s, Umberto Eco started teaching at Bologna University, and during the 1980s and 1990s, he was a visiting professor at Harvard and Columbia universities in the USA.

4 Umberto Eco is best known for his hugely successful novel *The Name of the Rose*, ⁴___. It was published in 1980 and made into a film six years later. The book, ⁵___, is set in a 14th-century Italian monastery. It made him an international literary star. However, Eco did not enjoy his fame – he said, 'I don't feel free any more'.

5 Umberto Eco died in 2016, on 19th February. He was 84 and had cancer.

c Read the biography again. Match the information to each paragraph.

childhood   death   family   first book   first job   fame
greatest achievement   illness   later life   studies

Paragraph 1: _____ _____
Paragraph 2: _____ _____
Paragraph 3: _____ _____
Paragraph 4: _____ _____
Paragraph 5: _____ _____

Using the correct preposition

In a biography, we often refer to specific times or places, so it is important to use the correct prepositions. Remember the rules:

Time: **in** with months and years, **on** with specific days or dates, **during** / **in** with periods of time
*Umberto Eco died **in** 2016, **on** 19th February.*

Place: **in** with specific buildings, towns, cities, and countries, **at** with generic places, e.g. school, university.
*They lived **in** an apartment **in** Milan. Umberto Eco started teaching **at** Bologna University.*

d Read the information box. Then complete the sentences with the correct preposition.

1 Louise Bourgeois was a French American artist. She was born _____ Paris _____ 1911, _____ Christmas Day.

2 After leaving school, she studied maths _____ Sorbonne University, but later studied art _____ the École des Beaux-Arts and the École du Louvre.

3 _____ 1938, she opened her own gallery _____ a building next door to where her father worked, and _____ the same year, she married Robert Goldwater, an American art professor.

4 They soon moved to New York, but _____ their early years there, for example, _____ the Second World War, Louise struggled to break into the art scene. Later, _____ the 1950s, she became friends with other famous artists such as Mark Rothko and Jackson Pollock, and became more confident.

5 One of her most famous works is a giant spider sculpture called *Maman*, which stands outside the Guggenheim Museum _____ Bilbao.

e Plan a short biography of an interesting or successful person who has died this century. Plan five paragraphs. Make notes on the information in **c**.

f Now write your biography. Use your notes in **e** and the language in the information box. Include some of the highlighted phrases, which are typical in a biography of this kind.

g Check your biography for mistakes in spelling, grammar, and punctuation.

p.99

Listening

🔊 **6.6**

Part 1

Interviewer So tell me, how did you get involved in the film, Dagmara?

Dagmara Well, as you probably know, *Schindler's List* was shot in Krakow, in Poland, which is where I live. I was a university student at the time, studying English. And the film company set up their production office here three months before they started shooting the film and I got a job there as a production assistant, preparing and translating documents and the script.

Interviewer But how did you get the job as Steven Spielberg's interpreter?

Dagmara Well, it was a complete coincidence. Just before the shooting started, there was a big party in one of the hotels in Krakow for all the actors and the film crew, and I was invited, too. When I arrived at the party the Polish producer of the film came up to me and said, 'The woman who was going to interpret for Steven Spielberg can't come, so we need you to interpret his opening speech.'

Interviewer How did you feel about that?

Dagmara I couldn't believe it! I was just a student – I had no experience of interpreting – and now I was going to speak in front of hundreds of people. I was so nervous that I drank a couple of glasses of champagne to give myself courage. I must have done a pretty good job though, because soon afterwards Spielberg came up to me to say thank you and then he said, 'I'd like you to be my interpreter for the whole film.' I was so stunned I had to pinch myself to believe that this was happening to me.

🔊 **6.8**

Part 2

Interviewer So what exactly did you have to do?

Dagmara I had to go to the film set every day and translate Spielberg's instructions to the Polish actors, and also to the extras. I had to make them understand what he wanted them to do. It was really exciting, and I often felt as if I was a director myself.

Interviewer So, was it a difficult job?

Dagmara Sometimes it was really hard. The worst thing was when we had to shoot a scene again and again because Spielberg thought it wasn't exactly right. Some scenes were repeated as many as 16 times – and then sometimes I would think that maybe it was my fault – that I hadn't translated properly what he wanted, so I'd get really nervous. I remember one scene with lots of actors in it which we just couldn't get right and Spielberg started shouting at me because he was stressed. Eventually, we got it right and then he apologized, and I cried a little, because I was also very stressed – and after that it was all right again.

Interviewer So, was Spielberg difficult to work with?

Dagmara Not at all. I mean, he was very demanding, I had to do my best every day, but he was really nice to me. I felt he treated me like a daughter. For instance, he was always making sure that I wasn't cold – it was freezing on the set most of the time – and he would make sure that I had a warm coat and gloves and things.

Interviewer Did you ever get to be an extra?

Dagmara Yes, twice! I was going to be in two party scenes, and I got to wear beautiful long dresses and high heels. Unfortunately, one scene didn't make it to the final cut of the film, and before we started shooting the other one, I tripped walking down some stairs and twisted my ankle really badly. I was in so much pain that I couldn't take part in the filming. And that was the end of my 'acting career'. I still have the photos of me looking like a girl from the 40s, though!

Interviewer Have you ever worked with Spielberg again?

Dagmara Yes. A year later he invited me to interpret for him again, this time during the premiere of *Schindler's List* in Poland, which was broadcast live on national television! Before that, he had also asked me to come to work as a production assistant on his next movie in Hollywood. I was very tempted and thought really hard about it, but I hadn't finished my studies yet, and all my family and friends were in Poland – so in the end, I decided not to go.

Interviewer Do you regret it?

Dagmara Not at all. I had my moment, and it was unforgettable, but that was it!

🔊 **6.16**

Danish Sheikh tells me that people with charisma do two basic things. They project their own personality, but at the same time they also make other people feel important. Sheikh's lessons are designed to help me to do both of these things, and in the next 48 hours I learn a lot.

Projecting your own personality is difficult to learn. Nobody likes people who talk about how fantastic they are, but nobody remembers people who don't say anything about themselves. Sheikh says the solution is to talk about yourself enough, but not too much.

People with charisma also feel confident. Sheikh gives me advice to help me feel more confident, for example, when I walk into a meeting or a party. He tells me to remember a time in the past when I was successful. This positive memory will stop me from feeling afraid or anxious.

Body language is also important. We practise it together, including how to stand like a gorilla, with your feet apart and your arms wide – this shows that you're an important person. Sheikh also tells me how to enter a room. You have to have your chin up and your shoulders back. He tells me to make eye contact with the people I'm talking to, but not for too long – maximum four seconds – it's important not to stare. We also study hand gestures – you shouldn't use them too much.

Finally, conversation. I learn that it's important not to speak too fast or too slowly. You need to vary your speed to keep your listener's attention. But the most important thing of all is listening carefully. If you show interest in people, it makes them feel special. But if you're not really listening, the person you're talking to notices very quickly, so you need to make sure you really concentrate on what they're saying.

At the end of the two days, I have a practical test...

🔊 **6.17**

At the end of the two days, I have a practical test. I go to a pub with Sheikh, and I have to talk to strangers. I start talking to people and it goes OK. I don't think English people really like it when a stranger starts speaking to them, but we laugh and I have some interesting conversations. Occasionally, Sheikh gives me advice. He reminds me to make eye contact with everyone I'm talking to, and tells me not to cross my arms, that kind of thing.

As we leave the pub, we shake hands. He says that the course has been good for me, and he gives me a thumbs-up. So have I changed? Am I more charismatic? Not exactly – I'm never going to stand like a gorilla again, for example. But perhaps charisma is simpler than that anyway; it's about understanding who you are better, and showing the best version of yourself.

🔊 **7.7**

Episode 2: the 1920s–1930s

In this episode the children learn Esperanto. This language of international communication was invented in the 19th century and became popular in the period between the two World Wars. It was called 'the language of peace'. To help them learn it, teachers use the latest technology – a record player, or 'gramophone' as it was called then. There are school medical checks, and the children have to take a spoonful of a medicine called cod liver oil every day, for extra vitamins – they all hate it! Children of all ages also have to have a sleep every afternoon, as it's considered important for their health. In lessons, the girls aren't happy when they discover that the boys are studying science, while they have to look after dolls to teach them how to look after babies when they have them! And it's not just the female pupils who are treated differently; female teacher Sue must leave when she gets married.

Episode 3: the 1940s–1950s
The Second World War has ended, and a revolution in education has begun. There is a new exam for children called the 11 plus which separates the academic and less academic children. Health is still very important, and children get a free bottle of milk every day. Learning is all based on memorizing facts. The girls now do some academic subjects like English and history, but they also do some 'girls' subjects; for example, they have 'deportment' lessons, where they practise balancing books on their heads to learn how to walk gracefully. For the boys, on the other hand, apart from doing all their academic subjects, they also go cross-country running – a sport where they run long distances in the countryside. This is because being athletic was now considered very important.

Episode 4: the 1960s
In the 60s, the class try out a different school called a Secondary Modern. Education is now less formal, and they study vocational subjects to prepare them for certain types of jobs. Boys and girls are separated again: typewriting for girls and bricklaying for boys. Then there's cookery for girls, and the boys learn to drive, something that is considered a vital skill for male school leavers. They still have to do maths, though, and this is one of the few lessons where boys and girls are mixed.

Episode 5: the 1970s
In the 1970s, the children are at a new type of school called a Comprehensive. Finally, boys and girls are mixed for all lessons. The curriculum expands to include new subjects like business and air travel – they even have a life-size model plane in the classroom. Although education now is more experimental, school rules are still strict, especially as regards uniform and appearance, and the children rebel. The girls want to wear short skirts and the boys want to have long hair, both of which are forbidden. Three of the pupils in the programme are kept in after school as a punishment for breaking the rules!

Episode 6: the 1980s
The pupils arrive in the 1980s, where technology is changing fast. In the maths class, they try out a computer for the first time. School meals have also changed. Fast food is now served in a canteen, and children can choose what they want to eat – for the very first time they can have chips! The only area where boys and girls do different things is in PE lessons. Boys still have to do cross-country running, for example, but the girls can take part in a new sport – rhythmic gymnastics.

Episode 7: the 1990s
By the 1990s, many of the changes at school are to do with extra-curricular activities and how pupils spend their free time. The children raise money for charity by performing a fashion show for their friends and family. In break time, they exchange football stickers, or play with toys such as the Game Boy and their pet Tamagotchis. But the biggest change of all takes place in their computer class. They get the chance to use an early dial-up modem, and access the very first world wide website. Education will never really be the same again.

🔊 7.10
The topic I've chosen is 'All children should play a team sport at school'.
I completely agree for the following reasons. First of all, I think that doing any kind of sport is a really positive thing for children. It's good for their health and apparently, it helps children to learn better.
My second point is that team sports are good for building relationships. Children learn how to work together.
Another important point is that they can use the team skills they learn from sport in other areas of their life.
Finally, being part of a team is a great experience. It doesn't matter if you're not good at a sport – you can still enjoy playing the game with your friends.

🔊 8.8
Part 1

Interviewer Whose idea was it to go on the programme?
Joe It was my idea. I applied without telling my business partner Jake. Of course, I never really expected to get on it. But then they phoned me from the BBC and said, 'You're on the programme', so that's when I told him.
Interviewer Did you spend a long time preparing your pitch?
Joe Yes. We worked really hard, and we practised a lot so that we knew the pitch word for word. The evening before the show we actually went for a run – up in Manchester, where it's filmed – and we went running together just repeating the pitch over and over again.
Interviewer How did you feel when you arrived at the Den?
Joe Erm, well, we were told to get to the set at about 11.00 the night before, because you had to prepare everything in advance, like any furniture you need, things like that. It was freezing cold, and we were exhausted – we didn't get back to our hotel until the middle of the night – and a car came to pick us up a few hours later, at half five in the morning.
Interviewer What time did you actually do your pitch?
Joe Erm, 11.30. So we were lucky because we were the first in that particular programme.
Interviewer Why lucky?
Joe Because we didn't have to wait too long. The other contestants spent ages just waiting around. Some of them – the ones who are on last – had to wait 12 hours!
Interviewer Did you meet the Dragons before you went in to do the pitch?
Joe No. You're not allowed to. Like, if you go to the toilet before you go on, someone has to escort you in case you meet a Dragon. So the first time you see them is when you go into the Den.

🔊 8.9
Part 2

Interviewer What were the Dragons like?
Joe Well, they're obviously told by the producers to be really unfriendly and aggressive. So I remember thinking, when the doors opened and we walked in, what I wanted to do was just to smile at one of them. That was my way of making myself relaxed. And I looked at Deborah Meaden, because she was in the middle, and I smiled at her, but she just, you know, stared at me, stony-faced, to make me feel nervous. And it worked.
Interviewer Did you think you did a good presentation?
Joe Yeah, we did. But Jake, who usually never gets anything wrong, he forgot his first words, and he just never does that. So we both thought, when he got the introduction wrong, that it was going to go badly, but it didn't.
Interviewer So what happened after you'd done your pitch?
Joe Yeah, well, four of the Dragons said, 'I'm out'. They said they weren't interested. So we were feeling pretty depressed, pretty negative.
Interviewer And then?
Joe The last Dragon was Peter. And he's quite scary – he's incredibly tall, over two metres. And at first he really criticized us. But then he told us he had a big chain of camera shops called Jessops and they were starting online printing and photo framing as part of their business. And then he said, 'I've got 15 guys in Hong Kong (SAR) trying to do what you guys are doing, but you guys are doing it better. I'm going to offer you both a job.'
Interviewer Were you very surprised?
Joe Totally, because it had never happened on Dragons' Den before. In ten years, they'd never offered someone a job.
Interviewer So he offered you jobs just like that?
Joe Well, his offer was that he wanted to have our business, and for us to work with him at Jessops.
Interviewer With a good salary?
Joe Very.
Interviewer So what did you do?

🔊 8.10
Part 3

Joe It was very stressful because we knew we had to make a decision immediately. So Jake said, 'Yes, let's take the jobs', but I said, 'You don't want to work for Jessops'. And he stayed silent and I said, 'I don't want to work for Jessops'. I mean,

neither of us were in a position where we could have dropped everything and gone and worked for Jessops full-time. It was completely..., it was ridiculous.
Interviewer So you said no?
Joe That's right.
Interviewer Have you ever regretted saying no?
Joe No, not for a second. It was still early days for us then, so we were still kind of having fun and enjoying running our own business. And things worked out well for us. Frame Again was successful, and eventually we sold the business.
Interviewer But not to one of the Dragons?
Joe No, but that would have been perfect!

🔊 8.14

Hello and welcome to *How's Business?* Today we're going to look at how social media can make a big difference for some businesses. And I'd like to start with the story of Dave Carroll, a Canadian singer-songwriter, who had a very bad experience with United Airlines.

Dave and his band were flying with United Airlines from Halifax, in Nova Scotia, to Omaha, in Nebraska, with a stopover in Chicago. As they were waiting to get off the plane in Chicago, they heard another passenger say, 'My God! They're throwing guitars out there!'

One of the band members looked out of the plane window, and saw that the baggage handlers, who were taking the luggage off the plane, weren't being careful with the band's guitars – they were throwing them. The band were very worried and they immediately complained to United Airlines, but nobody listened to them.

When they arrived in Omaha, Dave discovered that part of his very expensive Taylor guitar had been damaged. It cost him $1,200 to get it repaired. For nine months he tried to claim compensation from United Airlines. He phoned and emailed their offices in Halifax, Chicago, and New York without success. In the end he even suggested that instead of money, they could give him $1,200 of flight tickets. But after all his complaints and suggestions, United simply said, 'No'.

So, what else could a singer-songwriter do? Dave wrote a song about his experience, and produced a music video to go with it. The song was called 'United Breaks Guitars'. He posted the video on YouTube and it was a huge hit. The song reached number 1 on the iTunes music store within a week. Dave decided to produce two more videos, which he also posted on YouTube.

Four days later, after one million views of the first video, United Airlines contacted Dave and offered him a payment – they said he had one chance to accept, and he wouldn't get a better offer from them. He refused, and suggested they gave the money to charity. Of course, the impact of Dave's song went far beyond YouTube. Soon newspapers, websites, TV, and radio stations all over North America were doing stories about the song. Dave was interviewed on many radio and TV shows where, of course, he retold the story of how 'United Breaks Guitars'. He did over 200 interviews in the first three months!

Dave Carroll's favourite guitar was damaged, but in the end United Airlines were the bigger losers. After the bad publicity, the BBC reported that United Airlines' share price had dropped by 10% within four weeks, which means that the company lost an incredible $180 million. It would have been much cheaper to repair Dave's guitar. Since, then, Dave's first music video has had over 22 million views.

🔊 9.1

Here are three of the best stories people sent to me at Solo Traveler. First, Katya. Katya was in Argentina to see the famous Iguazu Falls. She'd just arrived in Puerto Iguazu, the nearest town to the falls. It was 10 p.m. at night. She'd booked a room in a hostel, but when she tried to find it, it just didn't seem to exist. She walked around town for a long time, but she had no luck, and in the end, she stopped at a bar and asked the owner and his wife for help. It turned out that the hostel had given her the wrong address. The kind bar owner ended up driving her around town at two o'clock in the morning to try to find the hostel. In the end, they found the place, but the front desk was closed for the night. So then the bar owner drove her to a small hotel that was still open, so she could get a room for the night. He even negotiated the price for her as he was worried it would be too expensive, so it only cost her the same as the hostel. Katya says she can't believe how incredibly kind he was.

What a great story. Now, this is Gerry's story.

Gerry was on a solo trip to France. While he was in Paris, one day he was in a hurry. He ran across the street and tripped on the kerb. He fell flat on his face on the sidewalk and cut his face badly – it was bleeding a lot. He was lying on the sidewalk, and a group of boys, about 13 or 14 years old, came over to him. They helped him to stand up and they took him to sit down on a bench. One of the boys gave him some tissues to stop the bleeding. Then another boy ran to a nearby school to ask the school nurse to have a look at Gerry, and all the other boys helped him to walk slowly along the road to the school. They couldn't go in with him, so they waved goodbye and ran off. Gerry says that the whole experience could have been much worse, but the kindness of those young men really cheered him up.

And finally, this is what happened to Jenn. Jenn was at the airport in Lisbon. She was on her way first to London and then back to the US. She thought she'd allowed plenty of time to check in, but when she got to the airport, there was a huge line, of several hundred people. She was absolutely convinced that she would miss her flight – she was panicking, and talking aloud to herself, saying, 'What am I going to do?' Then a man in the line asked her, in English, if he could help. She explained that she had a flight to London and the man told her she was actually in the line for a flight to Brazil. He wasn't sure where she needed to be, but he stepped out of his line, found the line she needed to be in, which was much shorter, and showed her where to go. The person behind him saved his place while he made sure Jenn was OK. Jenn says if it wasn't for the kindness of this man, she would have had a complete panic attack! I love these stories of the kindness of strangers. Keep sending your stories in – we love to hear from all those solo travelers out there.

🔊 9.9

We're more dependent on power than ever before, thanks to our phone addiction, and because many people work from home more often, using laptops. So how difficult would life be for 24 hours without power? I decided to find out.

7 a.m. – 9 a.m.
Laptop battery: 95% Phone battery: 100% Tablet battery: 65%
It's ten minutes since my alarm went off. I set it on my phone, which I charged overnight – my last blast of electricity for the next 24 hours. Already I'm realizing quite how dependent we are on power. My usual morning shower isn't possible. Neither is breakfast. I look sadly at the electric kettle. I can't even boil some water in a saucepan. My hob needs power. My toaster needs power. Everything in my modern home seems to need power. I read the news on my tablet and the battery life drops from 65% to 55% in a few minutes. Uh-oh.

9 a.m. – midday
Laptop battery: 72% Phone battery: 91% Tablet battery: 55%
I sit down to work at my laptop. By 10 a.m., it's down to 72% battery. Someone gets in touch to ask me to Skype, but Skype calls really drain the power. I close down unnecessary programs and turn the brightness of my screen down to its lowest level. I can't use the wi-fi because my internet router is turned off. I can only use my mobile data, but I decide not to use it because I'm worried that it will use up my phone battery very quickly. A researcher at Queensland University of Technology, who has studied 'battery anxiety', says that when our battery life drops to 20%, we start thinking about what we actually need to do compared to what we want to do. Do we need to scroll through TikTok? I think we all know the answer to that.

Midday – 2 p.m.
Laptop battery: 39% Phone battery: 86% Tablet battery: 54%
Normally for lunch, I'd reheat yesterday's pizza in the oven. But that's not possible, so I eat cold meats, and drink a warm Diet Coke, because the fridge is also off! I'm trying to avoid opening the fridge as much as possible; if the door is shut, food should be OK for four to six hours in the fridge, and 15 to 24 hours in the freezer before you need to throw it away.

2 p.m.–6 p.m.
Laptop battery: 0% Phone battery: 69%
Tablet battery: 36%
Finally, my laptop battery dies just after lunch. Thankfully, I can continue to work in the cloud on my phone. I do this for a while, but the small screen makes typing very difficult and I want to shout at the screen! I go for a walk – only I can't listen to music or the radio on my phone, as I usually would. I think nostalgically of the battery-operated Walkman of the 1980s…

6 p.m. onwards
Laptop battery: 0% Phone battery: 44%
Tablet battery: 26%
There's not much power left and it's getting dark. How on earth did people keep themselves busy in the evenings before electricity? I call a friend named Joel. Two and a half years ago, he decided to live off-grid and now he lives in a tent in a field. I ask Joel what to do with my long Friday evening. He thinks for a minute. 'Cook yourself a really nice meal,' he says, sounding very chilled. 'But I have an electric cooker,' I say. Joel's surprised – he cooks his food outside over a fire. Then I have a flash of inspiration. My car has enough petrol in it to get to a takeaway. As my phone charge drops to 20%, I drive out to pick up dinner. For the next hour, my girlfriend and I sit in the dark eating fried chicken. Then we decide to have an early night. And with hardly any phone battery left, I won't be able to rely on my alarm to wake me up tomorrow.

🔊 10.4

1 The red phone box
In 1924, the Post Office organized a competition to design a new phone box. The winner was the architect Giles Gilbert Scott, who also designed Liverpool Cathedral and the building that is now Tate Modern. The first phone box was built in London in 1926. It was painted red to make it easy to see at a distance, although Scott had originally suggested silver with a blue interior. With the arrival of mobile phones in the 21st century, people didn't need phone boxes any more, and most of them have now been removed. However, today they are considered design icons of historic importance, and several are now tourist attractions, including one of the original ones next to the Royal Academy of Arts in Piccadilly. Others have found new lives in local communities, as mini-libraries or art galleries, and a very few still survive as working phones.

2 The Anglepoise lamp
George Carwardine was an engineer, who specialized in suspension systems for cars. He worked for car manufacturers for several years, but when the company he was working for went bankrupt, he decided to set up a small company on his own. He had a little workshop in his garden, and there he designed a lamp which could be moved in different directions, inspired by the human arm. He licensed his design to a company which made the springs for his lamps, and in 1935 they brought out the three-spring Anglepoise desk lamp. It was an instant success, and the exact same model, the Anglepoise 1227, is still made today. Carwardine later developed many variations on the original design, including lamps for hospital operating theatres and for military aeroplanes. But it is the classic ever-popular Anglepoise 1227 which is today considered an iconic British design.

3 The Penguin book covers
Penguin books was started in 1935, although the classic cover was not designed until eleven years later. In 1935, publisher Allen Lane was at a bookstall on a railway platform looking for something to read, but he could only find magazines. He decided that people needed to be able to buy books that were good quality fiction, but cheap, and not just in traditional bookshops but also on railway stations and in chain stores. Lane wanted a dignified but amusing symbol for the new books and his secretary suggested a penguin, so graphic designer Edward Young was sent to London Zoo to make drawings of penguins. The first Penguin paperbacks appeared in the summer of 1935. They included the works of Agatha Christie and the American writer Ernest Hemingway. The classic book cover was designed by Young in 1946. The books were colour coded – orange for fiction, blue for biography, and green for crime. The way people thought about books had changed forever – the paperback revolution had begun.
The cover designs of Penguin books have changed a lot over the years, but the original 1946 cover, which is considered a design icon, was recently brought back, and is also used on mugs, notebooks, and other items.

4 The miniskirt
The 1960s was famous for many things from the Beatles to the first man on the moon, but the miniskirt remains one of the decade's most long-lasting icons. Mary Quant was a British fashion designer, who had a boutique called Bazaar in the King's Road, the most fashionable shopping street of the time. As a girl, she had always tried to make her school uniform skirt shorter, 'to be more exciting-looking'. In 1966, she saw a group of tap dancers at a nearby school in very short skirts, with socks and dance shoes. This inspired her to create the miniskirt, which she named after her favourite car, the Mini. However, the miniskirt was not popular with everyone. Coco Chanel described it as 'just awful'. But Quant's customers loved it. Before the 1960s, young women had been expected to dress like their mothers, but this was about young people looking young. Although 1960s fashion soon changed to the long hippy clothes of the 1970s, the miniskirt has never disappeared, and is still worn today by women of all ages all over the world.

🔊 10.7
Part 1

Interviewer Good morning and thank you for coming, Mr Morton – or should it be Inspector Morton – you were a detective with Scotland Yard, weren't you?
Morton Yes, that's right. For 25 years. I retired last year.
Interviewer People today are still fascinated by the identity of Jack the Ripper, over 130 years after the crimes were committed. It's incredible, isn't it?
Morton Well, it's not really that surprising. People are always interested in unsolved murders – and Jack the Ripper has become a sort of cult horror figure.
Interviewer So what can you tell us about some of the new theories about his identity?
Morton Well, a recent new theory was put forward by a crime historian called Jan Bondeson. He thinks that Jack the Ripper was a Dutch sailor called Hendrik de Jong.
Interviewer What evidence does he have?
Morton Well, de Jong was definitely a murderer. He killed four women in Holland and Belgium, including two of his ex-wives. He also travelled to London a lot, and he was there when the Jack the Ripper murders took place. He also matches the descriptions we have of Jack the Ripper.
Interviewer How credible is his theory?
Morton Well, even Dr Bondeson says that it's impossible to know for certain if de Jong was Jack the Ripper. I would say it's possible, but there isn't really enough conclusive evidence.

🔊 10.8
Part 2

Interviewer The next recent theory I'm interested in comes from the film director Bruce Robinson, who wrote a book in 2016 called *They All Love Jack*. What can you tell us about it?
Morton Bruce Robinson is convinced that Jack the Ripper was in fact Michael Maybrick, the brother of one of the original suspects, James Maybrick. He thinks that the style of the murders indicates that there was a connection with the Freemasons – which both brothers were.
Interviewer What did Michael do?
Morton He was a popular singer and composer of songs at the time, and Robinson thinks that the Ripper's letters are similar in style to some of his songs, and the fact that they were posted from so many different parts of the UK makes sense because Michael was on tour at the time. Robinson thinks he was a psychopath, and was responsible for at least 16 more murders that took place in England later. He even thinks that Michael went on to murder his brother James.
Interviewer But he was never arrested, was he?
Morton No, he wasn't. However, Bruce thinks that by 1893 the police had begun to suspect him, but because many of the police themselves were Freemasons, they allowed him to escape to the Isle of Wight, where he lived for the rest of his life.
Interviewer And what do you do think?

Morton I think the book is well researched, but I don't really believe his conspiracy theory, that the police knew it was Michael and let him get away. I think the reason the Ripper was never caught was because the police were incompetent, not corrupt.

🔊 **10.9**
Part 3
Interviewer Finally, let's talk about Patricia Cornwell's research. In her 2002 book *Jack the Ripper – Case Closed,* she said that she had identified the murderer and that she was convinced that Jack the Ripper was in fact Walter Sickert, the painter. What evidence did she put forward to support this claim?
Morton Well, she mainly used DNA analysis. She actually spent over £2,000,000 buying 32 paintings by Sickert. She cut up one of them to get the DNA from it – people in the art world were furious.
Interviewer I can imagine.
Morton And then she compared the DNA from the painting with DNA taken from the letters that Jack the Ripper sent to the police. Patricia Cornwell said that she was 99% certain that Walter Sickert was Jack the Ripper.
Interviewer And now she's written a new book with more evidence.
Morton Yes, it's called *Ripper: The Secret Life of Walter Sickert.* She says she's found new evidence, including letters which were written by Jack the Ripper and by Walter Sickert on the same very unusual type of paper. She also points out that some of his paintings are very violent and frightening.
Interviewer But you don't think she's right, do you?
Morton Well, I think she might be right. She has a lot of evidence, although I don't think it's completely reliable. And a lot of people think she's wrong!
Interviewer So, who do you think the murderer was?
Morton I can't tell you because I don't know.
Interviewer Do you think we'll ever solve the mystery?
Morton Yes, I think one day the mystery will be solved. Some new evidence will appear that proves 100% who Jack the Ripper was, and we'll be able to say that the case is finally closed. But at the moment it's still a mystery, and people like a good mystery.

🔊 **10.15**
Part 2
Holmes What do you think, Watson?
Watson said Holmes, when our visitor left. 'It's a mystery to me,' I answered. 'What are you going to do?'
Holmes Think. Don't speak to me for 50 minutes!
Watson Holmes settled himself in his chair and closed his eyes. Just when I thought he had fallen asleep, he suddenly jumped up out of his chair.
Holmes Come on, Watson, let's visit Coburg Square.
Watson We took the Underground and walked a short way to Coburg Square. It was a poor little place with small brick houses. On one house there was a sign with 'Jabez Wilson' in white letters. It was the shop of our red-haired client. Holmes looked it all over. He hit the pavement in front of the shop with his stick two or three times. He walked slowly up and down the street, looking carefully at the other houses. Finally, he went to the front door of the shop and rang the bell. It was opened by a young man with a pale face.
Holmes Can you tell me how to get to the Strand?
Watson asked Holmes.
Vincent Third right, fourth left.
Watson answered the man, closing the door. 'That was Mr Wilson's assistant, Vincent,' I said. 'Did you ask the way so that you could see him?'
Holmes Not him.
Watson said Holmes. 'What then?' I asked.
Holmes I wanted to see the knees of his trousers. Now let's explore what's in the next street.
Watson We turned the corner out of Coburg Square into one of the main streets in the City. It was difficult to believe that these expensive shops and businesses were immediately behind the buildings in the poor square.
Holmes Let me see.
Watson said Holmes.
Holmes Here we have a tobacconist, a newspaper shop, a vegetarian restaurant, and the City Bank...
Watson He looked thoughtful. Then he said,
Holmes I have some business to do. This case is serious. Be ready tonight at 10.00. I hope we will be in time to prevent a serious crime. There may be some danger, so bring your gun.
Watson He waved goodbye and disappeared into the crowd.

🔊 **10.17**
Part 4
Watson We waited and waited. From my position behind the box, I could see across the stone floor of the cellar. Suddenly I saw a thin line of light. A small hole opened in the floor and a hand appeared. Then one of the stones was pushed up, and we could see the light from a lantern. A pale face appeared, and then a young man climbed out of the hole and pulled up after him another man with bright red hair. It was Vincent and the manager from the office of the Red-Headed League! Sherlock Holmes jumped out from his hiding place and he caught Vincent. He had a gun, but Holmes hit his hand and the gun fell to the floor. The second man quickly went back down the hole.
Holmes He won't escape.
Watson cried Holmes.
Holmes The police are waiting for him.
Vincent Oh really?
Watson said Vincent.
Vincent Congratulations. You have been very clever.
Holmes You too.
Watson said Holmes.
Holmes Your red-headed idea was very new and effective.
Watson Vincent was taken to the police station, and Mr Merryweather thanked Holmes for catching the bank robbers. Back at Baker Street, Holmes explained everything.
Holmes You see, Watson, the only possible reason for The Red-Headed League was to get Mr Wilson out of his shop for a few hours every day. They put in the advertisement, they set up the office of The Red-Headed League and then Vincent went to work for Mr Wilson. He needed to persuade him to apply for the job. When I heard that Vincent was working for half pay and spent a lot of time in the cellar, I realized that he was doing something there which took many hours a day for several months. It had to be a tunnel to another building. When I hit the pavement with my stick, I discovered that the shop's cellar was behind the shop, not in front. When I looked at Vincent's knees, I saw that they were dirty from hours of digging. I walked round the corner and saw that the City Bank was directly behind Mr Wilson's shop. Then I felt I had solved the problem. So I called the police and the bank director.
Watson 'But how did you know that they were planning to do the robbery tonight?' I asked.
Holmes Well, when they closed the office of The Red-Headed League, it was a sign that they didn't care about Mr Wilson any more, so I was sure that they had completed the tunnel. But they needed to act quickly before the tunnel was discovered.
Watson 'You solved it beautifully!' I exclaimed.
Holmes Thank you, Watson. It saved me from being bored.

6A

Grammar Bank

passive (all tenses)

1 A lot of films **are shot** on location. 🔊 6.4
   When **is** our car **being repaired**?
   Artem's bike **has been stolen**.
   The director died when the film **was being made**.
   You**'ll be picked up** at the airport by one of our staff.
   This bill **must be paid** tomorrow.
   I love **being given** a massage.
2 The new concert hall **will be opened** by the King.
   Napoleon **was directed** by Ridley Scott.

1 We often use the passive (*be* + past participle) when it isn't said, known, or important who does an action.
   Artem's bike has been stolen. (= somebody has stolen Artem's bike, but we don't know who). In passive sentences, the object of the verb becomes the new subject.

2 If we want to say who did the action, we use *by*.
   - We can often say things in two ways, in the active or in the passive. Compare:
   Napoleon *was directed by Ridley Scott.* (= we want to focus more on the film)
   Ridley Scott directed Napoleon. (= we want to focus more on the director)
   - We form negatives and questions in the same way as in active sentences.
   Some films **aren't shot** on location.
   Is your car **being repaired** today?
   - We often use the passive to talk about processes, e.g. scientific processes, and in formal language, such as news reports.
   Then the water **is heated** to 100 degrees...
   Many buildings in the city **have been damaged** by the earthquake.

---

a Circle the correct form, active or passive.

   The college *built / was built* in the 16th century.
1 The costumes for the show *are making / are being made* by hand.
2 The story *inspired / was inspired* him to make a film.
3 This castle *hasn't inhabited / hasn't been inhabited* for nearly a century.
4 His latest film *set / is set* in Vietnam in the 1960s.
5 The film *will shoot / will be shot* in the autumn.
6 The actors *aren't recording / aren't being recorded* the dialogue until next week.
7 The house *wasn't using / wasn't being used* by the owners during the winter.
8 The make-up artist *has transformed / has been transformed* the actor into a monster.
9 They *hadn't owned / hadn't been owned* the company for very long before they went bankrupt.
10 The photo *took / was taken* by my husband on the balcony of our hotel.

b Complete with the passive so that the meaning is the same. Only use *by* if necessary.

   People don't use this room very often.
   This room *isn't used very often*.
1 They subtitle a lot of foreign films.
   A lot of foreign films _____.
2 García Márquez wrote *Love in the Time of Cholera* in 1985.
   Love in the Time of Cholera _____ in 1985.
3 Someone is repairing my laptop at the moment.
   My laptop _____ at the moment.
4 They haven't released the DVD of the film yet.
   The DVD of the film _____.
5 They won't finish the film until the spring.
   The film _____ until the spring.
6 You have to collect the tickets from the box office.
   The tickets _____ from the box office.
7 They hadn't told the actor about the changes in the script.
   The actor _____ about the changes in the script.
8 Damien Chazelle directed *La La Land*.
   La La Land _____.
9 They've already recorded the soundtrack.
   The soundtrack _____.
10 They were interviewing the director about the film.
   The director _____ about the film.

⬅ p.59

6B Grammar Bank

modals of deduction: *might*, *can't*, *must*

might (when you think something is possibly true)

Diego's phone is switched off. He **might** be on the plane now, or just boarding.
Laura **might not** like that skirt. It's not really her style.
🔊 6.10

can't (when you are sure something is impossible / not true)

Daniel **can't** earn much money in his job. He's still living with his parents.
That woman **can't** be Bruno's wife. Bruno's wife has dark hair.
🔊 6.11

must (when you are sure something is true)

The neighbours **must** be out. There aren't any lights on in the house.
Your sister **must** have a lot of money if she drives a Porsche.
🔊 6.12

- We often use *might*, *can't*, or *must* to say how sure or certain we are about something (based on the information we have).
- In this context, the opposite of *must* is *can't*. Compare:
  The neighbours must be out. There aren't any lights on in the house.
  The neighbours can't be out. All the lights are on in the house. **NOT** ~~The neighbours mustn't be out.~~
- We can use *may* instead of *might* and we can use *could* in positive sentences.
  Jack could (or may) be at the party – I'm not sure.
- We don't use *can* instead of *might* / *may*. **NOT** ~~He can be on the plane now.~~
- We often use *be* + gerund after *might* / *must* / *can't*.
  They must be having a party – the music's very loud.

The neighbours must be out. There aren't any lights on in the house.   The neighbours can't be out. All the lights are on in the house.

a Match the sentences.

He might be American. D
1 He can't be a university student.
2 He must be cold.
3 He might be going to the gym.
4 He could be lost.
5 He must be married.
6 He must be a tourist.
7 He can't be enjoying the party.
8 He may not have a job.
9 He can't be a businessman.

A He's carrying a sports bag.
B He's carrying a camera and a guide book.
C He's looking at a map.
D ~~He's wearing a baseball cap.~~
E He's looking at job adverts online.
F He isn't talking to anybody.
G He isn't wearing a suit.
H He's wearing a wedding ring.
I He's wearing school uniform.
J It's freezing and he isn't wearing a jumper.

b Complete with *must*, *might* (not), or *can't*.

A What does Pete's new girlfriend do?
B I'm not sure, but she _might_ be a doctor. I think she works at the hospital.
1 A Do you know anyone who drives a Ferrari?
  B Yes, my nephew. I don't know his salary, but he _____ earn a fortune!
2 A Why don't you buy this dress for your mum?
  B I'm not sure. She _____ like it. It's a bit short for her.
3 A My sister works as an interpreter for the EU.
  B She _____ speak a lot of languages to work there.
4 A Did you know that Maxim's parents have split up?
  B Poor Maxim. He _____ be very happy about that.
5 A Are your neighbours away? All the curtains are closed.
  B I'm not sure. I suppose they _____ be on holiday.
6 A Where's your colleague today?
  B She _____ be ill. She called to say that she was going to the doctor's.
7 A I'm looking forward to seeing Carolina! I haven't seen her for years.
  B You _____ recognize her – she's lost a lot of weight.
8 A My daughter has been out every night this week.
  B She _____ be working very hard.
9 A Why is Tina so happy?
  B I'm not sure, but she _____ have a new partner.
10 A Where does your boss live?
   B I don't know, but he _____ live near the office because he commutes every day by train.

⬅ p.63

151

7A Grammar Bank

first conditional and future time clauses + *when*, *until*, etc.

first conditional sentences: *if* + present simple, *will* / *won't* + infinitive

- We use first conditional sentences to talk about a possible / probable future situation and its consequence.

> 1 If you **work** hard, you**'ll pass** your exams. 🔊 7.8
> The teacher **won't be** very pleased if we**'re** late for class.
> 2 **Come** and see us next week if you **have** time.
> 3 Alison **won't get** into university unless she **gets** good grades.
> I **won't go** unless you **go**, too.

1 We use the present tense (**NOT** the future) after *if* in first conditional sentences. **NOT** *If you'll work hard, you'll pass all your exams.*
2 We can also use an imperative instead of the *will* clause.
3 We can use *unless* + present simple + instead of *if...not* in conditional sentences. Compare: *Alison won't get into university if she **doesn't get** good grades.*

future time clauses

> We**'ll have** dinner when your father **gets** home. 🔊 7.9
> As soon as you **get** your exam results, **call** me.
> I **won't go** to bed until you **come** home.
> I**'ll have** a quick lunch before I **leave**.
> After I **finish** university, I**'ll** probably **take** a year off and travel.

- We use the present tense (**NOT** the future) after *when*, *as soon as*, *until*, *before*, and *after* to talk about the future.

---

a Complete with the present simple or future with *will* and the verbs in brackets.

If I fail my exams, I*'ll take* them again next year. (take)

1 That girl _____ into trouble if she doesn't wear her uniform. (get)
2 If you give in your homework late, the teacher _____ it. (not mark)
3 Don't write anything unless you _____ sure of the answer. (be)
4 Matias will be expelled if his behaviour _____. (not improve)
5 They'll be late for school unless they _____. (hurry)
6 Ask me if you _____ what to do. (not know)
7 Johnny will be punished if he _____ at the teacher again. (shout)
8 My sister _____ university this year if she passes all her exams. (finish)
9 I _____ tonight unless I finish my homework quickly. (not go out)
10 Call me if you _____ some help with your project. (need)

b Circle the correct word or expression.

I won't go to university *if* / *unless* I don't get good results.

1 Don't turn over the exam paper *after* / *until* the teacher tells you to.
2 Please check the water's not too hot *before* / *after* the kids get in the bath.
3 Your parents will be really happy *when* / *unless* they hear your good news.
4 I'll look for a job in September *before* / *after* I come back from holiday.
5 The schools will close *unless* / *until* it stops snowing soon.
6 The job is very urgent, so please do it *after* / *as soon as* you can.
7 We'll stay in the library *as soon as* / *until* it closes. Then we'll go home.
8 Nicolas will probably learn to drive *when* / *until* he's 18.
9 You won't be able to speak to the head teacher *unless* / *if* you make an appointment.
10 Give Mummy a kiss *before* / *after* she goes to work.

← p.70

7B Grammar Bank

second conditional, choosing between conditionals

second conditional sentences: *if* + past simple, *would / wouldn't* + infinitive

🔊 7.12

1 If I **had** a job, I**'d get** my own flat.
   If Tomas **spoke** good English, he **could get** a job in that new hotel.
   I **would get on** better with my parents **if** I **didn't live** with them.
   I **wouldn't do** that job **unless** they **paid me** a really good salary.
2 If your sister **were** here, she**'d know** what to do.
   If it **was** warmer, we **could have** a swim.
3 If I **were** you, I**'d buy** a new computer.

- We use the second conditional to talk about a hypothetical / imaginary present or future situation and its consequence. *If I had a job...* (= I don't have a job, I'm imagining it)
1 We use the past simple after *if* and *would / wouldn't* + infinitive in the other clause.
- We can also use *could* instead of *would* in the other clause.
2 After *if*, we can use *was* or *were* with *I*, *he*, and *she*.
3 We often use second conditionals beginning *If I were you, I'd...* to give advice. We don't normally use *If I was you...*

Choosing between the first or second conditional

Using a first or second conditional usually depends on how probable you think it is that something will happen.
If I have time, I'll help you. (= this is a real situation, it's possible that I'll have time – first conditional)
If I had time, I'd help you. (= this is a hypothetical / imaginary situation, I don't have time – second conditional)

would / wouldn't + infinitive

We also often use *would / wouldn't* + infinitive (without an *if* clause) when we talk about imaginary situations.
*My ideal holiday **would be** a week in the Bahamas.*
*I'd never **buy** a car as big as yours.*

---

a Write second conditional sentences and questions.

I <u>wouldn't live</u> with my parents if I <u>didn't have to</u>. (not live, not have to)
<u>Would</u> you <u>work</u> from home if your company <u>allowed</u> it? (work, allow)

1 Ricardo _____ commute every day if he _____ from home. (not have to, work)
2 If they _____ such a noisy dog, they _____ better with their neighbours. (not have, get on)
3 I _____ that bike if I _____ you – it's too expensive. (not buy, be)
4 _____ we _____ our house if somebody _____ us enough money? (sell, offer)
5 If we _____ in the country, we _____ for more walks. (live, go)
6 _____ you _____ a flat with me if I _____ half the rent? (share, pay)
7 If my sister _____ her room more often, it _____ such a mess. (tidy, not be)
8 You _____ me like this if you really _____ me. (not treat, love)
9 If we _____ the kitchen white, _____ it _____ bigger? (paint, look)
10 I _____ a house with a garden if I _____ gardening so much. (not buy, not enjoy)

b First or second conditional? Complete with the correct form of the verb in brackets.

I<u>'ll stay</u> with my sister if I have to go to Berlin for my job interview. (stay)
I'd buy my own flat if I <u>had</u> enough money. (have)

1 My kids _____ earlier if they didn't go to bed so late. (get up)
2 Where _____ you _____ if you go to university? (live)
3 If you _____ your exams, what will you do? (not pass)
4 I'd buy a bigger house if I _____ sure we could afford it. (be)
5 We couldn't have a dog if we _____ a garden. (not have)
6 How will you get to work if you _____ your car? (sell)
7 If we sit in the shade, we _____ sunburnt. (not get)
8 If you could change one thing in your life, what _____ it _____ ? (be)
9 He won't be able to pay next month's rent if he _____ a job soon. (not find)
10 If she made less noise, her neighbours _____ so often. (not complain)

⬅ p.73

153

8A Grammar Bank

choosing between gerunds and infinitives

gerund (verb + -ing)

1 I'm not very **good at working** in a team.
  Katie's **given up smoking**.
2 **Looking for** a job can be depressing.
  Shopping is my favourite thing to do at weekends.
3 I **hate not being** on time for things.
  I **don't mind getting up** early.

🔊 8.5

- We use the gerund (verb + -ing)
1 after prepositions and phrasal verbs.
2 as the subject of a sentence.
3 after some verbs, e.g. *hate, don't mind*.
- Common verbs which take the gerund include: *admit, avoid, deny, dislike, enjoy, feel like, finish, hate, keep, like, love, mind, miss, practise, prefer, recommend, spend time, stop, suggest,* and some phrasal verbs, e.g. *give up, go on,* etc.
- The negative gerund = *not* + verb + *-ing*.

> **like, love, and hate**
> In American English, *like, love,* and *hate* are followed by the infinitive with *to*. This is becoming more common in British English too, e.g. *I like to listen to music in the car.*

the infinitive with *to*

1 My flat is very **easy to find**.
2 Liam is saving money **to buy** a new car.
3 My sister has never **learned to drive**.
  Try not to make a noise.

🔊 8.6

- We use the infinitive + *to*:
1 after adjectives.
2 to express a reason or purpose.
3 after some verbs, e.g. *want, need, learn*.

- Common verbs which take the infinitive include: (*can't*) *afford, agree, decide, expect, forget, help, hope, learn, need, offer, plan, pretend, promise, refuse, remember, seem, try, want, would like*. More verbs take the infinitive than the gerund.
- The negative infinitive = *not to* + verb.
- These common verbs can take either the infinitive or gerund with no difference in meaning: *start, begin, continue. It started to rain. It started raining.*

> **Verb + person + infinitive with *to***
> We also use the infinitive with *to* after some verbs + person, e.g. *ask, tell, want, would like.*
> Can you ask the manager **to come**?
> She told him not **to worry**.
> I want you **to do** this now.
> We'd really like you **to come**.

the infinitive without *to*

1 I **can't drive**.
  We **must hurry**.
2 She always **makes** me **laugh**.
  My parents didn't **let** me **go** out last night.

🔊 8.7

- We use the infinitive without *to*:
1 after most modal and auxiliary verbs.
2 after *make* and *let*.

> **Verbs that can take a gerund or an infinitive, but the meaning is different**
> **Try to be** on time. (= make an effort to be on time)
> **Try doing** yoga. (= do it to see if you like it)
> **Remember to phone** him. (= don't forget to do it)
> I **remember meeting** him years ago. (= I have a memory of it)

---

a Circle the correct form.

I'm in charge of *recruiting* / *to recruit* new staff.
1 It's important for me *spending* / *to spend* time with my family.
2 *Applying* / *Apply* to go to university abroad can be complicated.
3 I want *to do* / *doing* my shopping this morning.
4 My boss wants *open* / *to open* a new office.
5 Be careful *not asking* / *not to ask* her about her boyfriend – they've split up.
6 We went on *working* / *to work* until we finished.
7 Mehmet is very good at *solving* / *to solve* problems.
8 The best thing about weekends is *not going* / *not to go* to work.
9 Layla gave up *modelling* / *to model* when she had a baby.
10 I went on a training course *to learning* / *to learn* about the new software.

b Complete with a verb from the list in the correct form.

not buy   commute   do   leave   lock
not make   retire   ~~set up~~   wear   not worry

I'd like <u>to set up</u> my own company.
1 My parents are planning _____ before they are 65.
2 Ela spends three hours _____ to work and back every day.
3 Markus and his wife agreed _____ about the problems he had at work.
4 Did you remember _____ the door?
5 In the end, I decided _____ the shoes because they were very expensive.
6 The manager lets us _____ work early on Fridays.
7 All employees must _____ a jacket and tie at work.
8 Please try _____ any more mistakes in the report.
9 I don't mind _____ overtime during the week.

← p.79

8B

Grammar Bank

reported speech: sentences and questions

reported sentences

direct statements	reported statements	🔊 8.11
'**I like** shopping.'	She said (that) **she liked** shopping.	
'**I'm** leaving **tomorrow**.'	He told her (that) **he was** leaving **the next day**.	
'**I'll** always love **you**.'	He said (that) **he would** always love **me**.	
'**I passed** the exam!'	She told me (that) **she had passed** the exam.	
'**I've** forgotten **my** keys.'	He said (that) **he had** forgotten **his** keys.	
'**I can't** come.'	She said (that) **she couldn't** come.	
'**I may** be late.'	He said (that) **he might** be late.	
'**I must** go.'	She said (that) **she had to** go.	

- We use reported speech to report (i.e. to tell another person) what someone said.
- When the reporting verb (*said*, *told*, etc.) is in the past tense, the tenses in the sentence which is being reported usually change like this:
  present → past
  will → would
  past simple / present perfect → past perfect

> **When tenses don't change**
> When you report what someone said very soon after they said it, the tenses often stay the same as in the original sentence.
> **Adam** '*I can't come tonight.*'
> I've just spoken to Adam and he said that he **can't come** tonight.
> **Tomas** '*I really enjoyed my trip.*'
> Tomas told me that he **really enjoyed** his trip.

- Some modal verbs change, e.g. *can* → *could*, *may* → *might*, *must* → *had to*. Other modal verbs stay the same, e.g. *could*, *might*, *should*, etc. '*I might come back next week.*' He said he **might** come back next week.
- We usually have to change the pronouns.
  '*I like jazz.*' Rebecca said that **she** liked jazz.
- Using *that* after *said* and *told* is optional.

- If you report what someone said on a different day or in a different place, some other time and place words can change, e.g. *tomorrow* → *the next day*, *here* → *there*, *this* → *that*, etc.
  '*I'll meet you **here tomorrow**.*' He said he'd meet me **there the next day**.

> **say and tell**
> Be careful – after *said*, <u>don't</u> use a person or an object pronoun.
> *Sarah said that she was tired.* **NOT** *Sarah said me that she was tired.*
> After *told*, you <u>must</u> use a person or object pronoun.
> *Sarah told **me** that she was tired.* **NOT** *Sarah told that she...*

reported questions

direct questions	reported questions	🔊 8.12
'**Are you** married?'	She asked him if **he was** married.	
'**Did** Lucy **phone**?'	He asked me whether Lucy **had phoned**.	
'**What's your** name?'	I asked him what **his** name **was**.	
'**Where do you live**?'	She asked me where **I lived**.	

- When we report a question, the tenses change as in reported statements.
- When a question doesn't begin with a question word, we add *if* (or *whether*).
  '*Do you want a drink?*' He asked me **if / whether** I wanted a drink.
- We also have to change the word order to subject + verb and not use *do / did*.

---

a Complete using reported speech.

'I'm in love with you.'
My boyfriend told me <u>he was in love with me</u>.

1 'I'm selling all my books.'
  My friend Luis said _____.
2 'I've booked the flights.'
  Georgia told me _____.
3 'Your new dress doesn't suit you.'
  My mother told me _____.
4 'I may not be able to go to the party.'
  Juan said _____.
5 'I won't wear these shoes again.'
  Cristina said _____.
6 'I didn't buy you a present.'
  My brother told me _____.
7 'I can't find anywhere to park.'
  Luke told me _____.

b Complete using reported speech.

'Why did you break up?'
My friend asked me <u>why we had broken up</u>.

1 'When are you leaving?'
  My parents asked me _____.
2 'Have you ever been married?'
  She asked him _____.
3 'Will you be home early?'
  Anna asked Christof _____.
4 'Where do you usually buy your clothes?'
  My sister asked me _____.
5 'Did you wear a suit to the job interview?'
  We asked him _____.
6 'Do you ever go to the theatre?'
  I asked Lisa _____.
7 'Can you help me?'
  Sabrina asked the policeman _____.

← p.83

9A

Grammar Bank

third conditional

> If I **'d known** you had a problem, I **would have helped** you.
> If Paul **hadn't gone** to Brazil, he **wouldn't have met** his wife.
> **Would** you **have gone** to the party if you**'d known** Lisa was there?
> You **wouldn't have lost** your job if you **hadn't been** late every day.
>
> 🔊 9.2

- We normally use third conditional sentences to talk about hypothetical / imaginary situations in the past, i.e. how things could have been different in the past. Compare:

  Yesterday I got up late and missed my train. (= the real situation)

  If I hadn't got up late yesterday, I wouldn't have missed my train. (= the hypothetical or imaginary past situation)

- To make a third conditional, we use *if* + past perfect and *would have* + past participle. **NOT** ~~If I would have known you had a problem...~~

- The contraction of both *had* and *would* is *'d*.

  If I'd known you had a problem, I'd have helped you.

- We can use *might* or *could* instead of *would* to make the result less certain.

  If she'd studied harder, she might have passed the exam.

a Match the sentence halves.

Billy wouldn't have injured his head — **D**
1. If I hadn't seen the speed camera,
2. Albert might have got the job
3. She would have hurt herself badly
4. If Suzanna and Rory hadn't caught the same train,
5. What would you have studied
6. How would you have got to the airport
7. If you'd worn a warmer coat,
8. Your parents would have enjoyed the trip
9. Would you have been annoyed

A if you'd gone to university?
B you wouldn't have caught a cold.
C if she'd told you the truth?
D ~~if he'd worn his helmet~~.
E they wouldn't have met.
F if he'd been on time for his interview.
G if they'd come with us.
H if she'd fallen down the stairs.
I I wouldn't have slowed down.
J if the trains had been on strike?

b Complete the third conditional sentences with the correct form of the verbs in brackets.

If Tom *hadn't gone* to university, he *wouldn't have got* a job with that company. (not go, not get)
1. If you _____ me to the station, I _____ my train. (not take, miss)
2. We _____ the match if the referee _____ us a penalty. (not win, not give)
3. You _____ the weekend if you _____ with us. (enjoy, come)
4. If I _____ the theatre tickets online, they _____ more expensive. (not buy, be)
5. Andreas _____ his wife's birthday if she _____ him. (forget, not remind)
6. If the police _____ five minutes later, they _____ the thief. (arrive, not catch)
7. If you _____ me the money, I _____ to go away for the weekend. (not lend, not be able)
8. That girl _____ in the river if you _____ her arm! (fall, not catch)
9. We _____ the hotel if we _____ the signpost. (not find, not seen)
10. If I _____ about the job, I _____ for it. (know, apply)

← p.89

9B

Grammar Bank

quantifiers

large quantities

1 My daughter has **a lot of apps** on her phone.
  Nina has **lots of clothes**.
  I've been there **loads of times**.
2 James eats **a lot**.
3 There aren't **many cafés** near here.
  Do you have **many** close **friends**?
  Do you watch **much TV**?
  I don't eat **much chocolate**.
4 Don't run. We have **plenty of time**.

🔊 9.11

1 We use *a lot of* or *lots of* in ➕ sentences. We can also use *loads of*, but it's more informal.
2 We use *a lot* when there is no noun, e.g. *He talks a lot.* NOT *He talks a lot of.*
3 *much* / *many* are normally used in ➖ sentences and ❓, but *a lot of* can also be used.
4 We use *plenty of* in ➕ sentences. (= more than enough)

small quantities

1 **A** Do you want some more ice cream?
  B Just **a little**.
  The town only has **a few cinemas**.
2 I'm so busy that I have **very little time** for myself.
  Sarah isn't popular and she has **very few friends**.
3 I have **less free time** than I used to have.
  There are **fewer flights** in the winter than in the summer.

🔊 9.12

1 We use *little* + uncountable nouns, *few* + plural countable nouns.
• *a little* and *a few* = some, but not a lot.
2 *very little* and *very few* = not much / many.
3 The comparative of *little* is *less* and the comparative of *few* is *fewer*.

more or less than you need or want

1 I don't like this city. It's **too big** and it's **too noisy**.
  You're speaking **too quietly** – I can't hear you.
2 There's **too much traffic** and **too much noise**.
  There are **too many tourists** and **too many cars**.
3 There aren't **enough parks** and there aren't **enough trees**.
  The buses aren't **frequent enough**.
  The buses don't run **frequently enough**.

🔊 9.13

1 We use *too* + adjective or adverb.
2 We use *too much* + uncountable nouns and *too many* + plural countable nouns.
3 We use *(not) enough* before a noun, e.g. *(not) enough eggs / milk*, and after an adjective, e.g. *It isn't big enough*, or an adverb, e.g. *You aren't walking fast enough*.

zero quantity

1 There **isn't any milk** in the fridge.
  We **don't have any eggs**.
2 There's **no milk** in the fridge. We **have no eggs**.
3 **A** How many eggs do we have?
  B **None**. I've used them all.

🔊 9.14

1 We use *any* + uncountable or plural noun for zero quantity with a ➖ verb.
2 We use *no* + uncountable or plural noun with a ➕ verb.
3 We use *none* (without a noun) in short answers.

---

a Circle the correct word or phrase. Tick (✓) if both are possible.

My husband has *too much* / *too many* gadgets.

1 I just have to reply to *a few* / *a little* emails.
2 Do you spend *much* / *many* time on social media?
3 My bedroom is a nice size. There's *enough room* / *plenty of room* for a desk.
4 I know *very few* / *very little* people who speak two foreign languages.
5 My brother has downloaded *a lot of* / *lots of* apps onto his new phone.
6 I have some cash on me, but not *a lot* / *a lot of*.
7 Their new TV is *too* / *too much* big. It hardly fits in the living room.
8 *There aren't any* / *There are no* potatoes. I forgot to buy some.
9 My niece isn't *old enough* / *enough old* to play with a games console.
10 I don't have *a lot of* / *many* close friends.

b Are the highlighted phrases right (✓) or wrong (✗)? Correct the wrong ones.

My nephew got lots of video games for his birthday. ✓
I don't post much photos online. *many photos*

1 'How many presents did you get?' 'A lot of!'
2 I buy fewer e-books than I used to because I prefer physical books.
3 There isn't no time to walk there. We'll have to get a taxi.
4 Please turn that music down. It's too much loud!
5 There aren't many good programmes on TV tonight.
6 My broadband isn't enough fast for me to download films easily.
7 I get too much emails at work. It takes me ages to read them all!
8 **A** How much fruit do we have? **B** Any. Can you buy some?
9 There are only a little people that I can talk to about my problems.
10 Katarina has plenty of money, so she always has the latest phone.

⬅ p.94

10A Grammar Bank

relative clauses: defining and non-defining

defining relative clauses (giving essential information)

1 Prince is the singer **who** (**that**) wrote *Purple Rain*. 🔊 10.1
 I'm looking for a book **which** (**that**) teaches you how to relax.
 That's the house **where** I was born.
2 Is Frank the man **whose** brother plays for Manchester United?
 It's a tree **whose** leaves change colour in autumn.
3 I've just had a text from the girl (**who** / **that**) I met on the flight to Peru.
 This is the phone (**which** / **that**) I bought yesterday.

- We use a defining relative clause (= a relative pronoun + verb phrase) to give essential information about a person, place, or thing.
1 We use the relative pronoun *who* for people, *which* for things / animals, and *where* for places.
- We can use *that* instead of *who* or *which*.
2 We use *whose* to mean 'of who' or 'of which'.
3 In some relative clauses, the verb after *who*, *which*, or *that* has a different subject, e.g. *She's the girl who I met on the train* (the subject of *met* is *I*). In these clauses, *who*, *which*, or *that* can be omitted.
 She's the girl I met on the train.
- *where* and *whose* can never be omitted. **NOT** ~~Is that the woman dog barks?~~
- We can't omit *who* / *which* / *that* / *where* if it's the same subject in both clauses. **NOT** ~~Julia's the woman works in the office with me.~~

non-defining relative clauses (giving extra non-essential information)

This painting, **which** was painted in 1860, is worth millions of pounds. 🔊 10.2
Last week I visited my aunt Jacinta, **who**'s nearly 90 years old.
Burford, **where** my grandfather was born, is a beautiful little town.
My neighbour, **whose** son goes to my son's school, has just remarried.

- We use a non-defining relative clause to give extra (often non-essential information) in a sentence. If this clause is omitted, the sentence still makes sense.
 This painting, which was painted in 1860, is worth millions of pounds.
- Non-defining relative clauses must go between commas (or a comma and a full stop).
- In these clauses, we <u>can't</u> leave out the relative pronoun (*who*, *which*, etc.).
- In these clauses, we <u>can't</u> use *that* instead of *who* / *which*.
 NOT ~~This painting, that was painted in 1860, is worth millions of pounds.~~

---

a Complete with *who*, *which*, *where*, or *whose*.

 Minneapolis is the city <u>where</u> Prince was born.
1 Rob and Corinna, _____ have twins, often need a babysitter.
2 Downing Street, _____ the British Prime Minister lives, is in central London.
3 The sandwich _____ you made me for lunch was delicious.
4 The woman _____ lived here before us was a writer.
5 David Bowie, _____ songs inspired us for nearly 50 years, died in 2016.
6 My computer is a lot faster than the one _____ I used to have.
7 The *Mona Lisa*, _____ has been damaged several times, is now displayed behind glass.
8 Look! That's the woman _____ dog bit me last week.
9 On our last holiday we visited Prague, _____ Kafka was born.
10 We all went to the match except Angela, _____ doesn't like football.
11 That man _____ you saw at the party was my boyfriend!
12 That's the park _____ I learned to ride a bike.

b Look at the sentences in **a**. Tick (✓) the ones where you could use *that* instead of *who* / *which*. Ⓒircle the relative pronouns which could be left out.

c Add commas (,) where necessary.

 Stephanie, who lives next door to me, is beautiful.
1 This is the place where Jon crashed his car.
2 The castle that we visited yesterday was amazing.
3 Beijing which is one of the world's biggest cities has a population of over 25 million.
4 Adele's *25* which was released in 2015 is one of the best-selling albums of the last ten years.
5 These are the shoes which I'm wearing to the wedding tomorrow.
6 Danielle and Bruce who got married last year are expecting their first baby.

← p.99

10B

Grammar Bank

question tags

positive verb, negative tag
It's cold today, **isn't it**?
You're Polish, **aren't you**?
They live in Athens, **don't they**?
The match finishes at 8.00, **doesn't it**?
Your sister worked in the USA, **didn't she**?
We've met before, **haven't we**?
You'll be OK, **won't you**?
You'd lend me some money, **wouldn't you**?

negative verb, positive tag   🔊 10.11
She isn't here today, **is she**?
You aren't angry, **are you**?
They don't eat meat, **do they**?
Lucy doesn't drive, **does she**?
You didn't like the film, **did you**?
Mike hasn't been to Las Vegas before, **has he**?
You won't tell anyone, **will you**?
Blanca wouldn't resign, **would she**?

- Question tags (*is he?*, *aren't they?*, *do you?*, *did we?*, etc.) are often used to check something you already think is true.
  Your name's Maria, isn't it?
- To form a question tag, we use:
  – the correct auxiliary verb, e.g. *be / do / have / will / would*, etc. in the correct form, e.g. *do / don't*, etc. for the present, *did / didn't* for the past, *will / won't*, etc. for the future.
  – a pronoun, e.g. *he*, *it*, *they*, etc.
  – a negative auxiliary verb if the sentence is positive and a positive auxiliary verb if the sentence is negative or with *never*, e.g. *You never do the washing-up, do you?*

a Match the question halves.

	You know that man,	G	A didn't you?
1	You're going out with him,	☐	B will you?
2	You haven't told your family about him,	☐	C did you?
3	You met him last month,	☐	D won't you?
4	You were at the same party,	☐	E have you?
5	You didn't know he was a criminal,	☐	F weren't you?
6	You aren't happy in the relationship,	☐	G ~~don't you?~~
7	You never want to see him again,	☐	H are you?
8	You'll tell us the truth,	☐	I aren't you?
9	You won't tell any lies,	☐	J don't you?
10	You understand what I'm saying,	☐	K do you?

b Complete with a question tag (*are you*, *isn't it*, etc.).

   Your name's Leonardo, _isn't it_?
1 Your brother works at the police station, _____?
2 They don't have any proof, _____?
3 That man isn't the murderer, _____?
4 You were a witness to the crime, _____?
5 The police have arrested someone, _____?
6 The woman wasn't dead, _____?
7 That girl took your handbag, _____?
8 He won't go to prison, _____?
9 You haven't seen the suspect, _____?
10 They couldn't find enough evidence, _____?

← p.103

Cinema

Vocabulary Bank

1 Kinds of film

a Match the kinds of films and photos.

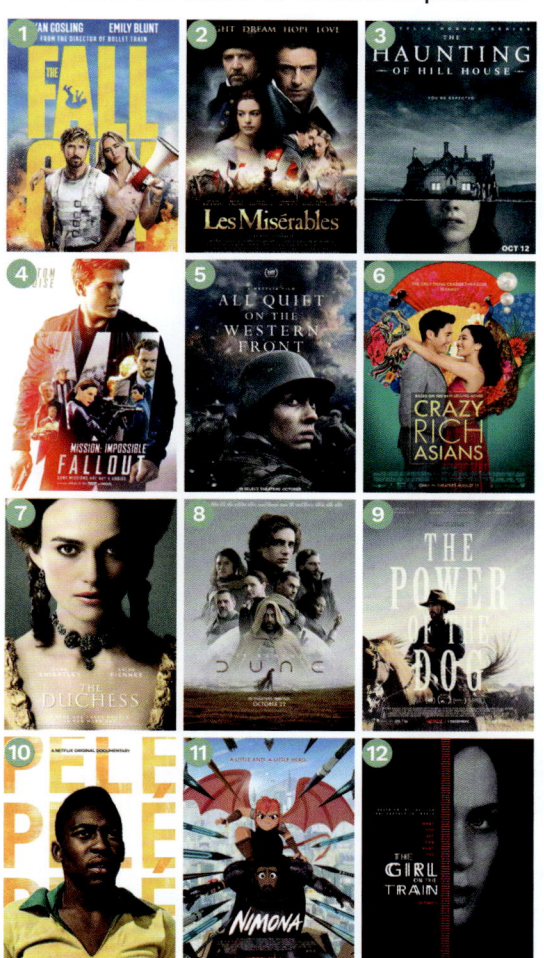

- [ ] an **ac**tion film /ˈækʃn fɪlm/
- [ ] an ani**ma**tion /ˌænɪˈmeɪʃn/
- [ ] a **bio**pic /ˈbaɪəʊpɪk/
- [x] a **co**medy /ˈkɒmədi/
- [ ] a **pe**riod **dra**ma /ˈpɪəriəd drɑːmə/
- [ ] a **ho**rror film /ˈhɒrə fɪlm/
- [ ] a **mu**sical /ˈmjuːzɪkl/
- [ ] a **rom**-com /ˈrɒm kɒm/ (romantic comedy)
- [ ] a **sci**ence **fic**tion film /ˌsaɪəns ˈfɪkʃn fɪlm/
- [ ] a **thri**ller /ˈθrɪlə/
- [ ] a **war** film /ˈwɔː fɪlm/
- [ ] a **wes**tern /ˈwestən/

b 🔊 6.1 Listen and check.

✅ **ACTIVATION** Talk to a partner. Think of a famous film for each kind of film in **a**. What kind of films do you / don't you like? Why?

2 People and things

a Match the nouns and definitions.

audience /ˈɔːdiəns/   ~~cast~~ /kɑːst/   **cri**tic /ˈkrɪtɪk/   **ex**tra /ˈekstrə/
plot /plɒt/   prop /prɒp/   re**view** /rɪˈvjuː/   scene /siːn/
script /skrɪpt/   **se**quel /ˈsiːkwəl/   set /set/   **sound**track /ˈsaʊndtræk/
special e**ffects** /ˈspeʃl ɪˈfekts/   star /stɑː/   **sub**titles /ˈsʌbtaɪtlz/
trailer /ˈtreɪlə/

1 *cast* all the people who act in a film
2 _____ (also *verb*) the most important actor in a film
3 _____ the music of a film
4 _____ the story of a film
5 _____ a part of a film which happens in one place
6 _____ the people who watch a film in a cinema
7 _____ a film which continues the story of an earlier film
8 _____ images often created by a computer
9 _____ a series of short scenes from a film, shown in advance to advertise it
10 _____ the words of a film
11 _____ a person who is employed to play a very small part in a film, usually as a member of a crowd
12 _____ the translation of the dialogue of a film on screen
13 _____ an article which gives an opinion about a new film
14 _____ the place where a film is being shot
15 _____ an object used by actors during a performance
16 _____ a person who writes film reviews for the press

b 🔊 6.2 Listen and check.

3 Verbs and verb phrases

a Match sentences 1–6 to sentences A–F.
1 [ ] The film **is based on** the life of an opera singer.
2 [ ] It **is set in** New York during the 1940s.
3 [ ] It **is directed by** Stephen Frears.
4 [ ] Hugh Grant **plays the part of** Florence's husband and manager.
5 [ ] It **was shot** (or **filmed**) **on location** in Liverpool.
6 [ ] It **is dubbed** into other languages.

A It is situated in that place at that time.
B He is the director.
C This is his role in the film.
D The words are spoken in a different language by foreign actors.
E The film is an adaptation of a true story.
F It was filmed outside the studio.

b 🔊 6.3 Listen and check.

✅ **ACTIVATION** Cover 1–6 and look at A–F. Remember 1–6. Then think of another film you know well and say sentences 1–6 about the film.

⬅ p.58

The body

Vocabulary Bank

1 Parts of the body

a Match the words and photos.

- arms /ɑːmz/
- back /bæk/
- chin /tʃɪn/
- ears /ɪəz/
- eyes /aɪz/
- face /feɪs/
- feet /fiːt/ (sing foot /fʊt/)
- fingers /ˈfɪŋɡəz/
- hands /hændz/
- head /hed/
- knees /niːz/
- legs /leɡz/
- lips /lɪps/
- mouth /maʊθ/
- neck /nek/
- nose /nəʊz/
- shoulders /ˈʃəʊldəz/
- stomach /ˈstʌmək/
- teeth /tiːθ/ (sing tooth /tuːθ/)
- thumb /θʌm/
- toes /təʊz/
- tongue /tʌŋ/

b 🔊 6.13 Listen and check.

✓ **ACTIVATION** In pairs, point to a part of the body for your partner to say the word.

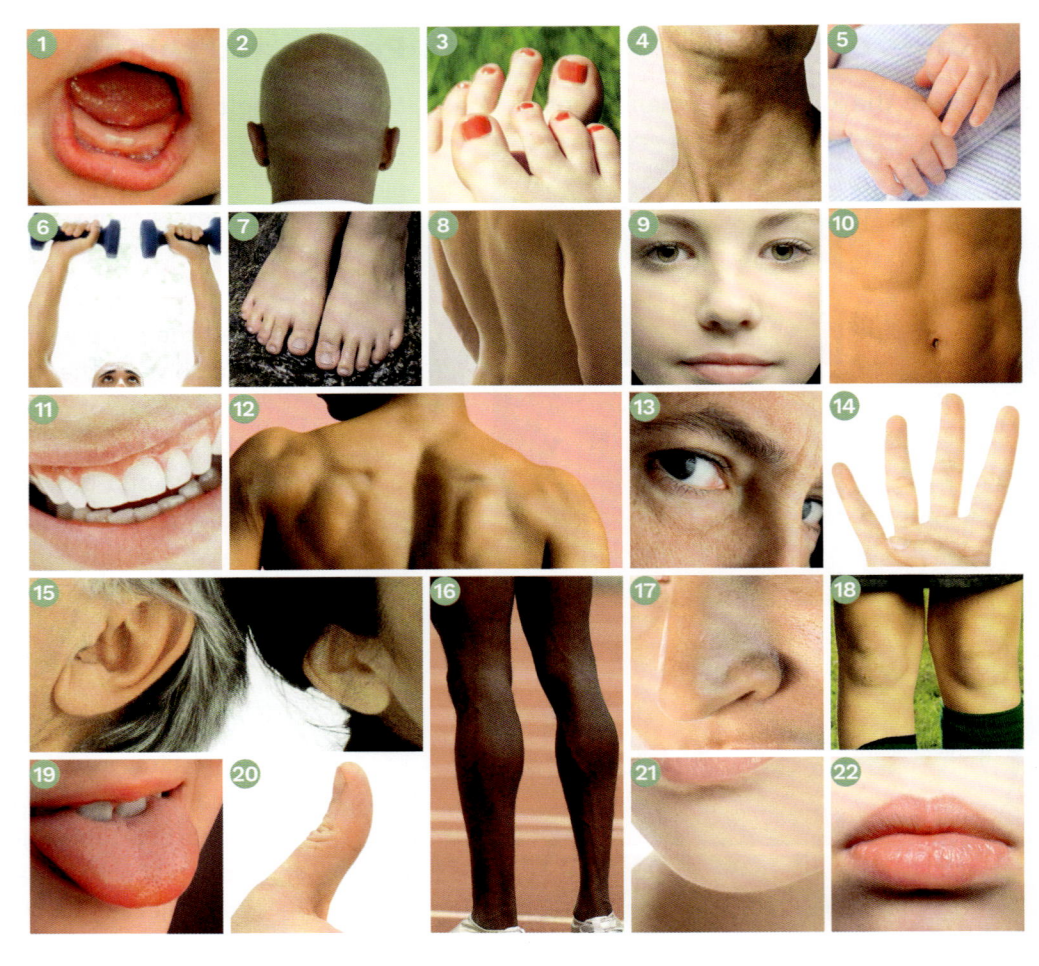

> **Possessive pronouns with parts of the body**
> In English, we use possessive pronouns (*my*, *your*, etc.) with parts of the body.
> *Give me your hand.* **NOT** ~~Give me the hand.~~

2 Verbs related to the body

a Complete the sentences with a verb from the list in the correct tense.

~~bite~~ /baɪt/	clap /klæp/	kick /kɪk/
nod /nɒd/	point /pɔɪnt/	smell /smel/
smile /smaɪl/	stare /steə/	taste /teɪst/
touch /tʌtʃ/	whistle /ˈwɪsl/	

1 Don't be frightened of the dog. He won't <u>bite</u>.
2 Jason _____ the ball too hard and it went over the wall into the next garden.
3 Mmm! Something _____ delicious! Are you making a cake?
4 The stranger _____ at me for a long time, but he didn't say anything.
5 Can you _____ the sauce? I'm not sure if it needs more salt.
6 My dog always comes back when I _____.
7 Don't _____ the oven door! It's really hot.
8 The audience _____ when I finished singing.
9 The teacher suddenly _____ at me and said, 'What's the answer?' I hadn't even heard the question!
10 He's a very serious person – he never _____.
11 Everybody _____ in agreement when I explained my idea.

b 🔊 6.14 Listen and check. Which parts of the body do you use to do the things in **a**?

⬅ p.64

Education

Vocabulary Bank

1 The school system in the UK and the US

a Complete the text about the UK with words from the list.

boarding /ˈbɔːdɪŋ/ degree /dɪˈɡriː/ head /hed/
nursery /ˈnɜːsəri/ primary /ˈpraɪməri/ private /ˈpraɪvɪt/
pupils /ˈpjuːplz/ secondary /ˈsekəndri/ state /steɪt/
students /ˈstjuːdnts/ terms /tɜːmz/

In the UK

Children start ¹*primary* school when they're five. Before that, many children go to ²_____ school, e.g. between the ages of two and four, but this is not compulsory. From 11–18, children go to ³_____ school. The majority of schools in the UK (about 90%) are ⁴_____ schools, which means that they are paid for by the government and education is free. The other ten per cent are ⁵_____ schools, where parents have to pay. A few of these are ⁶_____ schools, where children study, eat, and sleep. Children at primary school are often called ⁷_____ and children at secondary school are usually called ⁸_____, as are people who are studying at university. The person who is in charge of a school is called the ⁹_____ teacher. The school year is divided into three ¹⁰_____.

If you want to go to university, you have to take exams called A levels in your last year at school. If your results are good enough, you get a place. A person who has finished university and has a ¹¹_____ is called a graduate.

b 🔊 7.2 Listen and check.

c Complete the text about the US with words from the list.

college /ˈkɒlɪdʒ/ elementary /elɪˈmentri/
grades /ɡreɪdz/ high /haɪ/ kindergarten /ˈkɪndəɡɑːtn/
semesters /sɪˈmestəz/ twelfth grade /ˈtwelfθ ɡreɪd/

In the US

The school system is divided into three levels, ¹*elementary* school, middle school (sometimes called junior high school), and ²_____ school. Schoolchildren are divided by age groups into ³_____. The youngest children start in ⁴_____ (followed by first grade) and continue until ⁵_____, which is the final year of high school. The school year is divided into two ⁶_____. Higher education in the US is often called ⁷_____.

d 🔊 7.3 Listen and check.

✅ **ACTIVATION** Cover the texts. With a partner, remember the different types of school (starting from the lowest level) in both countries.

2 Discipline and exams

a Complete the texts with a verb from the list in the correct form.

~~not be allowed to~~ /nɒt biː əˈlaʊd tə/
be expelled /bi ɪkˈspeld/ be punished /bi ˈpʌnɪʃt/
cheat /tʃiːt/ let /let/ make /meɪk/
misbehave /mɪsbɪˈheɪv/

A Discipline is very strict in our school. We ¹*aren't allowed to* switch on our phones during class and they don't ²_____ us bring unhealthy food for lunch, like crisps or fizzy drinks. Most students behave well, but if you ³_____, for example, talk too much in class, you'll ⁴_____ and the teacher will probably ⁵_____ you stay behind after class. If you do something more serious, like ⁶_____ in an exam, you might even ⁷_____.

fail /feɪl/ pass /pɑːs/ get the result /ɡet ðə rɪˈzʌlt/
revise /rɪˈvaɪz/ take /teɪk/ (or *do*)

B Marc has to ¹_____ an important English exam next week. He hopes he'll ²_____, but he hasn't had much time to ³_____, so he's worried that he might ⁴_____. He won't ⁵_____ until July.

b 🔊 7.4 Listen and check.

✅ **ACTIVATION** Cover the texts and look at the verbs. Explain what they mean.

> **make, let, and allow**
>
> My French teacher **made me do** extra homework.
> Our IT teacher **lets us play** games every Friday.
> The head does**n't allow us to take** our phones to school.
>
> We use *make* and *let* with an object pronoun and the infinitive without *to*. We use *allow* with an object pronoun and the infinitive + *to*.
>
> *let* and *allow* have a similar meaning. We often use *allow* in the passive, e.g. *We're allowed to play games every Friday*, but we can't use *let* in the passive NOT ~~We're let play games...~~

⬅ p.68

169

Houses

Vocabulary Bank

1 Where people live

a Complete the **Preposition** column with *in* or *on*.

		Preposition
1	I live ☐ **the country**, surrounded by fields.	*in*
2	I live ☐ **the outskirts** of Oxford, about three miles from the centre.	_____
3	I live ☐ **a village** (**a town** / **a city**).	_____
4	I live in Cromer, a small town ☐ **the east coast**.	_____
5	I live ☐ **the second floor** of a large block of flats.	_____
6	I live ☐ Croydon, a **suburb** of London about 15 miles from the city centre.	_____

b 🔊 **7.14** Listen and check.

c Cover the **Preposition** column. Say the sentences with the correct preposition.

✅ **ACTIVATION** Talk to a partner. Describe where you live.

2 Parts of a house

a Match the words and pictures.

- ☐ attic /ˈætɪk/
- ☐ balcony /ˈbælkəni/
- ☐ basement /ˈbeɪsmənt/
- ☐ chimney /ˈtʃɪmni/
- ☐ entrance /ˈentrəns/
- ☐ gate /ɡeɪt/
- ☐ ground floor /ɡraʊnd ˈflɔː/ (*AmE* first floor)
- ☐ path /pɑːθ/
- ☐ roof /ruːf/
- ☐ steps /steps/
- ☐ terrace /ˈterəs/ (patio /ˈpætiəʊ/)
- ☐ top floor /tɒp ˈflɔː/
- ☐ wall /wɔːl/

b 🔊 **7.15** Listen and check.

3 Describing a house or flat

a Match the descriptions and photos.

☐ I live in a cottage in the country. It's old and made of stone and the rooms have very low ceilings. There's an open fire in the living room and it's very cosy in the winter.

☐ I live in a modern flat in the city centre. It's spacious and very light, with wooden floors and big windows.

b 🔊 **7.16** Listen and check. Focus on how the highlighted words and phrases are pronounced.

chimney or fireplace?
In English, *chimney* only refers to the structure on the roof of the house.
Fireplace is the place where you burn wood or coal. For some nationalities, *chimney* is a 'false friend'.

roof or ceiling?
Roof is the top part of a house. *Ceiling* is the top part of a room.

✅ **ACTIVATION** Cover the descriptions and look at the photos. Describe the rooms.

← p.74

Work

Vocabulary Bank

1 Verb phrases

a Complete the sentences with a verb or verb phrase from the list.

| applied for /əˈplaɪd fɔː/ | do /duː/ | do overtime /duː ˈəʊvətaɪm/ | got promoted /gɒt prəˈməʊtɪd/ | resign /rɪˈzaɪn/ | retire /rɪˈtaɪə/ |
| run /rʌn/ | set up /set ʌp/ | was made redundant /wəz meɪd rɪˈdʌndənt/ | was sacked /wəz sækt/ | work shifts /wɜːk ʃɪfts/ |

1 Dan has to _do overtime_. — He has to work extra hours.
2 Matt _____ last week. — He was given a more important job.
3 Most nurses have to _____. — Sometimes they work during the day and sometimes at night.
4 A man in our department _____ yesterday. (or *be fired*) — The boss told him to leave.
5 Paolo _____. — He lost his job because the company didn't need him any more.
6 The director of the company is going to _____. (*AmE* quit) — He has decided to leave his job.
7 Lilian is going to _____ next month. — She's 65 and she's going to stop working.
8 Isobel has _____ a business selling clothes online. — She had the idea and has started doing it.
9 Everyone in the office has to _____ a training course. — They need to learn how to use the new software.
10 Mandy _____ a job online. — She replied to an advert and sent in her CV.
11 My parents _____ a language school in Brighton. — They employ six teachers, who teach English to foreign students.

b 🔊 **8.1** Listen and check. Cover the first sentence and look at the second. Can you remember the verb?

✅ **ACTIVATION** Do you know anybody who has applied for a job / got promoted / been made redundant / resigned / been sacked (fired) / retired recently?

2 Saying what you do

a Match the adjectives and definitions.

freelance /ˈfriːlɑːns/   part-time /pɑːt ˈtaɪm/
self-employed /ˌself ɪmˈplɔɪd/   temporary /ˈtemprəri/
unemployed /ˌʌnɪmˈplɔɪd/

talking about people

1 I'm _____. — without a job
2 He's _____. — working for himself
3 He's a _____ designer. — working for different companies

talking about a job or work

4 It's a _____ job. (*opp* permanent) only a short contract, e.g. for six months
5 It's a _____ job. (*opp* full-time) only a few hours a day

b Complete the sentences with *at, for, in,* or *of*.

1 I **work** _for_ (in) a multinational company.
2 I'm _____ **charge** _____ the Marketing Department.
3 I'm **responsible** _____ customer loans.
4 I'm _____ school (university).
5 I'm _____ my third year at university.

c 🔊 **8.2** Listen and check **a** and **b**.

3 Word building

a Make nouns from the verbs by adding *-ment, -ion,* or *-ation*. Make any other necessary changes.

	Verb	Noun		Verb	Noun
1	pro<u>mote</u>	promotion	4	em<u>ploy</u>	
2	a<u>pply</u>		5	<u>qual</u>ify	
3	re<u>tire</u>		6	re<u>sign</u>	

b Make nouns for the people who do the jobs by adding *-er, -or, -ian,* or *-ist*. Make any other necessary changes.

	Noun			Noun	
1	<u>sci</u>ence		4	<u>phar</u>macy	
2	law		5	farm	
3	<u>mu</u>sic		6	trans<u>late</u>	

c 🔊 **8.3** Listen and check **a** and **b**. Under<u>line</u> the stressed syllable in the new words.

✅ **ACTIVATION** Cover the **Noun** columns and look at 1–6 in **a** and **b**. Remember the nouns. Then think of two more jobs ending in *-er, -or, -ian,* or *-ist*.

↩ p.78

Word building

Vocabulary Bank

1 Making nouns from verbs

a Make nouns from the verbs in the list and write them in the correct column.

> ~~achieve~~ /əˈtʃiːv/   agree /əˈɡriː/   argue /ˈɑːɡjuː/
> attach /əˈtætʃ/   choose /tʃuːz/
> compensate /ˈkɒmpənseɪt/   complain /kəmˈpleɪn/
> consider /kənˈsɪdə/   deliver /dɪˈlɪvə/
> demonstrate /ˈdemənstreɪt/   explain /ɪkˈspleɪn/
> fail /feɪl/   improve /ɪmˈpruːv/   lose /luːz/
> manage /ˈmænɪdʒ/   pay /peɪ/   respond /rɪˈspɒnd/
> sell /sel/   serve /sɜːv/   succeed /səkˈsiːd/
> tempt /tempt/   treat /triːt/   value /ˈvæljuː/

+ -ation	+ -ment	new word
	achievement	

b 🔊 8.15 Listen and check. Underline the stressed syllable in the nouns.

✓ **ACTIVATION** Test a partner. Then change roles.
A (book open) Say the verb.
B (book closed) Say the noun.

c Complete the questions with a noun from **a** in the singular or plural.
1. Have you ever been on a _demonstration_? What were you protesting about?
2. Have you ever opened an email _____ that contained a virus? What happened?
3. Do you often have _____ with your family? What about?
4. Do you prefer reading grammar _____ in your own language, or do you think it's better to read them in English?
5. Have you ever made a _____ to a company and got _____?
6. Do you think that there's too much _____ when you're shopping, e.g. for a new phone?
7. In a restaurant, what's more important for you, the food or the _____?

d 🔊 8.16 Listen and check.

✓ **ACTIVATION** With a partner, ask and answer the questions in **c**.   → p.84

2 Making adjectives and adverbs

> **Adjective prefixes and suffixes**
> We often make adjectives from nouns by adding a suffix. Some common suffixes are: -y, e.g. *sun – sunny*; -ate, e.g. *passion – passionate*; -able / -ible, e.g. *fashion – fashionable*; -ful, e.g. *use – useful*.
> Nouns which end in -ence often make the adjective with -ent, e.g. *violence – violent*.
> To make a negative adjective, we usually add a prefix, e.g. *un-, im-*, etc. (See **Vocabulary Bank** Personality *p.161*.) However, some adjectives that end in -ful make the negative by changing the suffix -ful to -less, e.g. *useful – useless, hopeful – hopeless*.

a Look at the adjectives and adverbs from the noun *luck* in the chart below. Complete the chart.

	adjectives		adverbs	
noun	+	−	+	−
luck	lucky	unlucky	luckily	unluckily
fortune	fortunate	unfortunate		
comfort				
patience				
care				

b 🔊 9.5 Listen and check.

c Complete the sentences with the correct form of the **bold** noun.
1. The beach was beautiful, but _unfortunately_ it rained almost every day. **fortune**
2. My new shoes are very _____. I wore them all day yesterday and they didn't hurt at all. **comfort**
3. He did the exam quickly and _____, and so he made lots of mistakes. **care**
4. We were really _____. We missed the flight by just five minutes. **luck**
5. Jack is a very _____ driver! He can't stand being behind someone who is driving slowly. **patience**
6. It was a bad accident, but _____ nobody was seriously hurt. **luck**
7. It was raining, but fans waited _____ in the queue to buy tickets for tomorrow's concert. **patience**
8. The roads will be very icy tonight, so drive _____. **care**
9. The temperature dropped to minus ten degrees, but _____, we were all wearing warm coats. **fortune**
10. The bed in the hotel was incredibly _____. I hardly slept at all. **comfort**

d 🔊 9.6 Listen and check.   → p.91

Irregular verbs

Infinitive	Past simple	Past participle
be /bi/	was /wɒz/ were /wɜː/	been /biːn/
beat /biːt/	beat	beaten /ˈbiːtn/
become /bɪˈkʌm/	became /bɪˈkeɪm/	become
begin /bɪˈgɪn/	began /bɪˈgæn/	begun /bɪˈgʌn/
bite /baɪt/	bit /bɪt/	bitten /ˈbɪtn/
break /breɪk/	broke /brəʊk/	broken /ˈbrəʊkən/
bring /brɪŋ/	brought /brɔːt/	brought
build /bɪld/	built /bɪlt/	built
buy /baɪ/	bought /bɔːt/	bought
can /kæn/	could /kʊd/	–
catch /kætʃ/	caught /kɔːt/	caught
choose /tʃuːz/	chose /tʃəʊz/	chosen /ˈtʃəʊzn/
come /kʌm/	came /keɪm/	come
cost /kɒst/	cost	cost
cut /kʌt/	cut	cut
do /duː/	did /dɪd/	done /dʌn/
draw /drɔː/	drew /druː/	drawn /drɔːn/
dream /driːm/	dreamt /dremt/ (also dreamed)	dreamt (also dreamed)
drink /drɪŋk/	drank /dræŋk/	drunk /drʌŋk/
drive /draɪv/	drove /drəʊv/	driven /ˈdrɪvn/
eat /iːt/	ate /eɪt/	eaten /ˈiːtn/
fall /fɔːl/	fell /fel/	fallen /ˈfɔːlən/
feel /fiːl/	felt /felt/	felt
find /faɪnd/	found /faʊnd/	found
fly /flaɪ/	flew /fluː/	flown /fləʊn/
forget /fəˈget/	forgot /fəˈgɒt/	forgotten /fəˈgɒtn/
get /get/	got /gɒt/	got
give /gɪv/	gave /geɪv/	given /ˈgɪvn/
go /gəʊ/	went /went/	gone /gɒn/
grow /grəʊ/	grew /gruː/	grown /grəʊn/
hang /hæŋ/	hung /hʌŋ/	hung
have /hæv/	had /hæd/	had
hear /hɪə/	heard /hɜːd/	heard
hit /hɪt/	hit	hit
hurt /hɜːt/	hurt	hurt
keep /kiːp/	kept /kept/	kept
know /nəʊ/	knew /njuː/	known /nəʊn/
learn /lɜːn/	learnt /lɜːnt/ (also learned)	learnt (also learned)
leave /liːv/	left /left/	left

Infinitive	Past simple	Past participle
lend /lend/	lent /lent/	lent
let /let/	let	let
lie /laɪ/	lay /leɪ/	lain /leɪn/
lose /luːz/	lost /lɒst/	lost
make /meɪk/	made /meɪd/	made
mean /miːn/	meant /ment/	meant
meet /miːt/	met /met/	met
pay /peɪ/	paid /peɪd/	paid
put /pʊt/	put	put
read /riːd/	read /red/	read /red/
ride /raɪd/	rode /rəʊd/	ridden /ˈrɪdn/
ring /rɪŋ/	rang /ræŋ/	rung /rʌŋ/
run /rʌn/	ran /ræn/	run
say /seɪ/	said /sed/	said
see /siː/	saw /sɔː/	seen /siːn/
sell /sel/	sold /səʊld/	sold
send /send/	sent /sent/	sent
set /set/	set	set
shine /ʃaɪn/	shone /ʃɒn/	shone
shut /ʃʌt/	shut	shut
sing /sɪŋ/	sang /sæŋ/	sung /sʌŋ/
sit /sɪt/	sat /sæt/	sat
sleep /sliːp/	slept /slept/	slept
smell /smel/	smelt /smelt/ (also smelled)	smelt (also smelled)
speak /spiːk/	spoke /spəʊk/	spoken /ˈspəʊkən/
spend /spend/	spent /spent/	spent
stand /stænd/	stood /stʊd/	stood
steal /stiːl/	stole /stəʊl/	stolen /ˈstəʊlən/
swim /swɪm/	swam /swæm/	swum /swʌm/
take /teɪk/	took /tʊk/	taken /ˈteɪkən/
teach /tiːtʃ/	taught /tɔːt/	taught
tell /tel/	told /təʊld/	told
think /θɪŋk/	thought /θɔːt/	thought
throw /θrəʊ/	threw /θruː/	thrown /θrəʊn/
understand /ʌndəˈstænd/	understood /ʌndəˈstʊd/	understood
wake /weɪk/	woke /wəʊk/	woken /ˈwəʊkən/
wear /weə/	wore /wɔː/	worn /wɔːn/
win /wɪn/	won /wʌn/	won
write /raɪt/	wrote /rəʊt/	written /ˈrɪtn/

Vowel sounds

Sound Bank

		usual spelling	! but also

fish		i bill dish
		   fit pitch
		   since ticket
			pretty decided
			women busy
			village physics

tree		ee beef speed ea peach team e refund sequel	people magazine key niece receipt

cat		a mango tram
		   tax bank
		   carry crash	

car		ar garden charge
		   starter
		a cast pass
		   drama
			aunt laugh
			heart

clock		o cost lorry
		   bossy plot
		   off on
			watch want
			sausage because

horse		(o)or score floor al bald wall aw draw prawns	warm course thought caught audience board
bull		u full put oo cook look foot good	could should would woman
boot		oo food moody cartoon u* rude argue ew few flew	suitcase juice move shoe soup through queue
computer		Many different spellings. /ə/ is always unstressed. other nervous about complain information camera	
bird		er term prefer ir dirty circuit ur turn nursery	learn work world worse journey

egg		e lemon lend
		   text spend
		   plenty cent
			friendly healthy
			jealous already
			many said

up		u public subject
		   unlucky duck
		   hurry rush
			money tongue
			someone couple
			touch enough

		usual spelling	! but also
train		a* save gate ai fail brain ay may say	break steak great weight grey they
phone		o* broke stone frozen slope oa coach roast	owe elbow although shoulders aubergine
bike		i* bite retire y cycle shy igh lights flight	buy eyes height
owl		ou hour mouth proud ground ow town brown	

boy		oi boiled noisy
		   coin spoilt
		oy enjoy
		   unemployed	

ear		eer beer engineer ere here we're ear beard appearance	really idea serious
chair		air airport upstairs fair hair are stare careful	their there wear pear area
tourist		Not a very common sound. euro furious plural sure	
/i/		A sound between /ɪ/ and /iː/. Consonant + y at the end of words is pronounced /i/. happy angry hungry	
/u/		Not a very common sound. education usually situation	

* especially before consonant + e

○ short vowels   ○ long vowels   ○ diphthongs

Consonant sounds

Sound Bank

		usual spelling	! but also			usual spelling	! but also

	parrot	p propose pupil
		    transport trip
		pp apply shopping
					thumb	th throw thriller
						     healthy maths
						     path teeth	

	bag	b beans bill
		    probably crab
		bb dubbed stubborn
					mother	th the that
						     with
						     further together	

	key	c court script k kind kick ck track lucky	chemist's school stomach account squid		chess	ch change cheat tch match pitch t (+ure) picture future	
	girl	g golf grilled forget colleague gg aggressive luggage			jazz	j jealous just g generous manager dge fridge judge	
	flower	f food roof ph pharmacy nephew ff traffic affectionate	laugh enough		leg	l limit salary reliable until ll sell rebellious	

	vase	v van vegetables
		    travel invest
		    private believe
			of		right	r result referee
						    primary fried
						rr borrow terrace
							written
							wrong

	tie	t taste tidy
		    stadium strict
		tt attractive cottage
			worked
			passed
					witch	w war waste
						    western motorway
						wh whistle which
							one once

	dog	d director graduate
		    comedy afford
		dd address middle
			bored
			failed
					yacht	y yet year
						    yoghurt yourself
						before u
						    university argue	

	snake	s steps likes ss boss assistant ce/ci ceiling cinema	scene science cycle		monkey	m mean romantic charming arm mm summer swimming	lamb

	zebra	z lazy freezing
		s, se cosy loves toes
		    lose nose
					nose	n neck honest
						    none chimney
						nn tennis winner
							knee knew

	shower	sh show punish
		     cash selfish
		ti (+ vowel)
		     ambitious explanation
		ci (+ vowel)
		     spacious sociable
			sugar
			sure
			chef
			machine
					singer	ng cooking going
						     bring spring
						before g / k
						     tongue think	

	television	Not a very common sound.
		confusion decision revision
		usually courgette
					house	h hands helmet
						    behave inherit
						    unhappy perhaps
							who
							whose
							whole

○ voiced   ○ unvoiced

175

English File

Intermediate

Workbook B Units 6–10 WITH KEY

fifth edition

Christina Latham-Koenig   Clive Oxenden
Jerry Lambert   Paul Seligson with Jane Hudson

Paul Seligson and Clive Oxenden are the original co-authors
of *English File 1* (published 1996) and *English File 2* (1997)

OXFORD
UNIVERSITY PRESS

Contents

6
- 40 **A** Extra information
- 43 **B** In the picture

7
- 46 **A** Term time
- 49 **B** House or home?
- 52 **Practical English** Episode 4 Together again?
- 53 **Can you remember…? 1–7**

8
- 54 **A** The right job for you
- 57 **B** Service with a smile?

9
- 60 **A** I was so lucky!
- 63 **B** Power cut
- 66 **Practical English** Episode 5 Ben's big show
- 67 **Can you remember…? 1–9**

10
- 68 **A** Idols and icons
- 70 **B** And the murderer is…

- 76 **Answer Key**

6A Extra information

G passive (all tenses)
V cinema
P regular and irregular past participles

1 VOCABULARY cinema

a Match the words from the list to definitions 1–12.

action film   animation   biopic   ~~comedy~~
horror film   musical   period drama   rom-com
science fiction film   thriller   war film   western

1 an amusing film that has a happy ending
   comedy

2 a film that has a lot of exciting events, e.g. fights and car chases
   _____

3 a film about imaginary events in the future
   _____

4 a film that is set in a time and place in the past
   _____

5 a film where the cast sing and dance
   _____

6 a film with an exciting story, often about a crime
   _____

7 a film about the life of a particular person
   _____

8 a scary film
   _____

9 a film about soldiers fighting battles
   _____

10 a film about life in the past in the US
   _____

11 a film which is made with pictures that appear to move
   _____

12 a funny film about love
   _____

b Complete the sentences.

1 The st_ar_____ of the film was a famous British actor.
2 I didn't understand the film because the pl_____ was very complicated.
3 The actor wanted to play the part as soon as she had read the sc_____.
4 Some of the a_____ were crying at the end of the film.
5 Most critics have given the film an excellent r_____.
6 They only had to shoot the sc_____ once.
7 It's a French film, but with English s_____.
8 You'll have to wait for the s_____ to find out what happens next.
9 My favourite s_____ is the music from _Guardians of the Galaxy_.
10 The best thing about the film was the sp_____ e_____. They were very realistic.
11 The director is looking for e_____ to act in the crowd scenes.
12 The c_____ was a mixture of British and American actors.
13 _The Times_ film cr_____ didn't like the film at all.
14 The two actors first met on the s_____ of the film _La La Land_.
15 I've seen the tr_____, and it looks like a really interesting film.
16 The actor is using an old handbag as a pr_____ in this part of the film.

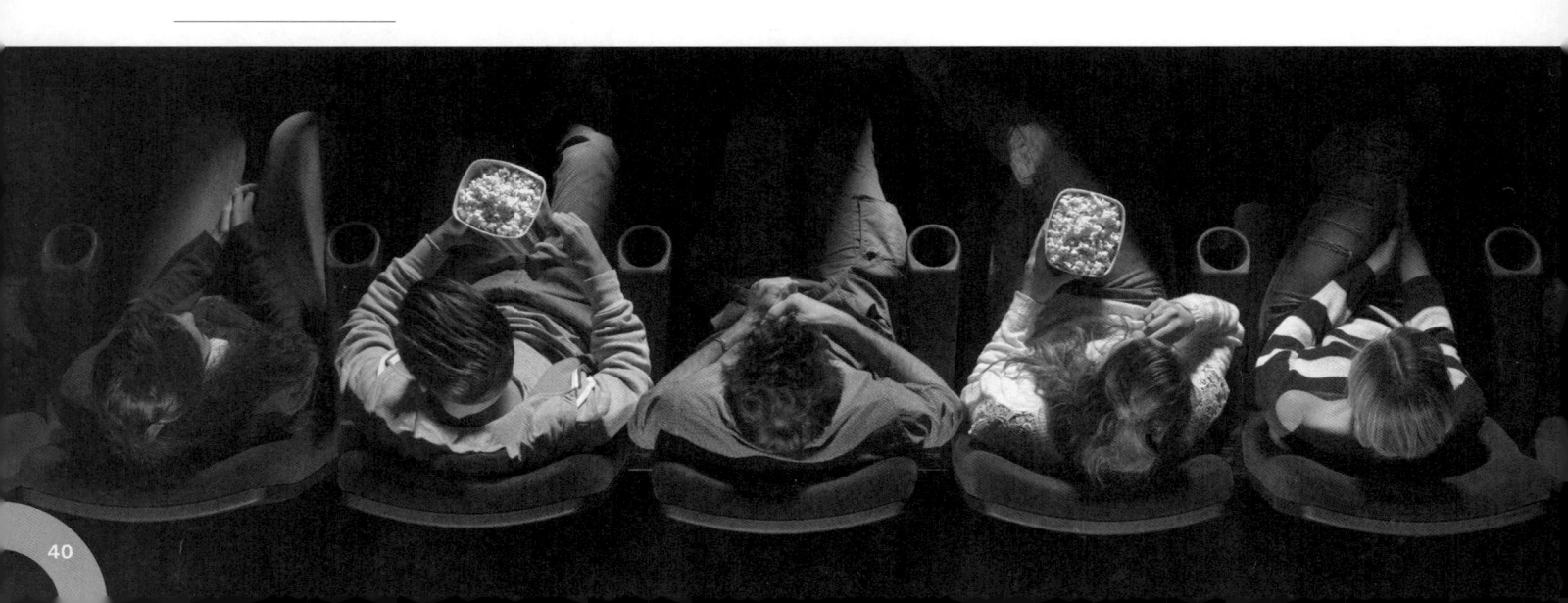

40

2 GRAMMAR passive (all tenses)

a Circle the correct form, active or passive.
1. The film *sets* / *is set* in Manchester in the 1980s.
2. A well-known comedy writer *wrote* / *was written* the script.
3. Special effects *will use* / *will be used* to create the monster.
4. Some of the extras *have invited* / *have been invited* to the film premiere.
5. Cinemas all over the country *are showing* / *are being shown* the musical.
6. The drama *is going to dub* / *is going to be dubbed* into other languages.
7. It was very windy while they *were filming* / *were being filmed* the final scenes.
8. Tickets for the show *can buy* / *can be bought* online.

b Complete the text with the phrases from the list.

is based on   is set in   plays the part of
was directed by   was dubbed into   was shot

c Complete the sentences with the correct passive form of the verbs in brackets.
1. The director's new film _____ on a true story. (base)
2. I've just read that Rachel Zegler _____ _____ for an Oscar. I hope she wins! (nominate)
3. The final scene _____ in Nigeria right now. (film)
4. The actor looked very different because he _____ into an old man by the make-up artist. (transform)
5. The first Star Wars films _____ by George Lucas. (direct)
6. The actors had time to learn the script while the set _____. (build)
7. The sequel _____ next year. (release)
8. The scene had to _____ several times before the director was satisfied. (shoot)

The Revenant

The Revenant is a 2015 American western. It [1] *was directed by* Mexican film director Alejandro G Iñárritu. The film [2] _____ the north-western part of the US. It [3] _____ a novel about the experiences of Hugh Glass, a man who lived in the area in the early 1800s. *The Revenant* [4] _____ on location in Canada, the US, and Argentina. Leonardo DiCaprio [5] _____ Hugh Glass, and he won an Academy Award for his performance. *The Revenant* was made in English, but it [6] _____ other languages.

d Read the article. Circle a, b, or c.

Steven Spielberg
Four decades of film history

Steven Spielberg ¹____ films for over 50 years. The film that made him famous around the world was *Jaws*, which ²____ in 1975. *Jaws* ³____ the story of a holiday resort where swimmers ⁴____ by a huge great white shark. Spielberg had many problems with the mechanical sharks while the film ⁵____, but he managed to finish it in the end. *Jaws* was extremely successful, and it ⁶____ three Academy Awards. Since then, Spielberg ⁷____ many films which have since become classics, including *Close Encounters of the Third Kind*, *E.T.*, and *Jurassic Park*. He ⁸____ the Oscar for Best Director eight times and has won the award twice: for *Schindler's List* and *Saving Private Ryan*. Today, Spielberg ⁹____ to be one of the most popular directors and producers in film history. Both film studios and audiences ¹⁰____ him when he eventually retires.

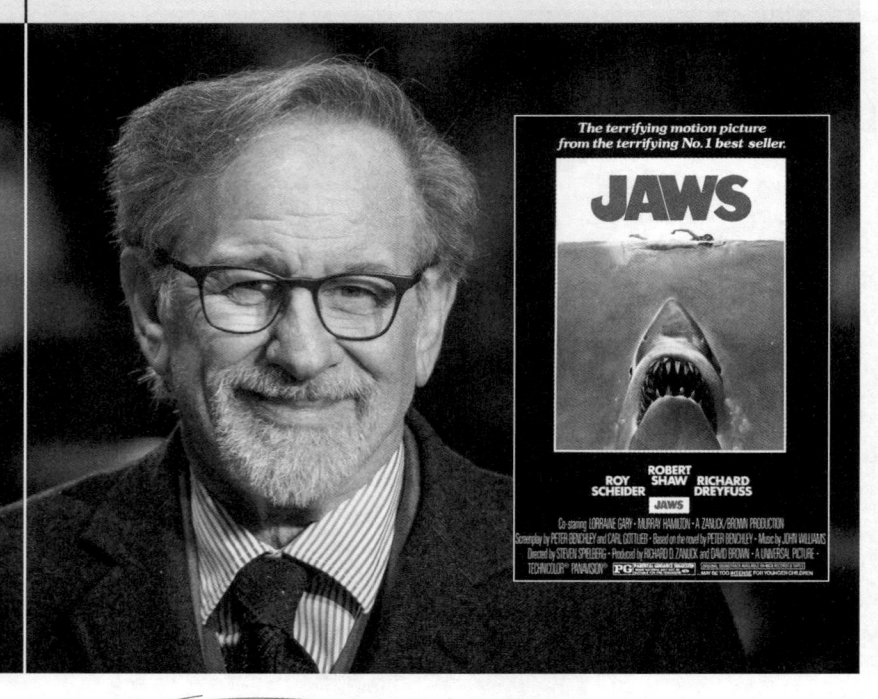

1 **a** has been making **b** has been made **c** is made
2 **a** is released **b** released **c** was released
3 **a** is told **b** tells **c** was told
4 **a** are being attacked **b** are attacking **c** attack
5 **a** was shot **b** shoot **c** was being shot
6 **a** was won **b** won **c** was being won
7 **a** has been directed **b** has directed **c** was directed
8 **a** has been nominated **b** has nominated **c** nominated
9 **a** considers **b** is considered **c** was considered
10 **a** will miss **b** will be missed **c** is missed

3 PRONUNCIATION regular and irregular past participles

a Look at the past participles. Which sounds do the letters in **bold** have? Write the words from the list in the correct column in the chart.

s**ai**d sh**o**t st**o**len t**a**ken us**ed** wait**ed** ~~watch**ed**~~ w**o**n w**o**rn wr**i**tten

tie	1	finish**ed** look**ed** *watched*
dog	2	film**ed** play**ed**
/ɪd/	3	add**ed** direct**ed**
fish	4	b**u**ilt g**i**ven
clock	5	c**o**st g**o**ne
horse	6	br**ough**t dr**aw**n
egg	7	f**e**lt l**e**ft
up	8	d**o**ne dr**u**nk
train	9	b**a**sed m**a**de
phone	10	ch**o**sen fl**ow**n

b 🔊 6.1 Listen and check. Then listen again and repeat the groups of words.

6B In the picture

G modals of deduction: might, can't, must
V the body
P diphthongs

1 GRAMMAR modals of deduction

a Circle the correct words.

1 That man *can't* / *must* be the new boss. Our new boss is a woman.

2 You *must* / *can't* be really tired. You've had a long trip.

3 I'm not sure what book to buy Oliver. He *might not* / *mustn't* like the same kind of things as me.

4 Paula *can't* / *could* be injured. She isn't running very well at all today. She's very slow.

5 Your neighbour *must* / *might not* have a good job. He has a very expensive car.

6 Arvin and Molly *must* / *can't* have much money. They never go out.

b Complete the sentences with *must*, *might*, *might not*, or *can't*.

1 He lived in Argentina for five years, so he _must_ speak good Spanish!
2 You _____ be very busy at work. You're always on Facebook!
3 I'm not sure what this fish is. It _____ be tuna.
4 Mark passed all his exams. His parents _____ be very proud.
5 A I think England will win tonight.
   B You _____ be serious! They have no chance!
6 Lucia wasn't feeling well this afternoon, so she _____ come to the party tonight. She said she'd let us know later today.
7 I thought our neighbour was away on holiday, but she _____ be – I've just seen her in her garden.
8 It's very cold and cloudy this evening. I think it _____ snow.

c Rewrite the highlighted sentences. Use *might (not)*, *can't*, or *must*.

1 They've been knocked out of the tournament. I'm sure they're disappointed.
   They _must be disappointed_.
2 Emily's late. It's possible that she has a meeting.
   She _____.
3 It's 8.30 and Tom's still in bed. I'm sure he isn't going to work today.
   He _____.
4 Don't buy that jumper for Ruth. It's possible that she won't like it.
   She _____.
5 We've only walked three kilometres. I'm sure you aren't tired already.
   You _____.
6 Susie's been studying all night. I'm sure she has an exam tomorrow.
   She _____.
7 We've been waiting ages for the lift. It's possible that it isn't working.
   It _____.
8 My brother isn't answering his phone. It's possible that he's driving home from work.
   He _____.

43

2 VOCABULARY the body

a Label the pictures.

1 h_ead_
2 n_____
3 b_____
4 a_____
5 l_____
6 fe_____
7 f_____
8 n_____
9 ch_____
10 st_____
11 f_____
12 kn_____

b Label the pictures with a word from the list.

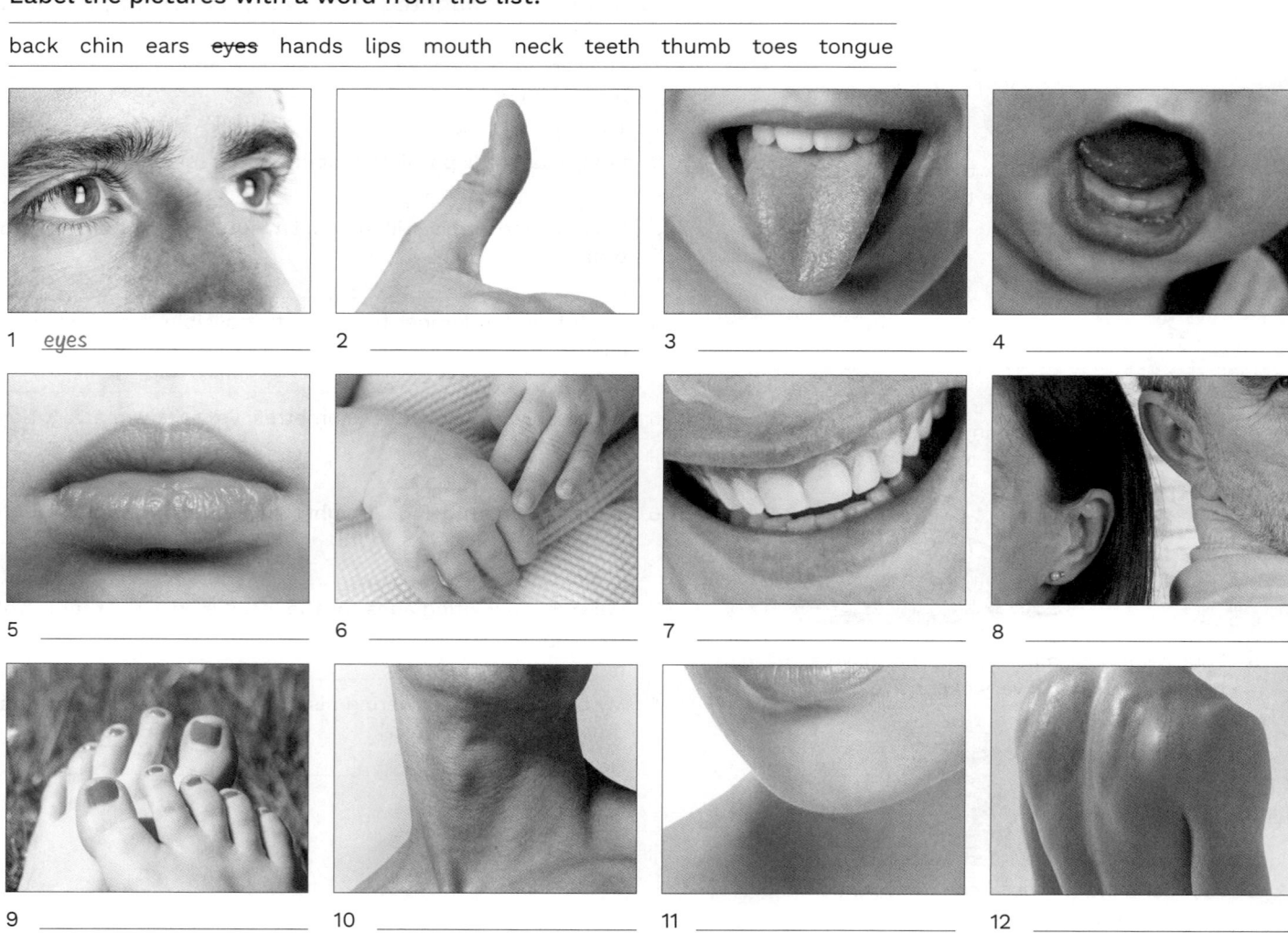

back   chin   ears   ~~eyes~~   hands   lips   mouth   neck   teeth   thumb   toes   tongue

1 _eyes_
2 _____
3 _____
4 _____
5 _____
6 _____
7 _____
8 _____
9 _____
10 _____
11 _____
12 _____

c Complete the sentences with a verb from the list.

bite clap kick nod point smell
smile ~~stare~~ taste touch whistle

1 It's rude to _stare_ at people. It can make them feel uncomfortable.
2 You'll have to _____ the ball harder to score a goal.
3 Don't _____ that plant with your hand – it's poisonous.
4 If you're in another country and don't speak the language, you can _____ at the thing you want in a shop or café.
5 I can _____ something burning. Did you turn off the oven?
6 My grandparents always look unhappy in photos because they never _____ at the camera.
7 He was too embarrassed to speak, but he was able to _____ his head to show he had understood.
8 Did the audience _____ much at the end of the concert?
9 Lisa doesn't like dogs because she's afraid they'll _____ her.
10 I often _____ my favourite song when I'm in the shower.
11 Can you _____ the soup? Do you think it's spicy enough?

d Complete the sentences with a part of the body.
1 You kick with your _foot_.
2 You point with your _____.
3 You smile with your _____.
4 You taste with your _____.
5 You nod with your _____.
6 You stare with your _____.
7 You smell with your _____.
8 You touch with your _____.
9 You whistle with your _____.
10 You bite with your _____.
11 You clap with your _____.

3 PRONUNCIATION diphthongs

a (Circle) the word with a different sound.

bike	1	bite smile he**igh**t (w**eigh**t)
train	2	f**a**ce gr**ea**t **eye**s t**a**ste
phone	3	n**o**se t**o**ngue thr**ow** t**oe**s
owl	4	s**ou**nd cr**ow**d m**ou**th sh**ou**lders
chair	5	h**air** h**ere** st**are** w**ear**

b 🔊 6.2 Listen and check. Then listen again and repeat the words.

7A Term time

G first conditional and future time clauses + *when*, *until*, etc.
V education
P the letter *u*

1 VOCABULARY education

a Complete the sentences.
1. Ph*ysics* is the scientific study of natural forces such as light, sound, heat, electricity, pressure, etc.
2. G_____ is the study of the world's surface, physical qualities, climate, countries, products, population, etc.
3. B_____ is the scientific study of living things.
4. L_____ is the study of poetry, drama, and fiction.
5. Ch_____ is the scientific study of substances and what happens to them in different conditions.
6. H_____ is the study of past events.
7. C_____ is the study of computers for collecting, storing, and sending out information.
8. M_____ is the study of numbers, quantities, and shapes.

b Match the words from the list to definitions 1–11 about schools in the UK.

boarding school   degree   head teacher   nursery school
primary school   private school   ~~pupils~~
secondary school   state school   students   term

1. children in school
   pupils
2. a school for children aged four to eleven
   _____
3. the person in charge of a school
   _____
4. a school controlled by the government
   _____
5. a qualification that students gain by successfully completing a course at university
   _____
6. a school that parents pay for
   _____
7. a period of time that the school year is divided into
   _____
8. a school that children live at while they're studying
   _____
9. a school for children aged from about two to four
   _____
10. people who are studying at school or university
    _____
11. a school for teenagers aged from 11 to 18
    _____

c Complete the sentences about schools in the US.
1. Very young children often go to k*indergarten*.
2. Children start e_____ sch_____ when they're six.
3. Schoolchildren are divided by age group into gr_____.
4. The school year is divided into s_____.
5. After middle school, students go on to h_____ sch_____.
6. Students finish school in tw_____ gr_____.
7. When they leave school, some students go to c_____ to continue their education.

d Complete the texts with the past simple form of the verbs from the list.

~~be expelled~~ be punished cheat let make misbehave (not) be allowed to

At my secondary school, discipline was very strict. Students who behaved badly ¹were expelled, so very few students ²_____ in class. We ³_____ talk during lessons, and the teacher ⁴_____ us stand up every time another teacher came into the classroom. We had to wear a uniform, and we ⁵_____ if we wore something different. We had to study a lot, and nobody ⁶_____ in exams. In the final year, the teachers weren't as strict with us, and they ⁷_____ us leave the school during the lunch break.

fail pass revise take

I was very nervous before my final exams at university. I ⁸_____ for several weeks, and I didn't go out at all. I ⁹_____ eight exams, and I was very relieved when I had finished. In the end, I ¹⁰_____ all of them, but my friends weren't so lucky. They ¹¹_____ some of the exams, so they had to do them again.

2 PRONUNCIATION the letter *u*

a Circle the word with a different sound.

boot	1	fruit (lunch) scooter true
up	2	couple mussels pull tongue
bull	3	cut full push put
/juː/ you	4	musical stupid subtitles tuna

b 🔊 7.1 Listen and check. Then listen again and repeat the words.

3 GRAMMAR first conditional and future time clauses + *when*, *until*, etc.

a Match the sentence halves.

1 Will you buy a car __e__
2 Mike's parents will be furious ____
3 I'll have more time to help you ____
4 You'll have to go to a new school ____
5 He won't pass his exams ____
6 Nina won't go back to work ____
7 You'll need to buy the book ____
8 I'll stay at home ____

a unless he revises more.
b after I come back from my holiday.
c if he fails his exam again.
d before the classes start.
e ~~if you pass your driving test?~~
f when your family moves house.
g if I still don't feel well in the morning.
h until her daughter starts school.

47

b Complete the sentences with a word from the list.

after   before   if   ~~unless~~   until   when

1 They won't be able to leave the school <u>unless</u> the teacher gives them permission.
2 The teacher won't start the class _____ all the pupils are quiet.
3 I'll talk to my teachers _____ I choose my exam subjects.
4 Ella will be disappointed _____ she doesn't get good marks.
5 I'll have a long holiday _____ the course finishes.
6 They'll have to wear a uniform _____ they go to secondary school.

c Complete the sentences with the correct form of the verbs in brackets. Use the present simple or future (*will / won't*).

1 <u>I'll do</u> my homework as soon as I <u>get</u> home. (do, get)
2 We _____ late unless we _____. (be, hurry)
3 I _____ a shower before I _____. (have, go out)
4 The school bus _____ for you if you _____ on time. (not wait, not be)
5 If the teacher _____, we _____ the exam. (not come, not have)
6 James _____ home until he _____ a job. (not leave, find)
7 Amelia _____ buy a car unless her parents _____ her the money. (not be able to, lend)
8 As soon as my boyfriend _____ his results, he _____ me. (get, call)
9 She _____ primary school until she _____ five years old. (not start, be)
10 You _____ better if you _____ every day. (play, practise)

d Complete the sentences with your own ideas.

1 I'll charge my phone <u>when I get home tonight</u>.
2 I'll go out tonight if _____.
3 I won't watch TV later unless _____.
4 I'll do my homework before _____.
5 I won't buy a (new) phone until _____.
6 I'll go to bed after _____.

7B House or home?

G second conditional, choosing between conditionals
V houses
P sentence stress, the letter c

1 GRAMMAR second conditional, choosing between conditionals

a Match the sentence halves.
1 If we had the time, _d_
2 I'd like my flat more ____
3 You'd be able to find a job ____
4 If my sister didn't live abroad, ____
5 If we bought a bigger house in the country, ____
6 If they could live anywhere they wanted to, ____
7 We'd get on better ____
8 I wouldn't want to live in London, ____

a she could visit us more often.
b they'd move to France.
c if you spoke better English.
d we'd do the housework ourselves.
e if we didn't have to share an office.
f unless I earned a lot of money.
g if it was on the top floor.
h we'd be able to have a dog.

b Complete the sentences with the correct form of the verbs in brackets. Use the second conditional.
1 If Mateo _had_ more time, he _'d paint_ his room himself. (have, paint)
2 Lucy _____ happier if her flatmate _____ the kitchen more often. (be, clean)
3 I _____ to work if I _____ a parking space. (not drive, not have)
4 _____ you _____ working if you _____ a lot of money? (carry on, win)
5 I'm sure Evie _____ better if she _____ so much coffee. (sleep, not drink)
6 My parents _____ me the money if I _____ to buy a new car. (lend, need)
7 I _____ surprised if it _____ tonight. (not be, snow)
8 If our house _____ so small, you _____ all stay the night. (not be, can)
9 _____ you _____ if you _____ your alarm? (wake up, not set)
10 If we _____ another bathroom, there _____ a queue for the shower. (have, not be)

c Complete the sentences with the words in brackets. Use the first or second conditional.
1 If they offer me the job, _I'll take it_. (I / take it)
2 If my car wasn't being repaired, _I'd give you a lift_. (I / give you a lift)
3 If I had Emily's number, _____. (I / call her)
4 You'll miss the train if _____. (you / not hurry up)
5 If I see Jon, _____. (I / tell him the news)
6 It wouldn't be so cold if _____. (you / not open the windows)
7 If my mother didn't live on her own, _____. (she / be happier)
8 If it rains on Saturday, _____. (they / cancel the match)
9 You wouldn't spend so much money if _____. (you / not eat out every night).
10 Rita won't go to work tomorrow if _____. (she / not feel better)

2 PRONUNCIATION sentence stress, the letter c

a 🔊 7.2 Listen and complete the sentences.
1 If I _did_ more _exercise_, I'd be a _lot fitter_.
2 I'd _____ my own _____ if I had a _____.
3 Would you _____ a _____ if you _____?
4 If it were _____, I _____ the _____.
5 I _____ a _____ if I _____ in the _____.

b Listen again and repeat the sentences. Copy the rhythm.

c Say the pairs of words. Do the letters in **bold** have the same pronunciation or are they pronounced differently? Write **S** (same) or **D** (different).

1 **c**arpet   lo**c**ation   S
2 **c**abin   **c**eiling   D
3 **c**entre   **c**osy   ___
4 spa**ci**ous   spe**ci**al   ___
5 **c**ity   **c**entre   ___
6 **c**astle   musi**ci**an   ___
7 de**c**ide   entran**ce**   ___
8 firepla**ce**   bal**c**ony   ___

d 7.3 Listen and check. Then listen again and repeat the words.

3 VOCABULARY houses

a Complete the sentences with *in* or *on*.
1 We're looking for a flat *in* a suburb. We don't want to live in the city centre.
2 I'd love to live by the sea, maybe ____ the south coast.
3 All the bedrooms are ____ the first floor.
4 Sara bought a beautiful cottage ____ the country, where she can ride her horse.
5 Yusuf lives ____ the outskirts of the city, so he has to commute to the centre every day.
6 My grandparents live ____ a town north of Manchester called Blackburn.

b Label the pictures.

1 st eps_____
2 b_____
3 en_____
4 p_____
5 g_____
6 ch_____
7 w_____
8 t_____ fl_____
9 a_____
10 r_____
11 t_____
12 b_____

c Complete the adverts. Circle a, b, or c.

JUST ADDED

FOR SALE

This ¹___ flat is on the top floor of a building with magnificent views of Regent Park. All the rooms are very ²___. It has three bedrooms, a bathroom, and a large ³___ kitchen. The living room has a ⁴___ floor, and there are carpets in all the bedrooms.

1	**a** modern	**b** recent	**c** young
2	**a** clear	**b** light	**c** lit
3	**a** big	**b** spacious	**c** tiny
4	**a** board	**b** rug	**c** wooden

VILLAGE LOCATION

FOR SALE

This 18th-century cottage is situated in a quiet village. It has a kitchen, bathroom, living room, and two small but ⁵___ bedrooms. All the rooms have low ⁶___, and the walls are made ⁷___ stone. There is an open ⁸___ in the living room, but the house also has central heating.

5	**a** cosy	**b** safe	**c** soft
6	**a** ceilings	**b** roofs	**c** walls
7	**a** by	**b** in	**c** of
8	**a** chimney	**b** fire	**c** heating

3 BEDROOMS

FOR SALE

This recently built house is located on the ⁹___ of the city, with good public transport links. Downstairs there's a kitchen, a living room, and a dining room, while on the ¹⁰___ floor there are three bedrooms and a stylish bathroom. At the back of the house there are four ¹¹___ down to a small garden with a ¹²___ which is perfect for outdoor entertaining.

9	**a** suburbs	**b** outskirts	**c** centre
10	**a** ground	**b** first	**c** second
11	**a** steps	**b** stairs	**c** paths
12	**a** terrace	**b** basement	**c** balcony

Practical English
Together again?

EPISODE 4 PICTURES OF YOU

making suggestions

1 MAKING SUGGESTIONS

a Re-order the words to make phrases for making and responding to suggestions.

1 not / why
   Why not?
2 go / could / we / there
   _____.
3 a / idea / great / that's
   _____.
4 pub / don't / to / we / why / a / go
   _____?
5 shall / that / go / we / where / for / drink
   _____?
6 going / what / to / about / Giovanni's
   _____?
7 Red / The / how / Lion / about
   _____?
8 there / go / we / shall
   _____?

b Complete the conversation with the phrases from **a**.

Jess ¹*Where shall we go for that drink*?
Phil There's a really nice tea shop up the road.
² _____.
Jess Actually, I'd prefer a cold drink.
Phil OK, ³_____?
Jess Good idea, ⁴_____?
I've heard it's a really nice pub and it's quite near here.
Phil Thinking about it, I'm quite hungry.
⁵_____?
Jess ⁶_____. They have excellent pizzas.
Phil And it isn't very far. ⁷_____?
Jess Yes, ⁸_____?

2 VERB FORMS

Complete the sentences with the correct form of a verb from the list.

eat out   go   meet   ~~order~~   play   watch

1 We could *order* a pizza.
2 Shall we _____ a film?
3 What about _____ outside the train station?
4 Why don't we _____ cards?
5 How about _____ to the theatre?
6 Let's _____ tonight.

3 SOCIAL ENGLISH

a Complete the highlighted phrases in the conversations with a word from the list.

ahead   done   ~~forget~~   forward   over

1 **A** Do you remember when Max came jogging with us?
   B How could I *forget*?
2 **A** I finished my course last month.
   B Well _____!
3 **A** Well, it's been really nice seeing you again.
   B Yes, it has. I'm looking _____ to working with you.
4 **A** I wanted to ask you something about work.
   B Sure, go _____.
5 **A** So, what did you want to talk to me about?
   B I'll tell you _____ a drink.

b Complete the conversation with the highlighted phrases from **a**.

1 **A** I've just passed my driving test.
   B *Well done*! That's fantastic news.
2 **A** I hope you have a lovely holiday.
   B Thanks. _____ having a break.
3 **A** Do you remember the first time you met my parents?
   B _____?
4 **A** I wanted to ask you something about your new car.
   B Sure, _____.
5 **A** So, what do you think I should do about my relationship?
   B I can't chat now. Let's talk about it _____.

52

1-7 Can you remember...?

1 GRAMMAR

Circle the correct words.

1 John and Mary are delighted because their son *gets / 's getting / will get* married next year.
2 He *plays / 's playing / 's been* playing tennis for ten years.
3 You *don't have to / ought to / mustn't* send text messages when you're driving. It's against the law.
4 I'd love to *can / be able to / could to* play the piano, but I can't.
5 If I *have / had / will have* time tonight, I'll send you those photos.
6 If I knew the answer, I *'ll tell / tell / 'd tell* you.

2 VOCABULARY

Circle the word that is different.

1 dishonest   irresponsible   sympathetic   unkind
2 borrow   charge   invest   mortgage
3 boarding   primary   state   head
4 circuit   coach   pitch   track
5 cast   extra   plot   star
6 lips   shoulder   teeth   tongue

3 PRONUNCIATION

Circle the word with a different sound.

key	1 **c**arpet **c**ast **c**inema **c**ritic
snake	2 **c**eiling **c**entre **c**osy terra**c**e
shower	3 **c**ity musi**c**ian spa**c**ious spe**c**ial
train	4 st**a**re st**a**te t**a**ste tr**a**iler
bike	5 **eye**s f**ai**l h**igh** sm**i**le

4 GRAMMAR & VOCABULARY

Read the article. Circle a, b, or c.

Alternative schooling

Sue Cowley is an experienced teacher and author of many books on how to give children ¹____ education. These days, teachers ²____ insist that children must be educated at school, not at home. However, Sue doesn't agree. That's why, when her children were young, she decided to take them out of school for six months to go on a road trip. The route the family took ³____ by the children themselves – Alvie and Edite, who were eleven and eight at the time.

Sue and her children ⁴____ in the family car and headed for the Netherlands, where they stayed in a mobile home on the ⁵____ of Amsterdam. They visited Anne Frank's house and the Rijksmuseum. From there, they drove all around Europe before making their way to China. While their ⁶____ were studying hard at school, Alvie and Edite ⁷____ giant pandas at Beijing Zoo.

The children ⁸____ get up early or study on their trip, but their mother ⁹____ them write a page in their travel diary every day. Alvie and Edite learned a lot on their travels, including how to draw an accurate map of Europe, and what to do if you become separated from your family on the Underground.

¹⁰____ more than ten years since their road trip, but Sue and her children will never forget the experience.

1	a better	b best	c the best
2	a usually	b are used to	c used to
3	a chose	b was chose	c was chosen
4	a set down	b set off	c set up
5	a coast	b outskirts	c suburbs
6	a classmates	b colleagues	c partners
7	a have visited	b had visited	c were visiting
8	a can't	b didn't have to	c mustn't
9	a allowed	b let	c made
10	a It's	b It's been	c It was

8A The right job for you

G choosing between gerunds and infinitives
V work
P word stress

1 VOCABULARY work

a Complete the text with words from the list.

applied ~~overtime~~ promoted ran redundant resign
retire sacked set up shifts training course

My father's first job was in a small local company. He had to do a lot of ¹ _overtime_, which he really hated, but he knew he would be ² _____ if he didn't do it. One day, he decided to ³ _____ from the job. He ⁴ _____ for a new job with a multinational company. At first, he worked ⁵ _____ in a factory. Then, he got ⁶ _____ to supervisor. Later, he was made ⁷ _____ because business was bad. After that, my dad did a ⁸ _____ in Business Management, and he ⁹ _____ his own business. He ¹⁰ _____ the company for 20 years, and he didn't ¹¹ _____ until he was 68 years old. This photo shows the party they organized for him on his last day.

b Complete each sentence with a preposition and a word from the list.

freelance full-time part-time permanent
~~self-employed~~ temporary unemployed

1 Maxine is a _self-employed_ mechanic. She loves working _for_ herself
2 My niece is still _____ school, but she has a _____ job. She only works on Friday evenings and Saturdays.
3 Oliver is _____ his third year at university. This summer, he hopes to get a _____ job as a waiter to earn some money.
4 Laura is _____ charge of IT at the public library. It's a _____ job – she works from 8 a.m. to 6 p.m. every day.
5 My cousin used to work _____ a large multinational company, but he's been _____ since he was made redundant last year.
6 My boyfriend has a _____ job in a bank, and he hopes to stay there until he retires. He's responsible _____ customer loans.
7 My sister is a _____ software developer. She works _____ lots of different companies.

54

c Complete the sentences with a noun form of the word in **bold**.

1. A <u>musician</u> plays **music** for a living.
2. They're looking for a _____ to **translate** some documents into Polish.
3. The company **employs** 200 staff – 150 are in full-time _____.
4. Helen studied **pharmacy** because she wanted to be a _____.
5. When we **retire**, we'd like to spend our _____ with our grandchildren.
6. They're going to **promote** someone, but we don't know who's going to get the _____.
7. Jamal's interested in **law**, so he'd like to be a _____.
8. My daughter is good at all the **sciences**, so I'm sure she'll be a _____ when she's older.
9. My colleague tried to **resign**, but our boss wouldn't accept his _____.
10. I **applied** for the job, but I sent in the _____ too late.
11. A _____ has to get up early to look after his **farm**.
12. He wasn't **qualified** for the job because he didn't have any _____.

d Complete the sentences with the correct form of a word from the list. Use each word twice.

company   fire   market   run   work

1. I like spending time with John. I enjoy his <u>company</u>.
2. The police officer _____ his gun.
3. I dropped my phone in the bath and now it doesn't _____.
4. I _____ five kilometres every evening.
5. Jane was _____ because she stole money from the company.
6. We always buy fruit and vegetables from our local _____.
7. My sister has applied for a job with an engineering _____.
8. There isn't a big _____ for this kind of product in Europe.
9. I _____ part-time in a café.
10. One day, I would like to _____ my own business.

2 PRONUNCIATION word stress

a Under<u>line</u> the stressed syllable.

1. ap|pli|<u>ca</u>|tion
2. ap|ply
3. em|ploy|ment
4. far|mer
5. free|lance
6. law|yer
7. mu|si|cian
8. per|ma|nent
9. phar|ma|cist
10. pro|mo|tion
11. qual|i|fi|ca|tion
12. qua|li|fy
13. re|dun|dant
14. re|sig|na|tion
15. re|tire
16. re|tire|ment
17. sci|en|tist
18. tem|po|ra|ry
19. trans|la|tion
20. un|em|ployed

b 🔊 8.1 Listen and check. Then listen again and repeat.

3 GRAMMAR choosing between gerunds and infinitives

a (Circle) a, b, or c.

1. It's difficult ____ a good job these days.
   a finding   (**b** to find)   **c** find
2. He isn't very good at ____ decisions.
   a making   **b** to make   **c** make
3. They promised ____ me at the end of the month.
   a paying   **b** to pay   **c** pay
4. I should ____. It's getting late.
   a going   **b** to go   **c** go
5. ____ an application form can take ages.
   a Filling in   **b** To fill in   **c** Fill in
6. My girlfriend told me ____ her later.
   a calling   **b** to call   **c** call
7. The film I saw last night made me ____.
   a crying   **b** to cry   **c** cry
8. Tim really enjoys ____ in a team.
   a working   **b** to work   **c** work
9. I went to the supermarket ____ some bread.
   a buying   **b** to buy   **c** buy
10. I gave up ____ basketball when I went to university.
    a playing   **b** to play   **c** play

b Correct any mistakes in the highlighted verbs. Tick (✓) the correct sentences.

1 I remember having my first job interview. I was really nervous! ✓

2 Lift heavy weights can give you back problems.
   Lifting heavy weights

3 The interviewer asked me wait in Reception.

4 I know you don't like my boyfriend, but please try to be nice to him.

5 Go on, tell me! I promise to not laugh.

6 The bus didn't come, so we started walking home.

7 Anna went on study until midnight.

8 It's impossible to read your writing!

9 If you are tired, I don't mind stay in tonight.

10 Everyone is afraid of being sacked.

c Complete the sentences with the correct form of the verbs in brackets.

1 I went to the bank *to get* some money. (get)
2 Try _____ to your boss. He might be able to help you. (talk)
3 I want you _____ me exactly what happened. (tell)
4 I didn't remember _____ the cooker, so the kitchen was full of smoke. (turn off)
5 Some couples can go on _____ to each other for days after an argument. (not speak)
6 I love hanging out with Lucas because he makes me _____. (laugh)
7 _____ drive is one of the requirements of the job. (be able to)
8 The service had been so bad that the manager agreed _____ us for our meal. (not charge)

8B Service with a smile?

G reported speech: sentences and questions
V making nouns from verbs
P the letters *ai* and *air*

1 GRAMMAR reported speech

a Circle the correct words.
1 Leo said yesterday that he *will* / **would** come shopping with me.
2 We asked the sales assistant how much *it was* / *was it*.
3 My brother *said me* / *told me* that he had spent all his money in the sales.
4 I asked Lily where *she bought* / *did she buy* her clothes.
5 You told me that you *may* / *might* go shopping on Saturday.
6 My sister asked me *if I can* / *if I could* lend her £50 until next weekend.
7 Hassan said that he *had to* / *must* go to the supermarket.
8 I asked my friend whether *suited me the dress* / *the dress suited me*, and she said I looked great!
9 Helena asked me what *I wanted* / *did I want* from the shops.
10 Marco said that he couldn't pay me back because he *'s forgotten* / *'d forgotten* his wallet.

b Complete the sentences with *said* or *told*.
1 Jackie _said_ that she was thinking of buying a new car.
2 My boyfriend _____ me he wanted to see his friends more often.
3 You _____ you'd check the price online.
4 I _____ you I might be late.
5 Ryan _____ me that he couldn't find his credit card.
6 My uncle _____ that he would buy me a new smartphone for my birthday.

c Report the conversations.
1 'Where do you buy your clothes?'
'I buy them online'.
I asked Kate _where she bought her clothes_.
She told _me (that) she bought them online_.

2 'Have you seen my wallet?'
'I don't know where it is.'
He asked me _____.
I said _____.

3 'Do your school shoes still fit you?'
'They fit me perfectly!'
I asked my daughter _____.
She told _____.

4 'How much did you pay for your jacket?'
'It was really cheap'.
I asked Oliver _____.
He said _____.

5 'Where are you going tomorrow?'
'I'm meeting some friends.'
Sofia asked me _____.
I told _____.

6 'Do you want anything from the shop?'
'I need some milk.'
I asked Ivan _____.
He said _____.

7 'Did you enjoy your stay?'
'It's been very enjoyable.'
She asked us _____.
We told _____.

8 'When are you going shopping?'
'I may go on Saturday.'
Holly asked me _____.
I said _____.

57

d Write the sentences and questions in direct speech.

1 Theo said that he couldn't afford to live on his own.
'I can't afford to live on my own.'
2 Kaya told me she had resigned from her job.
'_____.'
3 I asked my aunt when she was planning to retire.
'_____?'
4 My parents asked me if I was paid to do overtime.
'_____?'
5 Poppy told me she had gone to boarding school as a child.
'_____.'
6 We asked the artist how much the painting was worth.
'_____?'
7 Kristofer said he would take the tram to the city centre.
'_____.'
8 My uncle asked me where I had met my partner.
'_____?'
9 The tennis player said she expected to win the match.
'_____.'
10 My friend's parents asked me if I liked seafood.
'_____?'

2 VOCABULARY making nouns from verbs

a Complete the chart with verbs and nouns.

verb	noun
¹achieve	achievement
argue	2
3	choice
compensate	4
5	delivery
explain	6
7	failure
improve	8
9	loss
pay	10
11	sale
succeed	12

b Complete the sentences with the noun form of the verbs in brackets.

1 The company made a _loss_ of £2 million last year. (lose)
2 The _____ was very slow, so we didn't leave a tip. (serve)
3 I'm good friends with my manager, but she doesn't give me any special _____. (treat)
4 We couldn't reach an _____ with our boss about salaries. (agree)
5 My exam marks this term are a big _____ on last term. (improve)
6 They've had an _____, and they aren't talking to each other. (argue)
7 They had to get a _____ of their house before they could sell it. (value)
8 His greatest _____ was winning an Olympic gold medal. (achieve)
9 It's a difficult _____ to make between my best friend's wedding or my sister's birthday party. (choose)
10 The restaurant had to close as a result of bad _____. (manage)
11 There's a _____ on Saturday against the closure of the hospital. (demonstrate)
12 The _____ of alcohol is often prohibited at sports matches. (sell)
13 After careful _____, we've decided to sell the company. (consider)
14 My attempt to run a marathon ended in _____ when I fell and broke my leg after the first kilometre. (fail)
15 I had to resist the _____ to have another cake – they were delicious! (tempt)

c Complete the text with the noun form of the verbs in brackets.

A month ago, I bought a video game online for my son's birthday. I got a confirmation email back, which said that ¹_delivery_ (deliver) would take about ten days. Two weeks later, I began to worry. I knew the seller had received my ²_____ (pay), but the video game hadn't arrived. So I decided to make a ³_____ (complain). I sent an email to the seller, with a copy of the order confirmation as an ⁴_____ (attach). I received a ⁵_____ (respond) immediately, which said that the seller would look into the incident. After that, I heard nothing for three days, so I sent another email demanding an ⁶_____ (explain). This time I had more ⁷_____ (succeed), and the seller said he would send another copy of the game. If I don't receive it before my son's birthday, I'm going to ask for ⁸_____ (compensate).

3 PRONUNCIATION the letters *ai* and *air*

a Complete the chart with the words from the list.

airline   certain   ~~claim~~   complain   contain   email   explain   paid   repair   waiter

eɪ	tr**ai**n	claim
eə	ch**air**	
ə	comp**u**t**er**	

b 🔊 8.2 Listen and check. Then listen again and repeat the words.

9A I was so lucky!

G third conditional
V making adjectives and adverbs
P sentence rhythm, weak pronunciation of *have*

1 GRAMMAR third conditional

a Complete the sentences with *had* or *would have*.
1 If I'd known it was your birthday, I'*d have* bought you a present.
2 It _____ been quicker if we'd gone by train. Our flight was very delayed.
3 Harry wouldn't have been late for work if the bus _____ been on time.
4 I'm sure that if David _____ seen you, he would have said hello.
5 I _____ gone to their party if they'd invited me, but they didn't.
6 If you'd got up earlier, you _____ had time to make your bed.
7 If Kim _____ paid attention in class, she would have known about the exam.
8 You wouldn't have fallen asleep at the cinema if you _____ had a rest this afternoon.

b Complete the sentences with the correct form of the verbs in brackets.
1 If you'd told me you weren't staying for dinner, I *wouldn't have made* so much food. (not make)
2 We _____ on time if we'd left half an hour earlier. (arrive)
3 If we _____ a table, we wouldn't have been able to have dinner there. (not book)
4 You'd have seen my message if you _____ your mobile phone. (check)
5 I'd have enjoyed the party more if the music _____ so loud. (not be)
6 If you'd concentrated on what you were doing, you _____ so many mistakes. (not make)
7 If I _____ it was going to be so cold today, I would have worn a warmer coat. (know)
8 We _____ Jack to dinner, too, if we'd known you didn't like him. (not invite)
9 If you _____ so rude about my mother, I wouldn't have got so angry. (not be)
10 My sister _____ promoted if she'd refused to do overtime. (not get)

c Complete the second sentence so it has a similar meaning to the first sentence.
1 I got to the restaurant late because I went to the wrong place first.
If I hadn't gone to the wrong place first, *I wouldn't have got to the restaurant late*.
2 I passed my final exams, so I went to university.
I wouldn't have gone to university if _____.
3 Sofia didn't have the right qualifications, so she didn't get the job.
If Sofia had had the right qualifications, _____.
4 We had lunch before we left, so we weren't hungry.
We would have been hungry if _____.
5 We didn't play tennis this afternoon because it was so windy.
If it hadn't been so windy this afternoon, _____.
6 You got lost because you didn't follow my directions.
You wouldn't have got lost if _____.
7 I didn't win that game because you cheated.
If you hadn't cheated, _____.
8 Alex wasn't very careful with his glasses, so he broke them.
If Alex had been more careful with his glasses, _____.

2 PRONUNCIATION sentence rhythm, weak pronunciation of *have*

a 🔊 9.1 Listen and complete the sentences.

1 If they hadn't played so badly, they <u>would have won</u> the match.
2 If you'd told me about the meeting, I _____ _____.
3 She _____ the coat if it hadn't been so expensive.
4 If there had been room for us, we _____ _____ the night.
5 We _____ to the cinema on time if we'd taken a taxi.
6 If I'd known you were moving house, I _____ _____ you.

b Listen again and repeat the sentences. Copy the rhythm.

3 VOCABULARY making adjectives and adverbs

a Complete the chart with the two adjective forms of each noun from the list.

care <s>comfort</s> fortune luck patience

	+	−
adjective ending in *-able*	¹comfortable	²uncomfortable
adjective ending in *-ate*	3	4
adjective ending in *-ful / less*	5	6
adjective ending in *-ient*	7	8
adjective ending in *-y*	9	10

b Complete the sentences with the adverb form of the words in brackets. Use the negative form if necessary.

1 We were sitting <u>comfortably</u> on the sofa when there was a knock at the door. (comfort)
2 I was in a hurry, so I waited _____ for the lift to arrive. (patience)
3 She put down the glass _____, so it fell on the floor and broke. (care)
4 _____, I'd taken an umbrella, because it began to rain before I'd got to my office. (fortune)
5 The goalkeeper was injured so _____, she missed the final. (luck)

c Complete the charts with adjectives and adverbs.

	adjectives	
noun	+	−
success	¹successful	²unsuccessful
possibility	3	4
self	5	6
use	7	8
suit	9	10

	adverbs	
noun	+	−
success	¹¹successfully	¹²unsuccessfully
possibility	13	14
self	15	16
use	17	18
suit	19	20

d Complete the sentences with a word from the charts in **c**.

1 It's <u>possible</u> to see the English coast from France on a clear day.
2 She _____ took both of the biscuits that were left on the plate.
3 You should throw that old umbrella away – it's completely _____.
4 All of their children have been very _____ in their chosen careers.
5 It was a special occasion, so all the guests were dressed _____.

e Complete the text with the correct adjective or adverb form of the nouns in brackets.

Unlucky teen's meeting with an alligator

An American teenager made a ¹<u>careless</u> (care) mistake when he jumped into a river without checking the area for alligators before going swimming.

Kaleb Langdale was at the Caloosahatchee River in Florida with friends when he decided to go for a swim. The ²_____ (patient) young man soon found himself in the ³_____ (comfort) position of sharing the water with an alligator, which started to attack him. He was ⁴_____ (luck) enough to escape the first attack and began to swim to the bank, where his friends were waiting for him. ⁵_____ (fortune), the three-metre animal attacked again, and this time it held on to Kaleb's arm. ⁶_____ (luck), Kaleb managed to get away, but his arm was seriously injured in the process.

Kaleb is now recovering in hospital, and doctors say his condition is ⁷_____ (comfort) despite his injuries. Kaleb recommends that anybody who goes swimming in the Caloosahatchee River should check the area ⁸_____ (care) before going swimming.

9B Power cut

G quantifiers
V electronic devices
P linking, *ough* and *augh*

1 VOCABULARY electronic devices

a Complete the words.

1 k <u>e</u> y <u>bo a</u> r d
2 p _ _ _ _ t _ _ _
3 s _ _ _ k _ _ _
4 a _ _ p _ _ _ r
5 r _ _ _ _ _ _ _ _   c _ _ _ t _ _ _ l
6 s _ _ k _ _ _  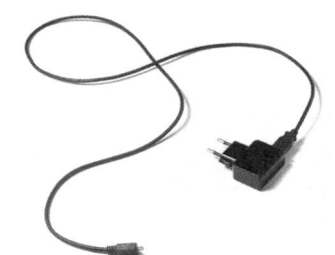   
7 ch _ _ _ g _ _ _
8 s _ _ _ t _ _ _
9 p _ _ _ g
10 U _ _ _ - _   c _ b _ _ _
11 m _ m _ _ _ _ _   s _ _ _ _ k    
12 r _ _ _ t _ _ _
13 w _ r _ l _ ss   m _ _ _ s _
14 v _ _ _ c _   _ ss _ st _ nt

b Complete the sentences with a word from **a**.

1 Let's turn the lights on. Where's the <u>switch</u>?
2 I've got the presentation on a _____ _____, so I don't need to take my laptop.
3 My battery's getting low. Can I borrow your _____?
4 Can I use your _____? I need to print out some documents.
5 You'll need a _____ _____ if you want to connect your phone to your laptop.
6 Where's the '@' symbol on this _____?
7 Who's got the _____ _____ for the TV? I want to change channels.
8 You can't use European plugs in the UK if you haven't got an _____.
9 If you turn on the _____, you might be able to hear something!
10 Is the _____ working? I haven't got an internet connection.
11 Never take a _____ out of a _____ with wet hands – you might get an electric shock.

63

c Replace the **bold** words with the past simple form of a verb from the list.

~~delete~~ install plug in set switch off switch on turn down turn up unplug update

1 I **removed** a video I didn't like.
   I _deleted_ a video.
2 I **programmed** the alarm on my phone for 7.30.
   I _____ the alarm for 7.30.
3 I **pressed the 'on' button** on the printer.
   I _____ _____ the printer.
4 I **put** some new software **on my laptop**.
   I _____ some new software.
5 I **put** my charger **into a socket**.
   I _____ _____ my charger.
6 I **pressed the 'off' button** on the router.
   I _____ _____ the router.
7 I **changed the volume** on the TV **from 20 to 15**.
   I _____ _____ the TV.
8 I **disconnected** the voice assistant.
   I _____ the voice assistant.
9 I **got the latest version** of the app.
   I _____ the app.
10 I **made the music** on the speaker **louder**.
   I _____ _____ the speaker.

2 GRAMMAR quantifiers

a Circle the correct answers. One, two, or three answers may be correct.

1 Do you eat ___ sweets?
   a many **b** a lot of
   c much
2 I sleep ___ when I'm on holiday.
   a a lot of **b** a lot
   c lots of
3 I don't drink ___ coffee.
   a many **b** a lot of
   c much
4 You can sit here. There's ___ room.
   a many **b** much
   c plenty of
5 My sister has ___ friends.
   a a lot of **b** lots of
   c loads of
6 Can I have ___ more cake, please? It's delicious!
   a a few **b** a little
   c very little
7 My phone has ___ games because I never play them.
   a a few **b** very few
   c very little
8 There are ___ young people living in the village than there used to be.
   a fewer **b** less
   c little
9 I can't hear you. There's ___ noise.
   a enough **b** too many
   c too much
10 You aren't working ___.
   a hard enough **b** enough hard
   c too much hard
11 There isn't ___ milk in the fridge.
   a any **b** much
   c some
12 **A** How much bread is there?
   B ___. I've just finished it all.
   a Any **b** None
   c No any

b Complete each pair of sentences so that they have the same meaning. More than one answer may be possible.

1 There aren't _enough_ chairs for everyone.
   There are _too few_ chairs for everyone.

2 He can't afford to buy a house. He doesn't have _____ money.
   He can't afford to buy a house. They're _____ for him.

3 We only had _____ sleep last night.
   We didn't have _____ sleep last night.

4 There are _____ cars in the car park.
   There aren't _____ parking spaces.

5 There's _____ petrol in the tank.
   There isn't _____ petrol in the tank.

6 She buys very _____ books these days.
   She doesn't buy _____ books these days.

c Complete the sentences with a quantifier and the words in brackets. Sometimes more than one answer is possible.

1 The party was quite quiet. There weren't _many people_. (people)
2 I didn't have _____, so I only ordered a plate of chips. (money)
3 We'll have to drive. There aren't _____ on a Sunday. (buses)
4 It's raining, so there are _____ on the beach – just one or two. (people)
5 He can't drive yet. He isn't _____. (old)
6 Amira's worried because she's a freelance photographer, and she has _____ at the moment. (work)
7 You can't move in their living room. There's _____. (furniture)
8 We can't use the printer. There's _____. (paper)
9 It took us ages to get here. There was _____. (traffic)
10 I couldn't sleep on the plane. There were _____. (noisy children)
11 I'll only be a moment. I have to make _____ before we leave. (phone calls)
12 This jacket doesn't fit me. It's _____. (small)

3 PRONUNCIATION linking, *ough* and *augh*

a 🔊 9.2 Listen and write the sentences.

1 I _switched it on_.   5 I _____.
2 I _____.   6 I _____.
3 I _____.   7 I _____.
4 I _____.   8 I _____.

b Listen again and repeat the sentences. Try to link the words.

c Circle the word with a different sound.

1 h**o**rse	2 **u**p	3 h**o**rse	4 h**o**rse
br**ough**t	alth**ough**	b**ough**t	c**augh**t
(c**ough**)	en**ough**	d**augh**ter	l**augh**ed
th**ough**t	t**ough**	thr**ough**	t**augh**t

d 🔊 9.3 Listen and check. Then listen again and repeat the words.

Practical English
Ben's big show

EPISODE 5 — PICTURES OF YOU

asking indirect questions

1 ASKING INDIRECT QUESTIONS

a Circle the correct words.
1. Can you tell me what time *it is* / *is it*, please?
2. Do you know if this bus *does go* / *goes* to Windsor?
3. Could you tell me where *can I* / *I can* buy a ticket?
4. I wonder where *Lola is* / *is Lola* today.
5. Do you know if this shirt *does come* / *comes* in a larger size?
6. I'd like to know where *are you* / *you're* going.
7. I wonder what time *the restaurant closes* / *does the restaurant close*.
8. I'd like to know who *did you speak to* / *you spoke to*.

b Make questions 1–6 more indirect by using the beginnings given.
1. What time is the next bus for Boston?
   I'd like to know _what time the next bus for Boston is_ .
2. What time does it arrive?
   Do you know _____?
3. Which stop does the bus go from?
   Could you tell me _____?
4. How much does a one-way ticket cost?
   Could you tell me _____?
5. Do I need to change buses?
   I wonder _____.
6. How much discount do I get with a student card?
   Can you tell me _____?

c Complete the conversation with the indirect questions from **b**. There is one question you do not need to use.

Ticket clerk	Can I help you?
Ali	Yes, please. ¹_I'd like to know what time the next bus for Boston is._
Ticket clerk	Well, the next bus leaves at 10 a.m.
Ali	Great. ² _____
Ticket clerk	Sure. It costs $35.95.
Ali	³ _____
Ticket clerk	With a student card you get a 20% discount on your ticket. That means it'll cost you $28.75.
Ali	OK. Here's my student card...and my bank card.
Ticket clerk	And here's your ticket.
Ali	Thanks. ⁴ _____
Ticket clerk	No, you don't. The bus goes straight through.
Ali	And ⁵ _____
Ticket clerk	Yes, it gets to Boston at 2.20 p.m.

2 SOCIAL ENGLISH

a Complete the highlighted phrases in the conversations with a word from the list.

actually ~~going~~ Hey think way

1. **A** You look exhausted.
   B Yeah. There's just been a lot _going_ on this week.
2. **A** By the _____, who was the photographer?
   B Oh, just an old friend.
3. **A** _____, bro!
   B Emma! It's great to see you!
4. **A** Do you think this is good enough?
   B I, um… Yes, _____, I do.
5. **A** So I went to Ben's exhibition.
   B Did you? What did you _____ of his photos?

b Complete the conversations with the highlighted phrases from **a**.

1. **A** _Hey, bro!_
   B Amara! It's great to see you!
2. **A** Do you think we've made enough food for the party?
   B Um… _____.
3. **A** So we stayed in the hotel you recommended.
   B Did you? _____ the rooms?
4. **A** You forgot my birthday last week.
   B Yeah, I'm sorry. _____ recently.
5. **A** _____, how are you planning to get home?
   B I'll take a taxi.

1-9 Can you remember...?

1 GRAMMAR

Complete the sentences with the correct form of the verbs in brackets.

1 I _____ my girlfriend for three years. We met when we were at university. (know)
2 When I was a child, I _____ like big dogs – they frightened me. (used to)
3 I'm not sure, but I think that man _____ Susan's brother. (be)
4 If I lived in the city centre, I _____ to work instead of driving. (walk)
5 Jake's room is a mess, and he refuses _____ it. (tidy)
6 The police officer asked the man where he _____ the day before. (be)

2 VOCABULARY

Circle the word or phrase that is different.

1 duck   mussels   prawns   squid
2 colleague   couple   flatmate   partner
3 comedy   script   thriller   western
4 degree   head   pupils   students
5 attic   basement   gate   ground floor
6 apply for   be made redundant   resign   retire

3 PRONUNCIATION

Circle the word with a different sound.

up	1	course enough lucky tongue
horse	2	bought keyboard loan wall
phone	3	although router throw toes
boot	4	floor roof suit through
clock	5	cough loss nose watch

4 GRAMMAR & VOCABULARY

Read the article. Circle a, b, or c.

DANGEROUS DEVICES

Most of us would agree that computers and smartphones ¹____ made life easier for us. However, there are a ²____ people who might not agree, because they've ³____ injured by their electronic devices. Experts are becoming increasingly worried ⁴____ this problem. One of the ⁵____ dangerous devices appears to be phone chargers. You probably ⁶____ be injured if you use the charger you got with your phone, but fake chargers are different. Fake chargers are sold at much lower prices than originals, and when customers choose ⁷____ them, they're often tempted to buy the cheaper of the two. It's thought that a Chinese woman died recently because of a fake charger. She had plugged ⁸____ the charger and attached her phone before she tried to make a phone call. Unfortunately, she received a massive electric shock from the charger, and she ⁹____ killed instantly. It was believed that she ¹⁰____ have died if she hadn't used a fake charger.

1	a are	b had	c have
2	a few	b less	c little
3	a be	b been	c was
4	a about	b in	c of
5	a less	b more	c most
6	a don't	b not	c won't
7	a between	b from	c to
8	a in	b on	c out
9	a is	b was	c were
10	a didn't	b won't	c wouldn't

10A Idols and icons

G relative clauses: defining and non-defining
V compound nouns
P word stress

1 GRAMMAR relative clauses

a Complete the sentences with a relative pronoun. Where two answers are possible, write both pronouns.

1. What's the name of the city _where_ you can see the Ponte Vecchio?
2. Apple is the company _which / that_ makes the iPhone.
3. Who's the actor _____ dress broke during the Oscars?
4. The thing _____ my son wants most for his birthday is a bike.
5. Helen Sharman was the first British woman _____ went into space.
6. That's the restaurant _____ we celebrated my dad's 80th birthday.
7. Alexander Graham Bell is the person _____ invented the telephone.
8. What's the name of your friend _____ parents have a huge house in the country?
9. Mountain View, California, is the city _____ Google is based.
10. Amazon is the company _____ has the largest number of online sales in the world.

b In which sentence in **a** can you leave out the relative pronoun?

c ~~Cross out~~ the extra word in each of the sentences.

1. Those are the students who ~~they~~ won the competition.
2. Isn't that the actor who he played the role of Sherlock Holmes?
3. Why don't we stay in the hotel where we stayed there last year?
4. I always use the supermarket which it is closest to where I live.
5. She's the woman whose her daughter went to the same school as me.
6. What's the name of the shop where you bought your jacket there?
7. That's the computer that it isn't working.
8. This is the series I was telling you about it.
9. These are the boots I bought them last Saturday.
10. That's the woman whose car we bought it.

d Complete the sentences with a relative pronoun and a phrase from the list. You will need to leave out one of the words in each of the phrases.

~~he played Jon Snow in *Game of Thrones*~~
her first name means 'love' in Albanian
it is in Tanzania
it was opened in 2011
she helped to free hundreds of slaves
the *Mona Lisa* can be seen there

1. Kit Harington, _who played Jon Snow in Game of Thrones_, was born in London.
2. The Louvre, _____, is in the centre of Paris 
3. Kilimanjaro, _____, is Africa's highest mountain. 
4. Jiaozhou Bay Bridge in China, _____, is the longest bridge in the world. 
5. Dua Lipa, _____, is an extremely successful singer. 
6. Harriet Tubman, _____, has been chosen to appear on the $20 note.

68

2 VOCABULARY compound nouns

a Complete the compound nouns.

1 r<u>emote</u> c<u>ontrol</u>
2 s_____ b_____ 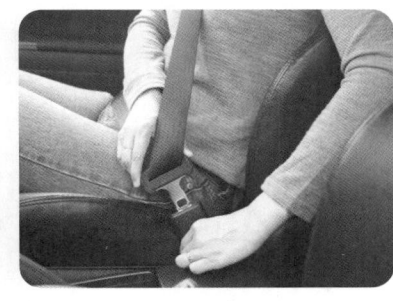
3 sp_____ e_____ 
4 m_____ st_____ 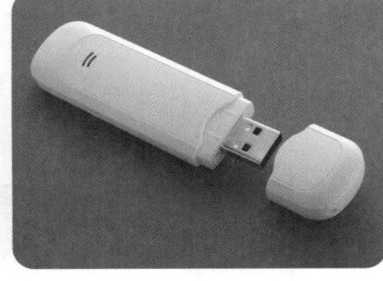
5 tr_____ j_____ 
6 gr_____ fl_____ 
7 f_____ p_____ 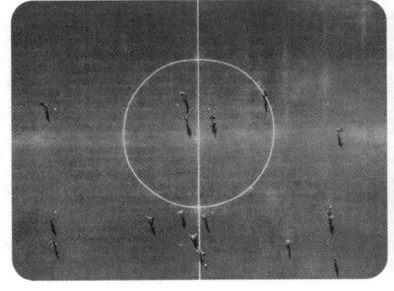
8 n_____ sch_____ 
9 d_____ l_____ 
10 r_____ 

b Match a word from **A** to a word from **B** to make compound nouns. Then complete the sentences.

A boarding   cycle   flat   rush   science   sound   speed   ~~sports~~   top   training

B camera   course   fiction   floor   ~~hall~~   hour   lane   mate   school   track

1 My basketball team practises three times a week in my local <u>sports hall</u>.
2 They live on the _____, so they've got a great view over the city.
3 I love the _____ of the latest Star Wars film – I listen to it all the time.
4 My brother has done a _____ to learn about health and safety.
5 Do you get on well with your _____, or do you argue about doing the housework?
6 Pupils at a _____ only see their families during the holidays.
7 Cyclists should use the _____ to keep away from traffic.
8 Commuters usually travel to work during the _____.
9 All the drivers are slowing down because there's a _____ up ahead.
10 I quite like fantasy films, but my favourite genre is _____.

3 PRONUNCIATION word stress

a Complete 1–8 with the words in the list to make compound nouns.

board   court   fine   lights   page   ~~products~~   school   tone

1 clean|ing <u>products</u>
2 key_____
3 pro|file _____
4 par|king _____
5 ring_____
6 se|con|dary _____
7 te|nnis _____
8 tra|ffic _____

b ◉ 10.1 Listen and check. Then listen again and repeat the words. Under<u>line</u> the stressed syllables.

10B And the murderer is...

G question tags
V crime
P intonation in question tags

1 VOCABULARY crime

a Complete the sentences.
1 A m<u>urder</u> was committed last night.
2 D_____ are investigating the crime.
3 They are hoping to s_____ it as soon as possible.
4 The v_____ was the wife of a millionaire.
5 The main s_____ are the woman's husband, their son, and their driver.
6 W_____ say they heard gunshots at around 10 p.m.
7 The police are convinced that the son is the m_____.
8 They're currently looking for more e_____.
9 They need to be able to pr_____ that they've caught the right person.

b Complete the text with the words from **a**.

NEWS   **ENTERTAINMENT**   **TECH**   **LIFESTYLE**   **SPORT**

Murder investigation after body found next to country road

Police appeal after murder of man in village north of Birmingham

¹<u>Detectives</u> are investigating a ²_____ in a village north of Birmingham. The ³_____ was a 26-year-old man, whose body was found last night next to a country road. No ⁴_____ was found at the scene, and police are appealing to ⁵_____ who saw the man yesterday to help them with their enquiries. They believe that the ⁶_____ was someone known to the man. The main ⁷_____ are the man's flatmate, his girlfriend, and a neighbour. These people are currently being interviewed by police in an attempt to ⁸_____ the crime. A police spokesperson said that they had a theory, but as yet they had been unable to ⁹_____ who had committed the crime.

2 GRAMMAR question tags

a Circle the correct words.
1. You live in Manchester, *don't you* / *aren't you*?
2. But you weren't born in Manchester, *weren't you* / *were you*?
3. You moved to Manchester when you were ten, *weren't you* / *didn't you*?
4. That means you've been living here for 20 years, *haven't you* / *have you*?
5. But you're emigrating to Canada next month, *won't you* / *aren't you*?
6. Your brother lives there, *doesn't he* / *does he*?
7. You've been in prison before, *aren't you* / *haven't you*?
8. I expect you'd like to call your lawyer now, *would you* / *wouldn't you*?

b Complete the question tags.
1. Adam's living with his parents, *isn't he*?
2. You don't like dogs, _____?
3. It isn't difficult, _____?
4. Anthony works in London, _____?
5. They left yesterday, _____?
6. Kathy hasn't come home yet, _____?
7. I'm late, _____?
8. You'll see him tomorrow, _____?
9. I wouldn't like that film, _____?
10. You haven't had lunch yet, _____?

c Rewrite the sentences using question tags.
1. I think your sister's in my class.
   Your sister's in my class, isn't she?
2. I'm sure you're younger than me.
   _____?
3. I have a feeling you don't like cheese.
   _____?
4. I heard your brother lives abroad.
   _____?
5. Is it right that you studied physics?
   _____?
6. I'm sure we've been here before.
   _____?
7. I'm sure you wouldn't do that.
   _____?
8. I'm hoping the flight won't be cancelled.
   _____?

3 PRONUNCIATION intonation in question tags

🔊 10.2 Listen and repeat the sentences. Copy the rhythm.
1. You **called** me **last night**, **didn't you**?
2. He's **older** than **you**, **isn't he**?
3. They **aren't coming tonight**, **are they**?
4. We've **missed** the last **bus**, **haven't we**?
5. She'll be **late**, **won't she**?
6. I **can't dance** very **well**, **can I**?
7. We **had** a **great holiday** in **Rio**, **didn't we**?
8. You've **never been** to the **opera before**, **have you**?
9. **That film** was **really boring**, **wasn't it**?

Answer Key

6A

1 VOCABULARY

a 2 action film, 3 science fiction film, 4 period drama, 5 musical, 6 thriller, 7 biopic, 8 horror film, 9 war film, 10 western, 11 animation, 12 rom-com

b 2 plot, 3 script, 4 audience, 5 review, 6 scene, 7 subtitles, 8 sequel, 9 soundtrack, 10 special effects, 11 extras, 12 cast, 13 critic, 14 set, 15 trailer, 16 prop

2 GRAMMAR

a 2 wrote
3 will be used
4 have been invited
5 are showing
6 is going to be dubbed
7 were filming
8 can be bought

b 2 is set in
3 is based on
4 was shot
5 plays the part of
6 was dubbed into

c 2 has been nominated
3 is being filmed
4 had / 'd been transformed
5 were directed
6 was being built
7 will be / is going to be released
8 be shot

d 2 c, 3 b, 4 a, 5 c, 6 b, 7 b, 8 a, 9 b, 10 a

3 PRONUNCIATION

a 2 used, 3 waited, 4 written, 5 shot, 6 worn, 7 said, 8 won, 9 taken, 10 stolen

6B

1 GRAMMAR

a 2 must, 3 might not, 4 could, 5 must, 6 can't

b 2 can't, 3 might, 4 must, 5 can't, 6 might not, 7 can't, 8 might

c 2 might have a meeting
3 can't be going to work today
4 might not like it
5 can't be tired already
6 must have an exam tomorrow
7 might not be working
8 might be driving home from work

2 VOCABULARY

a 2 neck, 3 back, 4 arms, 5 legs, 6 feet, 7 face, 8 nose, 9 chin, 10 stomach, 11 fingers, 12 knees

b 2 thumb, 3 tongue, 4 mouth, 5 lips, 6 hands, 7 teeth, 8 ears, 9 toes, 10 neck, 11 chin, 12 back

c 2 kick, 3 touch, 4 point, 5 smell, 6 smile, 7 nod, 8 clap, 9 bite, 10 whistle, 11 taste

d 2 finger, 3 mouth, 4 tongue, 5 head, 6 eyes, 7 nose, 8 fingers / hand, 9 lips / mouth, 10 teeth, 11 hands

3 PRONUNCIATION

a 2 eyes, 3 tongue, 4 shoulders, 5 here

7A

1 VOCABULARY

a 2 Geography
3 Biology
4 Literature
5 Chemistry
6 History
7 Computing
8 Mathematics

b 2 primary school
3 head teacher
4 state school
5 degree
6 private school
7 term
8 boarding school
9 nursery school
10 students
11 secondary school

c 2 elementary school
3 grades
4 semesters
5 high school
6 twelfth grade
7 college

d 2 misbehaved
3 weren't allowed to
4 made
5 were punished
6 cheated
7 let
8 revised
9 took
10 passed
11 failed

2 PRONUNCIATION

a 2 pull, 3 cut, 4 subtitles

3 GRAMMAR

a 2 c, 3 b, 4 f, 5 a, 6 h, 7 d, 8 g

b 2 until, 3 before, 4 if, 5 after, 6 when

c 2 will / 'll be, hurry
3 will / 'll have, go out
4 won't wait, aren't
5 doesn't come, won't have
6 won't leave, finds
7 won't be able to, lend
8 gets, will / 'll call
9 won't start, is / 's
10 will / 'll play, practise

d Students' own answers

7B

1 GRAMMAR

a 2 g, 3 c, 4 a, 5 h, 6 b, 7 e, 8 f

b 2 would be, cleaned
3 wouldn't drive, didn't have
4 Would…carry on, won
5 would sleep, didn't drink
6 would lend, needed
7 wouldn't be, snowed
8 wasn't / weren't, could
9 Would…wake up, didn't set
10 had, wouldn't be

c 3 I'd call her
4 you don't hurry up
5 I'll tell him the news
6 you didn't open the windows
7 she'd be happier
8 they'll cancel the match
9 you didn't eat out every night
10 she doesn't feel better

2 PRONUNCIATION

a 2 grow, vegetables, garden
3 buy, cottage, had enough money
4 my house, wouldn't make, kitchen bigger
5 wouldn't have, car, lived, city centre

c 3 D, 4 S, 5 S, 6 D, 7 S, 8 D

3 VOCABULARY

a 2 on, 3 on, 4 in, 5 on, 6 in

b 2 balcony, 3 entrance, 4 path, 5 gate, 6 chimney, 7 wall, 8 top floor, 9 attic, 10 roof, 11 terrace, 12 basement

c 2 b, 3 b, 4 c, 5 a, 6 a, 7 c, 8 b, 9 b, 10 b, 11 a, 12 a

Practical English 4

1 MAKING SUGGESTIONS

a 2 We could go there.
3 That's a great idea.
4 Why don't we go to a pub?
5 Where shall we go for that drink?
6 What about going to Giovanni's?
7 How about the Red Lion?
8 Shall we go there?

b 2 We could go there.
3 Why don't we go to a pub?
4 how about The Red Lion?
5 What about going to Giovanni's?
6 That's a great idea.
7 Shall we go there?
8 why not?

2 VERB FORMS

2 watch, 3 meeting, 4 play, 5 going, 6 eat out

3 SOCIAL ENGLISH

a 2 done, 3 forward, 4 ahead, 5 over

b 2 I'm looking forward to
3 How could I forget
4 go ahead
5 over a drink

Can you remember…? 1–7

1 GRAMMAR

1 's getting, 2 's been playing, 3 mustn't, 4 be able to, 5 have, 6 'd tell

Answer Key

2 VOCABULARY
1 sympathetic, 2 mortgage, 3 head, 4 coach, 5 plot, 6 shoulder

3 PRONUNCIATION
1 cinema, 2 cosy, 3 city, 4 stare, 5 fail

4 GRAMMAR & VOCABULARY
1 c, 2 a, 3 c, 4 b, 5 b, 6 a, 7 c, 8 b, 9 c, 10 b

8A

1 VOCABULARY
a 2 sacked, 3 resign, 4 applied, 5 shifts, 6 promoted, 7 redundant, 8 training course, 9 set up, 10 ran, 11 retire

b 2 at, part-time
3 in, temporary
4 in, full-time
5 for, unemployed
6 permanent, for
7 freelance, for

c 2 translator
3 employment
4 pharmacist
5 retirement
6 promotion
7 lawyer
8 scientist
9 resignation
10 application
11 farmer
12 qualifications

d 2 fired
3 work
4 run
5 fired
6 market
7 company
8 market
9 work
10 run

2 PRONUNCIATION
a 2 ap*ply*
3 em*ploy*ment
4 *farm*er
5 *free*lance
6 *law*yer
7 mu*si*cian
8 *per*manent
9 *phar*macist
10 pro*mo*tion
11 qualifi*ca*tion
12 *qual*ify
13 re*dun*dant
14 resig*na*tion
15 re*tire*
16 re*tire*ment
17 *sci*entist
18 *tem*porary
19 trans*la*tion
20 unem*ployed*

3 GRAMMAR
a 2 a, 3 b, 4 c, 5 a, 6 b, 7 c, 8 a, 9 b, 10 a

b 3 asked me to wait
4 ✓
5 I promise not to laugh
6 ✓
7 went on studying
8 ✓
9 I don't mind staying in
10 ✓

c 2 talking
3 to tell
4 to turn off
5 not speaking
6 laugh
7 Being able to
8 not to charge

8B

1 GRAMMAR
a 2 it was
3 told me
4 she bought
5 might
6 if I could
7 had to
8 the dress suited me
9 I wanted
10 'd forgotten

b 2 told, 3 said, 4 told, 5 told, 6 said

c 2 if I had / 'd seen his wallet, (that) I didn't know where it was
3 if her school shoes still fit her, me (that) they fit her perfectly
4 how much he had / 'd paid for his jacket, (that) it had / 'd been really cheap
5 where I was going the next day, her (that) I was meeting some friends
6 if he wanted anything from the shop, (that) he needed some milk.
7 if we had / 'd enjoyed our stay, her (that) it had / 'd been very enjoyable
8 when I was going shopping, (that) I might go on Saturday

d 2 I've resigned from my job.
3 When are you planning to retire?
4 Are you paid to do overtime?
5 I went to boarding school as a child.
6 How much is the painting worth?
7 I'll take the tram to the city centre.
8 Where did you meet your partner?
9 I expect to win the match.
10 Do you like seafood?

2 VOCABULARY
a 2 argument, 3 choose, 4 compensation, 5 deliver, 6 explanation, 7 fail, 8 improvement, 9 lose, 10 payment, 11 sell, 12 success

b 2 service
3 treatment
4 agreement
5 improvement
6 argument
7 valuation
8 achievement
9 choice
10 management
11 demonstration
12 sale
13 consideration
14 failure
15 temptation

c 2 payment
3 complaint
4 attachment
5 response
6 explanation
7 success
8 compensation

3 PRONUNCIATION
a train /eɪ/: claim, complain, contain, email, explain, paid, waiter
chair /eə/: airline, repair
computer /ə/: certain

9A

1 GRAMMAR
a 2 would have
3 had
4 had
5 would / 'd have
6 would / 'd have
7 had
8 had / 'd

b 2 would / 'd have arrived
3 hadn't booked
4 had / 'd checked
5 hadn't been
6 wouldn't have made
7 had / 'd known
8 wouldn't have invited
9 hadn't been
10 wouldn't have got

c 2 I hadn't passed my final exams
3 she would / 'd have got the job
4 we hadn't had lunch before we left
5 we would / 'd have played tennis
6 you had / 'd followed my directions
7 I would / 'd have won that game
8 he wouldn't have broken them

2 PRONUNCIATION
a 2 would have gone
3 would have bought
4 would have stayed
5 would have got
6 would have helped

3 VOCABULARY
a 3 fortunate, 4 unfortunate, 5 careful, 6 careless, 7 patient, 8 impatient, 9 lucky, 10 unlucky

b 2 impatiently, 3 carelessly, 4 Fortunately, 5 unluckily

c 3 possible, 4 impossible, 5 selfish, 6 unselfish, 7 useful, 8 useless, 9 suitable, 10 unsuitable, 13 possibly, 14 impossibly, 15 selfishly,

77

Answer Key

16 unselfishly, 17 usefully, 18 uselessly, 19 suitably, 20 unsuitably

d 2 selfishly, 3 useless, 4 successful, 5 suitably

e 2 impatient, 3 uncomfortable, 4 lucky, 5 Unfortunately, 6 Luckily, 7 comfortable, 8 carefully

9B

1 VOCABULARY

a 2 printer, 3 speaker, 4 adaptor, 5 remote control, 6 socket, 7 charger, 8 switch, 9 plug, 10 USB-C cable, 11 memory stick, 12 router, 13 wireless mouse, 14 voice assistant

b 2 memory stick, 3 charger, 4 printer, 5 USB-C cable, 6 keyboard, 7 remote control, 8 adaptor, 9 speaker, 10 router, 11 plug, socket

c 2 set, 3 switched on, 4 installed, 5 plugged in, 6 switched off, 7 turned down, 8 unplugged, 9 updated, 10 turned up

2 GRAMMAR

a 2 b, 3 b, c, 4 c, 5 a, b, c, 6 b, 7 b, 8 a, 9 c, 10 a, 11 a, b, 12 b

b 2 enough, too expensive / too much
3 a little, much
4 too many, enough
5 no, any
6 few, many

c 2 much money
3 any buses
4 very few people
5 old enough
6 very little / no work
7 too much / a lot of / lots of / loads of furniture
8 no paper
9 a lot of / lots of / loads of traffic
10 too many / a lot of / lots of / loads of noisy children
11 a few / some phone calls
12 too small

3 PRONUNCIATION

a 2 updated it
3 turned it down
4 deleted it
5 plugged it in
6 switched it off
7 unplugged it
8 turned it up

c 2 although
3 through
4 laughed

Practical English 5

1 ASKING INDIRECT QUESTIONS

a 2 goes
3 I can
4 Lola is
5 comes
6 you're
7 the restaurant closes
8 you spoke to

b 2 what time it arrives
3 which stop the bus goes from
4 how much a one-way ticket costs
5 if I need to change buses
6 how much discount I get with a student card

c 2 Could you tell me how much a one-way ticket costs?
3 Can you tell me how much discount I get with a student card?
4 I wonder if I need to change buses.
5 do you know what time it arrives?

2 SOCIAL ENGLISH

a 2 way, 3 Hey, 4 actually, 5 think

b 2 yes, actually, I do.
3 What did you think of
4 There's just been a lot going on
5 By the way

Can you remember...? 1–9

1 GRAMMAR

1 have / 've known
2 didn't use to
3 might / may / could be
4 would / 'd walk
5 to tidy
6 had / 'd been

2 VOCABULARY

1 duck, 2 couple, 3 script, 4 degree, 5 gate, 6 apply for

3 PRONUNCIATION

1 course, 2 loan, 3 router, 4 floor, 5 nose

4 GRAMMAR & VOCABULARY

1 c, 2 a, 3 b, 4 a, 5 c, 6 c, 7 a, 8 a, 9 b, 10 c

10A

1 GRAMMAR

a 3 whose
4 that / which
5 who / that
6 where
7 who / that
8 whose
9 where
10 that / which

b sentence 4

c 2 he, 3 there, 4 it, 5 her, 6 there, 7 it, 8 it, 9 them, 10 it

d 2 where the *Mona Lisa* can be seen
3 which is in Tanzania
4 which was opened in 2011
5 whose first name means 'love' in Albanian
6 who helped to free hundreds of slaves

2 VOCABULARY

a 2 seat belt
3 special effects
4 memory stick
5 traffic jam
6 ground floor
7 football pitch
8 nursery school
9 desk lamp
10 roadworks

b 2 top floor
3 soundtrack
4 training course
5 flatmate
6 boarding school
7 cycle lane
8 rush hour
9 speed camera
10 science fiction

3 PRONUNCIATION

a 2 keyboard
3 profile page
4 parking fine
5 ringtone
6 secondary school
7 tennis court
8 traffic lights

b 1 <u>cleaning</u> <u>products</u>, 2 <u>keyboard</u>, 3 <u>profile</u>, 4 <u>parking</u>, 5 <u>ringtone</u>, 6 <u>secondary</u>, 7 <u>tennis</u>, 8 <u>traffic</u>

10B

1 VOCABULARY

a 2 Detectives
3 solve
4 victim
5 suspects
6 Witnesses
7 murderer
8 evidence
9 prove

b 2 murder
3 victim
4 evidence
5 witnesses
6 murderer
7 suspects
8 solve
9 prove

Answer Key

2 GRAMMAR

a 2 were you
  3 didn't you
  4 haven't you
  5 aren't you
  6 doesn't he
  7 haven't you
  8 wouldn't you

b 2 do you, 3 is it, 4 doesn't he,
  5 didn't they, 6 has she, 7 aren't I,
  8 won't you, 9 would I, 10 have you

c 2 You're younger than me, aren't you
  3 You don't like cheese, do you
  4 Your brother lives abroad, doesn't he
  5 You studied physics, didn't you
  6 We've been here before, haven't we
  7 You wouldn't do that, would you
  8 The flight won't be cancelled, will it

OXFORD
UNIVERSITY PRESS

Great Clarendon Street, Oxford, OX2 6DP, United Kingdom

Oxford University Press is a department of the University of Oxford. It furthers the University's objective of excellence in research, scholarship, and education by publishing worldwide. Oxford is a registered trade mark of Oxford University Press in the UK and in certain other countries

© Oxford University Press 2025

The moral rights of the author have been asserted

First published in 2025

2029 2028 2027 2026 2025

10 9 8 7 6 5 4 3 2 1

No unauthorized photocopying

All rights reserved. No part of this publication may be reproduced, stored in a retrieval system, transmitted, used for text and data mining, or used for training artificial intelligence, in any form or by any means, without the prior permission in writing of Oxford University Press, or as expressly permitted by law, by licence or under terms agreed with the appropriate reprographics rights organization. Enquiries concerning reproduction outside the scope of the above should be sent to the ELT Rights Department, Oxford University Press, at the address above

You must not circulate this work in any other form and you must impose this same condition on any acquirer

Links to third party websites are provided by Oxford in good faith and for information only. Oxford disclaims any responsibility for the materials contained in any third party website referenced in this work

ISBN: 978 0 19 414451 3   Student Book with Exam Confidence Pack B
ISBN: 978 0 19 414405 6   Student Book B
ISBN: 978 0 19 414457 5   Student's Exam Confidence B
ISBN: 978 0 19 414468 1   Student's Online Resources B

Printed in China

This book is printed on paper from certified and well-managed sources

ACKNOWLEDGEMENTS

The authors would like to thank all the teachers and students round the world whose feedback has helped us to shape English File.

The authors would also like to thank: all those at Oxford University Press (both in Oxford and around the world) and the design team who have contributed their skills and ideas to producing this course.

Finally very special thanks from Clive to Maria Angeles, Lucia, and Eric, and from Christina to Cristina, for all their support and encouragement. Christina would also like to thank her children Joaquin, Marco, and Krysia for their constant inspiration.

The publisher and authors would also like to thank the following for their invaluable feedback on the materials: Paz Alonso, Cynthia Ebert, Philip Drury, Megan Watkins, Katherine Russen, Brian Brennan, Dagmara Lata, Gyula Kiss, Irene Iglesias, Jenny Holden, Marcos Norelle Ferreira Victor, Magdalena Muszynska, Jacqueline McCormack.

The publisher and authors would like to thank Jane Hudson for her work on the Revise and Check pages, Writing Bank, and Grammar Bank.

STUDENT BOOK

The authors and publisher are grateful to those who have given permission to reproduce the following extracts and adaptations of copyright material: p.9 Adapted from 'How you should eat: the new rules' by Peta Bee, 16 May 2022, The Times. © The Times/News Licensing. Reproduced by permission; p.10 Quotation reproduced by permission of Marianna Leivaditaki; p.19 Adapted from 'My no-spend year and how I survived' by Damian Whitworth, 18 January 2017, The Times. © The Times/News Licensing. Reproduced by permission; p.24 Excerpts adapted from 'Covid heroes 2020: From Sir Captain Tom Moore to Marcus Rashford, the faces that have inspired us' by Olivia Petter, 28 December 2020, The Independent. Reproduced by permission; p.27 Adapted from 'Leftover Pret a Manger baguettes go to homeless', Devon Live, www.devonlive.com. Reproduced by permission of Reach Publishing Services Limited; p.29 Adapted from 'Watch us race to London Heathrow by cab, the Heathrow Express and new Elizabeth Line' by Nicky Kelvin, 9 June 2022, The Points Guy, https://thepointsguy.com. Reproduced by permission; p.32 Adapted extracts from 'Understanding Generalizations and Stereotypes' by Sally Raskoff. Copyright © 2012 by W.W. Norton & Company, Inc., from Everyday Sociology Blog. Reproduced by permission of W. W. Norton & Company, Inc.; p.32 Illustration by DR Ink for Fawcett Society. Reproduced by permission of Fawcett Society; p.35 Interview with Dora Vanette has been written by our authors and audio is recorded with an actor voicing Dora Vanette. Included with permission; p.38 Extract from 'Michael Sheen stops performance to ask audience member to switch off phone' by Corrie David, 9 July 2021, WalesOnline. Reproduced by permission of Reach Publishing Services Limited; p.40 Extract abridged and adapted from Manners: A Modern Field Guide by Kay Plunkett-Hogge and Debora Robertson. © 2021 Kay Plunkett-Hogge and Debora Robertson. Reprinted by permission of HarperCollins Publishers Ltd; p.43 Abridged and adapted from 'Jason Arday: he learned to talk at 11 and read at 18 – then became Cambridge's youngest Black professor' by Charlie Brinkhurst-Cuff, 11 July 2023, The Guardian. Copyright Guardian News & Media Ltd 2024. Reproduced by permission; p.47 Adapted from 'How to be the Perfect Car Passenger' from www.autonational.co.uk. Reproduced by permission; p.52 Adapted from 'How we met: 'None of my Indian friends had girlfriends. But I liked her too much to say no' by Lizzie Cernik, 17 January 2022, The Guardian. Copyright Guardian News & Media Limited 2024. Reproduced by permission; p.58 Adapted from 'The secret life of an extra: don't talk, don't eat and don't go home till 2am' by Anonymous, 26 December 2026, The Guardian. Copyright Guardian News & Media Limited 2024. Reproduced by permission; pp.62–63 Extracts adapted from Francesca Tighinean's tips for choosing the right profile photo on social media, @ francescapsychology. Reproduced by permission; p.65 Adapted from 'I am not naturally magnetic': can you learn how to be charismatic?' by Colin Drury, 17 December 2016, The Guardian. Our audio recording uses an actor to voice Colin Drury. Copyright Guardian News & Media Limited 2024. Reproduced by permission; p.69 Extracts abridged and adapted from 'Back in Time for School – Episodes', www.bbc.co.uk. © Wall to Wall Media. Reproduced by permission; p.72 Adapted from '24 things you know if you still live with your parents' by Vicky Chandler, 10 February 2015, Metro. © dmg media licensing. Reproduced by permission; pp.74–75 information about Handel Hendrix House is included with permission; pp.82–83 Adapted extracts from 'Passengers treat me like a therapist': what the taxi driver hears at work' by Tobi Oredein, 8 December 2018, The Guardian. Copyright Guardian News & Media Limited 2024. Reproduced by permission; p.84 Adapted from 'United breaks guitars' by Dave Carroll, www.davecarrollmusic.com. Reproduced by permission; p.87 Extract from 'Breakthroughs, tips and trends: look, but don't touch' by Simon Crompton, 17 January 2009, The Times. © The Times/News Licensing. Reproduced by permission; p.88 Adapted from 'Strangers Helping Strangers: Locals Show Kindness to Solo Travelers' by Tracey Nesbitt, 17 May 2022, Solo Traveler, https://solotravelerworld.com. Our audio recording uses an actor to voice Tracey Nesbitt. Reproduced by permission; pp.90–91 Adapted from 'How to improve your luck and win the lottery twice (possibly)' by Richard Wiseman, 2 April 2015, The Guardian. Copyright Guardian News & Media Limited 2024. Reproduced by permission. p.93 Adapted from 'Could I survive a blackout? My day without power' by Chris Stokel-Walker, 10 October 2022, The Times. Our audio recording uses an actor to voice Chris Stokel-Walker © The Times/News Licensing. Reproduced by permission; p.95 Adapted extracts from '25 Areas of Digital Clutter to Minimize' by Joshua Becker, www.becomingminimalist.com. Reproduced by permission; p.107 Text about The London Dungeon is reproduced by permission; p.109 Adapted from 'How we met: 'He sent 40 Valentine's cards with all the different things he loved about me' by Lizzie Cernik, 6 February 2023, The Guardian. Copyright Guardian News & Media Limited 2024. Reproduced by permission; p.114 Adapted from 'How we met: 'She was giving out free footballs, and I thought she was really beautiful' by Lizzie Cernik, 21 February 2022, The Guardian. Copyright Guardian News & Media Limited 2024. Reproduced by permission; p.115 Adapted from 'Who needs uni? How to be successful without a degree' by Emily-Fleur Sizmur, 10 August 2014, originally published in Express. Reproduced by permission of Emily-Fleur Sizmur.

Sources: p.21 'Warning: WhatsApp 'mum and dad' scam continues' 2 March 2022, www.which.co.uk; p.30 www.pnas.org; p.34 information from www.jeongmeeyoon.com; p.85 story originally reported in www.huffpost.com; p.98 quotation from 'David Bowie did not know he was dying until final few months' by Hannah Ellis-Petersen, The Guardian, Jan 2017; p.100 'Short but sweet: The miniskirt' by Katya Foreman, Oct 2014, www.bbc.co.uk; pp.104–105 Adapted from 'The Red-Headed League' from The Adventures of Sherlock Holmes by Sir Arthur Conan Doyle, 1892.

Commissioned photography by: Dennis Kitchen Studio, Inc, Gareth Boden and MM Studios.

Pronunciation chart artwork by: Ellis Nadler

Illustrations by: Joelle Avelino, Peter Bull, Simon Clare, Jon Fletcher, Sarah Goodreau/Advocate Art, Joanna Kerr, Fabian Slongo/Advocate Art, Garry Walton/Meiklejohn, Kipper Williams.

Video stills: Digeo Productions

Video production by: Creative Listening (Pictures of you); Digeo Productions (all other videos).

The publisher would like to thank the following for their permission to reproduce photographs: 123RF (inbj, Jason Swalwell, Linda Cooke, Vyacheslav Ryaschikov); Aegean: Recipes from the Mountains to the Sea by Marianna Leivaditaki. Published by Kyle Books. Photography: Elena Heatherwick; Alamy (Aflo Foto Agency, Agencja Fotograficzna Caro, AKP Phot, Album, Alex Segre, Associated Press/Jim Cooper, BFA, Caspar Benson/fStop Images GmbH, Ceri Breeze, Chris Dorney, Clement Philippe, Corbis Super RF, D.Hurst, David Gee,

The manufacturer's authorised representative in the EU for product safety is Oxford University Press España S.A. el Parque Empresarial San Fernando de Henares, Avenida de Castilla, 2 – 28830 Madrid (www.oup.es/en)

David R. Frazier Photolibrary, Inc., DBURKE, Elizabeth Whiting & Associates/ Alamy Stock Photo, Ferenc Szelepcsenyi, FlixPix, Gastromedia, Granger, NYC./ Granger Historical Picture Archive, horst friedrichs, Ian Dagnall, imagebroker, Imagedoc, Ivan Vdovin, Jack Sullivan, James Marchington/LatitudeStock, Jonathan Larsen/Diadem Images, Justin Kase z12z, Karen Spencer, Kumar Sriskandan, Landmark Media, Lisa Top, Lusoimages, Marcin Rogozinski, Mark Davidson, Mark Henderson, Newscom, OnTheRoad, Oote Boe 2, PA Images, Pat Tuson, Paul Fearn, Paul Trinity, PBWPIX, Peter Titmuss, Photo12/7e Art/ See-Saw Films/New Zealand Film Commission, PhotoAlto, RGB Ventures/ SuperStock, Richard Heyes, Ringo H.W. Chiu, Silas Manhood, Stadium Bank, Tetra Images, The Print Collector, Universal/Courtesy Everett Collection, V&A Images, VPC Coins Collection, WARNER BROS. PICTURES, Yorkshire Pics, ZUMA Press); Anglepoise (Image courtesy of Anglepoise); ArenaPAL (Johan Persson); Dr Jan Bondeson; Dave Carroll; Cartoonstock (Elmer Parolini); John Evans; Diario de Navarro (Calleja); Emily Done; Denise Dorrance; Fawcett Society; Getty Images (ANDER GILLENEA, Chip Somodevilla, domoyega, Gary M. Prior, Hulton Deutsch, Ian Walton/Staff, Jean Catuffe, Michael Ochs Archives/Stringer, Michael Putland, Nigel French/Allstar, The Stanley Weston Archive, Theo Wargo, UroshPetrovic, UroshPetrovic, Vincenzo Lombardo, Andy Sacks/Photographer's Choice, Bill Varie/Corbis, Chris Ryan, Digital Vision, Flashpop, Fotosearch, Graham Chadwick, Issarawat Tattong, James Baylis – AMA, Jenna Woodward Photography/Flickr Open, JOCHEN LUEBKE, John Madere, Kevin C. Cox, Kris Timken/Digital Vision, Manu Vega, Matthew Stockman/Getty Images Sport, MEDITERRANEAN, Minas Panagiotakis/Stringer, monkeybusinessimages, Oliver Strewe, Philipp Nemenz/Lifesize, Pool, RgStudio, Roberto Serra – Iguana Press, Ryan McVay, Shane Anthony Sinclair/BAFTA, Steve Wisbauer/Photodisc, Stuart C. Wilson, tavor, Tom and Steve, Tony Anderson, track5, Travelpix Ltd, whitemay/ iStock Unreleased, Win Initiative); Becky Green (Wass); Guardian News & Media Ltd 2017; Savannah Hodge; JeongMee Yoon; Nick Jones; Chris Latham-Koenig; Mariana Leivaditaki; The London Dungeon; Tracey Nesbitt; Oppo; Oxford University Press (Andrew Scherbackov, BananaStock, Darko 1981, faungfupix, Masterfile, Maxim Lupascu/Dreamstime, Mikadun); Alex Parrish; Alex Rawlings; Graeme Robertson/Copyright Guardian News & Media Ltd 2024; Shutterstock (Andriy Blokhin, anna.spoka, Claudio Divizia, hamdi bendali, VectorIcon2003, Andrew Price, David Hartley, Ken McKay/ITV, Kevin Hodgson/SPP, Lucy Young, Mcpix Ltd, Nils Jorgensen, Shutterstock, Tottenham Hotspur FC); Emily-Fleur Sizmur; The Telegraph (Eddie Mulholland/The Telegraph, Julian Broad); The Times/News Licensing; Dagmara Walkowicz; Wonderbly.

WORKBOOK

The publisher would like to thank the following for their permission to reproduce photographs: Alamy (Gastromedia, Stanley Hare, Blend Images, Montgomery Martin, Jonathan Larsen/Diadem Images, Igor Kardasov, Alex Segre, Mk_Malin, Greg Balfour Evans, David Gee 4, Justin Kase, Peter Titmuss, imageBROKER, Bailey-Cooper Photography, PBWPIX, D. Hurst, Isabelle Plasschaert, Li Xin/Xinhua, Jeff Greenberg, James Schwabel, AKP Photos, Photo 12, Science History Images, George Impey, Newspix); Getty (Annabelle Breakey, Peter Muller/Cultura RF, Tetra Images, Tanya Constantine, Imgorthand, Richard Chapin Downs Jr, SolStock, NurPhoto, Ryan Pierse, Julian Finney, Caiaimage/Tom Merton, Ethan Miller/Getty Images for Keep Memory Alive, Samir Hussein/WireImage, Universal History Archive/UIG, Jenna Woodward Photography, Philipp Nemenz, SolStock, John Lund/Drew Kelly/Blend Images, FatCamera/Jonathan Long, Hispanolistic, Mike Coppola/ MG24); Oxford University Press (1996–98 AccuSoft Inc., Ocean/Corbis); Shutterstock (New Africa, norikko, Liv friis-larsen, Hong Vo, Eduardo Rgz, StockLite, bbernard, Vlada Tikhonova, panuwat phimpha, wavebreakmedia, DC Studio, Cast of Thousands, Ollyy, Martin Prochazkacz, colacat, DJTaylor, David Fowler, Ground Picture, kitzcorner, saiko3p, Syda Productions, spyarm, WAYHOME studio, stockfour, Phant, Bridget Calip, ESB Professional, romakoma, Christian Bertrand, Fedor Selivanov, kovop.58, fizkes, Zamrznuti tonovi, Stock-Asso, Minerva Studio, Malyugin, VaLiza, Shabby Datwin, Nenad Cavoski, Denys Kurbatov, Jack Frog, EF Stock, Creativa Images, bouybin, U.J. Alexander, 1000 Words, Ekkachai, Steve Mann, elegeyda, Alexander Lipko, Alexander Osenniy, Procreators, SARIN KUNTHONG, Artazum, A-photographyy, mubus7, Ewelina Wachala, Roman Chazov, Lucky Business, Halfpoint, Sabuhi Novruzov, StockLite, Resul Muslu, Bohbeh, Levon Avagyan, Kelvin Wong, Sonia Dubois, vitec, Marcelo Trad, Ruslan Ivantsov, aviemil, picturepixx, KOKTARO, Nattee Chalermtiragool, Volodymyr Burdiak, 4045, Petr Kopka, Tom Wang, Lauren Elisabeth, sabath, Ralf Gosch, Cegli, Samuel Naor, SpeedKingz, sirtravelalot, 1000 Words, Ground Picture, Mikadun); Shutterstock Editorial (20th Century Fox/Regency Enterprises/Kobal/ Shutterstock, IAN LANGSDON/EPA-EFE).

Illustrations by: Bill Brown/Illustration Division (p.15); John Haslam (pp.14, 15, 47, 68, 69, 79); Satoshi Hashimoto/Dutch Uncle (p.15); Roger Penwill (pp.21, 28, 39, 54, 73); Laura Perez/Anna Goodson Illustration Agency. (p.48).

Pronunciation chart artwork by: Ellis Nadler

Video stills: Creative Listening (Pictures of you).